COAL

Night shift, section 1, at Consolidation Coal's Mine No. 86, Carolina, West Virginia, 15 August 1940. Author's father, Clyde Lockard, is fourth from left in top row. (Photograph by "Tallent")

COAL

A Memoir and Critique

Duane Lockard

University Press of Virginia

Charlottesville & London

The University Press of Virginia

Printed in the United States of America

First published 1998

∞ The paper used in this publication meets the minimum requirements
of the American National Standard for Information Sciences—Permanence
of Paper for Printed Library Materials, ANSI Z39.48-1984.

Library of Congress Cataloging-in-Publication Data
Lockard, Duane. 1921–
Coal : a memoir and critique / Duane Lockard.
p.   cm.
Includes bibliographical references and index.
ISBN 0-8139-1784-0 (alk. paper)
1. Coal mines and mining—United States.
2. Coal trade—United States.
3. Social responsibility of business—United States.
I. Title.
TN805.A5L63   1998
338.2' 724' 0973—dc21   98-5196
                                                                CIP

To the memory of my parents
with thanks for a
good start

Contents

Illustrations

Preface

As the ideas of price system, market economy, and the privatization of state-run companies find favor around the world—even in countries where until recently overt belief in such heresies landed people in jail—it may seem an odd time to write a book expressing grave doubt about the role and power of capitalism's prime agent: the corporation. As Russia and China compete for capital investment from their erstwhile enemies, the industrialists and financiers of the Western world, and capitalism's ardent champions are singing "I told you so" over the demise of socialism, I have chosen this time to write about the pitfalls of corporate hegemony.

Or to put it more accurately I have just now completed a book that I began researching in the 1980s, several years before I retired from academic life and long before the Communist-bloc countries became tentatively converted to the doctrines of Adam Smith. In my teaching and writing for many years I expressed serious misgivings about the kind of sweeping discretionary power held by the modern corporation, and the coal industry was a prime example. The management and boards of directors of these independent principalities make life-determining decisions on a vast range of issues. They determine the condition of the environment not alone in the vicinity of the mines themselves—where dust, water contamination, gashed hillsides, silted stream beds, and polluted air all abound—but wherever downwind in the world acid rain may fall. To a significant degree they control land use, apportion tax burdens, endanger the lives of people who live downstream from unstable mine spoil dams that hold back the waste water used to clean coal. Coal companies characteristically long ignored the plight of miners slowly suffocating from black lung disease, and on corporate heads rests responsibility for thousands of lost fingers, for the empty sleeves and pant legs that are so common in coal country, for a history of needless deaths of many of the more than 100,000 miners who have been killed in mine accidents since record keeping began in the 1880s. The rate of fatalities has declined in recent decades, yet American miners are still several times more likely to die on the job than are their British counterparts. Coal companies manage to escape paying the bill for extinguishing raging fires in abandoned mines, the costs involved in the subsidence of land over mined-out underground coal seams, and the compensation of miners disabled by black lung. Coal corporations have shown little concern for the communities whence they drew their profits, leaving once mineral-rich regions to wither in poverty and despair. Coal barons have subverted the political systems of numerous states and municipalities through bribery and other tactics of corporate invasion and domination.

It is true that the situation today is better than it was yesterday: the miseries of company towns have gone the way of all obsolescence, and the number of miners killed annually is counted in dozens rather than the hundreds or, worse, the thousands of fifty years ago. But dozens *are* killed, black lung persists, hundreds of thousands are left unemployed, the environment sustains damage, and coal dust is still inhaled—the problems of the past haunt us still. And no one has proposed ways of dealing with the runaway power of the coal corporation.

I make no claim to impartiality in my observations; my recollections of coal company conduct are too negative for that. But coal mining has fascinated me as long as I can remember, for coal has been at the center of my family's history. It started with my maternal grandfather, John K. Walter, born in 1873, whose schooling stopped in grade school and who became a miner in the late 1880s. He met the requirements for certification as a section boss, then became a mine superintendent; I remember him best as an inspector of mines for the Consolidation Coal Company in northern West Virginia. My father, J. Clyde Lockard, became a coal loader for the same company during World War I in Owings, West Virginia, where Grandfather Walter was then superintendent. Dad spent the rest of his working life as a miner, and in the middle of his forty-year career underground I joined him "inside" in the summer of 1941. ("Inside" and "outside" are terms used in mine talk as they are in prison language, and for similar reasons.) A fourth generation of our family—my sister's daughter, Denise Santee—is currently a Consol employee in West Virginia.

So, my personal acquaintance with the coal industry serves my interest in investigating the development of a revealing slice of corporate Americana. My account of coal operators' conduct is critical of their abuse of power and decency, but that conduct is not so atypical as to be unrepresentative of corporate experience as a whole.[1] Even if it is a worst-case example—and in some respects it is—it nevertheless illustrates the freedom from restraints on corporate discretionary power that is certainly not restricted to the coal industry alone. The deaths of 100,000 miners and the abrupt layoffs of hundreds of thousands in the productivity revolution illustrate the corporate situation at the end of the twentieth century.

I propose some steps that might conceivably be taken to assert internal and external restraint on corporations in general and coal companies in particular, but I recognize that formidable barriers block the path to regulation of that outsized power. One is the mind-set favorable to corporate freedom to act independently, free from excessive restraint. Prevailing preconceptions and expectations set narrow parameters of possibility, and accomplishment of significant advances would necessitate some change of attitude on the part of the dominant thought-leaders of the nation. Changing that worshipful view of the corporation assuredly will not be easy to achieve.

Another limitation on the prospect of change is the fact that corporate leaders have in their hands something that opens doors and determines opinions—and that is money. Cash to invest; cash to provide jobs, positions of power, satisfaction of hopes—or, by withholding it, to assure loss of face, loss of jobs and income, failed election campaigns, failed dreams of power and glory and money. The total assets in the hands of corporate managers is staggering, a fact not lost on other businessmen, politicians, and institutional leaders (in education, religion, and information, for example) when policymaking conflict takes place. In a capitalist regime (but not there alone) control over investment is power indeed. The first step toward controlling corporate power is perhaps the recognition of its existence and how it functions.

A book in the making for fifteen years owes much to many, including some who unknowingly instructed me about coal mines and mining, coal town life, mine disasters, mining technology, and the political economy of coal. Among the libraries and museums to which I am indebted for books, journals, correspondence, and photographs, particularly helpful were the staffs of Firestone Library at Princeton University, the Brewster (Massachusetts) Ladies' Library, the West Virginia Collection at West Virginia University, the Eastern Regional Coal Archives and Coal Museum of Bluefield, West Virginia. I appreciate the support of Princeton University and the Ford Foundation for financing the leaves of absence from teaching that allowed me to conduct research. I owe thanks to numerous Princeton students who were members of research seminars on coal-related topics, and to those who wrote senior theses on coal under my supervision—they taught me more than they probably realized. For her professional photographic expertise and counsel and her enthusiastic support when my faith in the undertaking waned, as well as her editorial assistance, Lisa Little has my deepest gratitude. My late wife, Beverly, and my daughters, Linda, Jay, and Leslie, all contributed in special ways, most especially by untiring support and encouragement when I got a share of the blows that life deals to us all. To Mary Fishler-Fisk of New Pensmith I owe a special debt for introducing me to the intricacies of electronic reproduction of my thoughts. Copyeditor Patricia Sterling saved me from many errors and spared the reader countless unnecessary words.

I hesitate to name the legion of other individuals who helped in one way or another for fear of overlooking someone. But better to be embarrassed by memory lapse than fail to express my gratitude to those who aided with interviews, correspondence, and bibliographical suggestions or by reading all or parts of the manuscript or otherwise: Tom Bethel, Paul Boydoh, John Brass, John Brass Jr., Joseph Brennan, Arthur Brown, Keith Dix, Ben A. Franklin, John Gaventa, Fred Greenstein, Denver Johnson, Rosemary Little, Bill Love, Davitt McAteer, Eva McGuire, Charles A. Miller, Ralph Moyer, Betty Roberts Ritter, Denise Santee, Gerald Spragg, Sharon L. Tracy, David Ware, J. Randall Williams, and David Zielenziger.

COAL

Introduction

In the spring of 1941 when I was nineteen I pestered the superintendent of the mine where my father worked as a coal loader until he finally let me satisfy a curiosity I had harbored as far back as my memory could reach—to find out what it was like to work inside a coal mine. That curiosity had been whetted by hearing my father and grandfather converse, in the language of miners, about mine dangers, working conditions, accidents, tools and machinery, and the tragic or antic behavior of well-remembered buddies, dead and alive. I had some idea of what was meant by roof falls, black damp, blasting powder, entries and pillars, balky mules and swearing drivers, cutting coal by machine and by hand, building cribbing and setting timbers, bug dust, gob piles, ribs and faces—but I had never seen the inside of a mine. In a way I was still where I had been as a little boy when I draped blankets over kitchen chairs and crawled through the dark tunnels of my make-believe coal mine. Now at last I would see and experience the real thing.

The journey inside began with a trip to the company store, where I bought a number-four coal shovel, steel-toed safety shoes, a hard hat, leather gloves, heavy work socks, and a supersize dinner bucket suited to a young man's appetite. Mother would load it with sandwiches, fruit, and cake or cookies, leaving room for the near-gallon of water I would carry to slake the parched-throat dryness caused by the ubiquitous coal dust. Next, I paid a visit to the doctor's office for a perfunctory physical exam, and the doctor, having found me at least superficially sound, jabbed a needle in my arm to deliver a tetanus shot. Then he signed my work papers, and I was ready to go. I drove home to pick up my father, and by 4:00 P.M. we were off for the Carolina mine (officially, Consolidation Coal Company Mine No. 86), five or six miles from Monongah, where we lived. It was time

1

for my first work shift, going through the age-old initiation rites of father and son coal miners. In my father's place I would have talked about the meaning of such an occasion, but my father was a quiet man, and I can recall nothing being said about this momentous event; if he had thoughts about the danger involved and the exertion at hand, he kept them to himself. He was a taciturn Lockard, not a talkative Walter-descendant like his son.

The Carolina mine and its surrounding company town got their name from a daughter of the Watson family that had owned the mine when it opened. Like many coal mines in Appalachia it was on a hill, and our ancient Chevy had to shift down to climb the rough road past the ever burning, smoky slag heap that spilled into the valley, where severe fogs and the absence of barrier rails made driving hazardous. We crossed the tracks of the Norfolk and Western Railroad just ahead of the engine hauling away the day shift's output. High on the hill to our left was "Boss Row," where the families of mine foremen lived in substantial two-story residences standing in marked contrast to the small, four-room, square houses allotted to ordinary miners, regardless of the size of their families. The main street leading to the working facilities of the mine went by the company store, the recreation hall, the doctor's office, and the office of the clerk of the mine where you lined up to get your envelope with the cash—if you had any coming—on biweekly paydays. (There must have been a school, church, and union hall, but they don't appear on my memory map, and the mine having been closed for the better part of a half-century, the buildings themselves are gone.)

Just beyond these service structures were the mine's operational buildings, most of them constructed of brick, including the bathhouse, lamphouse, the blacksmith and repair shops; off to one side the small powder house where loaders bought their supplies of dynamite; the office of the superintendent where bosses gathered before shifts. The boiler to generate power for operations was nearby and, dominating the scene, the tipple, which transferred coal from the three-ton coal cars to the forty-ton railroad cars, and the mine shaft with its "cage," the elevator that transported miners, mules, and supplies to working areas more than five hundred feet below. High above the corrugated iron walls of the tipple and the superstructure of the shaft were huge wheels on which ran the cables that lifted coal and passengers from below—and, as I would soon discover, dropped them like rocks as it took man and beast down the chute.

In the lot beside the railroad tracks near the tipple I parked the car to accumulate its nightly coat of coal dust (not that that seemed unusual—the workers' houses spreading up the hillside got their double daily dustings too). The bathhouse was familiar territory to me; I had been there with my father and knew its steamy heat and its open clothes carriers hanging from the ceiling, where dirty work clothes dried out while one was at home and street clothes hung while one worked. I changed into work gear, ran my clean clothing to the roof by chain, and locked it in place. I grinned sheepishly as Dad's buddies kidded him about bringing in a green son to learn the ropes. Did I know where the skyhooks were stored? Had I brought a plug of Brown Mule? Most miners used either snuff or chewing tobacco—thickly shredded Mail Pouch or Red Man, or the cakes of sweet, dark Brown Mule—to counter the dustiness on the job. But I had tried them all out behind the barn, and without exception they made me sick. Loading coal was enough of a challenge; a jaw full of sickening "chew" would be too much. In time I turned to chewing gum, which helped.

Next I visited the lamphouse, where the man in charge gave me a battery-operated light that fitted on my hard hat; he also provided a freshly charged battery, which was carried in a holder attached to the back of the wide belt one wore for that purpose. At first the battery did not seem particularly heavy, but as the night went on it became a boulder that dragged me down. I gave the lampman one of my brass identification medallions (my number was 950), which he would keep until I returned my lamp at the end of the shift; this way, he had a record of who was inside—just in case. While we waited to take the cage down the shaft, we stood outside the bathhouse, listening to the banter of the younger miners; if anything about the work ahead bothered them, it was not apparent in their relaxed talk. The older men had less to say, and some of them searched for a place to sit as if they were weary by anticipation.

Then it was time for a patting-down search by Larry, a one-armed examiner whose job it was to see that no one took smoking materials inside—

for obvious reasons, it has always seemed to me; a cigarette company executive might agree that smoking in this workplace could be harmful to neighboring nonsmokers. (As recently as 1994, however, federal mine safety officials found it necessary to conduct a campaign to stop foolish miners who want to light up on the job.) As I waited my turn with Larry, I kept an eye on the cage. I didn't really expect anything untoward to happen, but the prospect of a 518-foot plunge in the clanking thing was frightening. Soon the cage popped up like a cork for our turn to board. It would hold about a dozen men, and I wasn't about to be separated from my father on this journey, so I stuck close to his side.

Unlike a conventional elevator this vehicle had no walls and was open to the shaft, which was cemented except where seams of coal were visible—that is, until the speed of the cage made the passing scene a blur. Suddenly I remembered the story I had heard about a drunken shaft operator who failed to apply the brakes, with crippling consequences for the passengers. We were going like the wind, and I wondered about the sobriety of our handler. But in good time the brakes were applied, and we decelerated so abruptly that I thought my knees would buckle. But my fears were those of the novice, and soon we were safely exiting the cage.

From the shaft bottom we followed a dark and confusing route of rail tracks to a waiting "mantrip," in this case a string of dozens of empty coal cars (pulled by a twenty-ton electric motor) being taken to the working face to be filled with three tons of coal each. It was called a mantrip, but it wasn't particularly man-oriented, since the cars had no springs, cushions, or any other concession to human comfort—better than walking the three miles, but not much; in fact, it was much worse if you boarded a car with a flat wheel, so called. A flat wheel was the result of locked brakes that at some point had worn down one section of the wheel, setting up a severe, bone-jolting vibration for the unsuspecting rider. One would prefer to walk, but once the train rolls it doesn't stop. One can't even crawl to another car, because the "top" (the mine's "ceiling") is low and uneven, and there is a high-voltage trolley wire to take into account. We had no flat wheels that night, however, and after a normal battering to the behind we arrived at 13 Left, as our section was designated on the mine map; it was totally black except for our personal lamps and finding my way at first was difficult and scary. (I know I keep saying that things are frightening, but above all that is what a coal mine is to the novice: frightening.)

Dad and I walked a few hundred yards to where we would load our quota of coal for the night. This "Pittsburgh Seam" (so named because it ran from western Pennsylvania to northern West Virginia) averaged six to seven feet thick, and the "entry" was ten to twelve feet wide, yielding about thirty tons of black, bituminous coal each work shift. (At that time two crews worked the entry, one by day and ours at night.) A cutting-machine crew of two had already prepared the "place" for us by undercutting the coal to a depth of several feet and about ten inches above the floor. This they did with an electrically powered cutting bar resembling a huge chain saw. Before that machine was invented, miners laboriously undercut the face of the coal themselves by lying on their sides and banging away with a pick, a tool with sharply pointed ends on a handle about the length of an axe handle.[1] Not only did the cutter crew save the work of manual undercutting; they could turn the bar on its side and cut a swath perpendicularly from floor to roof, thereby allowing coal to fall freely when dynamited. Cutting machines were also equipped with power drills, sparing a miner the lengthy task of cranking a hand drill to cut holes for the dynamite.

Because of full undercutting and deeply drilled holes, the blasting worked effectively to break the coal into manageable chunks. Blasting was risky business, though, and Dad took it with the seriousness it deserved (I never once fired a shot). He would put two sticks of dynamite in the average drilled hole, tamping it in securely with clay wrapped in newspaper (called a dummy; making those was my specialty) to prevent the blast from blowing out of the hole with a dangerous jet of fire. (Some miners who would not seek out clay used coal dust to tamp, and became dead miners as a result.) A cap or detonator was attached to the explosive and a long wire led back to Dad's lamp battery. After going around the corner from the entry he would shout, "Fiyah, fiyah, fire in the hole!" and, with that warning, press the wire ends into the terminals of the battery, setting off one hell of a noise.

The first shot he fired that night startled me, and I jumped like a scared rabbit. There is something special about the effect of dynamite set off underground; with nowhere to go, the sound reverberates menacingly, Dad thought my reaction was very funny, and he roared with laughter; at the time I couldn't see what was so humorous. But that was the only time I ever saw my father find anything amusing about blasting. He was a mild-mannered man, not given to telling people off, but once when a miner set off a blast near us without the conventional warning, Dad exploded in a tirade of abuse that left the offender shaken, apologetic, and unlikely to commit that blunder again.

The dust of the explosion and the pungent smoke from the blasting powder made breathing difficult. My throat burned, and I got a little dizzy from lack of oxygen—asphyxiation by blasting smoke, in effect. Yet well before the ventilation system brought fresh air into the cul-de-sac of the working face, we pushed an empty car into the room and got to work. First we gathered by hand all the large lumps that had blown free. Then standing at the front corners of the car we shoveled coal over our left or right shoulder respectively to load the front of the car. Next we threw coal over the opposite shoulder, aiming for the rear of the car. At first I missed the target area as often as I hit it; heaving coal six to eight feet and landing it in a predetermined place is not an inborn trait. My aim and delivery would improve with practice, but meantime I had to scoop a lot of coal twice.

At nineteen I was six feet tall, slender, accustomed to hard work, and under the impression that I was strong and able to endure exertion, but in loading coal I couldn't come close to matching my father. Although he was a bit smaller than I, his twenty-four years as a miner had given him not only the strength to go on and on at full steam for hour after hour but also the techniques required to make the difficult seem almost easy. I say "almost" advisedly, for the task never really becomes easy, however long you do it. The energy demanded and the sheer pain of that physical exertion was like nothing I ever experienced, before or since. In my early days, from gripping the shovel so long and so hard, I would awake after my day's sleep with my hands clenched in tight fists and so twisted that the only way I could open them was by using the curled knuckles of one hand to pry open the fingers of the other. My diary entry for my first day shows how impressed I was with the demands of the job (it also shows the writing of a naive youngster, but then that's what I was):

Friday, June 6, 1941. Well, my first nite in the mine. Man Oh Man! What work! Wow! I was so tired—so tired I didn't think I'd ever make it outside [meaning the three-mile walk to the cage after work]. In fact I didn't even have an apetite—& that's definitely in bad shape. I drug out of that mine. Loading that stuff is real work. . . . My feet, my back, my arms, my hands, Oh!

    To bed 4:00 A.M.

In time I adjusted to the demands on my energy reserves and was less exhausted than during those first weeks. In the beginning, however, I found the work so taxing that I failed to write regularly in my diary; that period has the only blank pages in eight years of daily notes. Otherwise, what I had begun as a high school junior I continued faithfully during the next eight years, even on days when I flew combat missions in Europe, 1943–45. So the demands of being an active coal miner stand out as uniquely preemptive of life's energy.

Perhaps I can give some measure of the exertion required to handload coal with this illustration. Assume that a miner swings his shovel five times a minute and that the average weight of a shovelful is 20 pounds—or 100 pounds a minute. Multiply that by fifty minutes per hour (allowing ten minutes in each hour for the necessary tasks of checking the top, blasting, moving cars in and out, and laying track) and then by six hours, and you have 30,000 pounds, or 15 tons (the traditional 16 tons requires still greater effort). Six hours of actual loading leaves time for eating lunch, setting timbers, or perhaps waiting for empties should some mishap cause a delay. But waiting for a string of empty cars to arrive is rarely restful, for one puts off all the housekeeping tasks possible for such downtime. And even when those jobs have been done, a rest period will be miserable because the steady underground temperature of 55 to 60 degrees feels uncomfortably cool to a sweat-soaked person.

Needless to say, six months of loading coal will put you in good physical condition—if some crippling accident doesn't negate the effect of all the effort.

But if exhaustion was the downside of loading coal, payday was the cheerful side—provided, of course, that the demand for coal brought steady work, as it did in 1941. We were paid on a piece-rate basis—then 74.5¢ a ton—calculated by the weighed tonnage of coal cars bearing your medallion. As each car was filled, one loader hung a brass check, as we called it, on the car; in our case, father and son tagged alternate cars. A shift's work of 15 tons brought $11.18, which doesn't sound like much today, but compared with other available jobs in West Virginia in that era it was a good wage. It was better than "day" work in the mine: maintenance jobs such as track work or haulage, which paid less than a dollar an hour. And loading coal paid nearly as much per day as I had been able to earn in a week during the summer of 1940, when I was getting under 14¢ an hour for an 84-hour week as a waiter in an all-night restaurant.

Back in 13 Left that first night wore on—and wore me down. The battery hanging on my belt got heavier by the hour. The stooping and straining to scoop up and heave coal revealed and exhausted muscles I never knew I had. Here and there the vein of coal dipped, lowering the roof, and I repeatedly banged my head on cross timbers. The hard hat absorbed part of the impact, but since the collisions were always unexpected, they jolted not just my head but my whole body. I was also learning what gritty coal dust felt like down the neck and around the belt line; the best analogy I can think of is sandpaper underwear.

My worst problem, however, was none of the above: more serious was the response of my left arm to that tetanus shot administered the previous afternoon. About midnight the arm stiffened and became so intensely painful that I couldn't lift it, far less use it for shoveling. At first I didn't know what was happening, but then I realized it was the effect of the shot. As a result, it was left for Dad to do the remaining cars alone while I sat on a gob pile (debris separated from the coal) shivering with cold. The stumbling three-mile walk from our place to the cage, tripping over coal beside the tracks, weary beyond belief, was a fitting finale to a day of unprecedented adventure.

Many years later I told our next-door neighbor in Monongah, Paul Boydoh, about that horrendous first night in Carolina mine, and he in turn related the story of his own initiation—in 1929 at age eighteen—and of how he had been scared "half to death," terrified that the top would cave in on him, frightened by the impenetrability of the blackness surrounding him; his first day remained vividly in his memory. "We used carbide lamps then and they didn't give much light." When that first shift ended, he said, he was "about wore out." He recalled that he got 19¢ a ton. "But that was better than the days when you would get to your place and find there was no work because of a slatefall or something like that; maybe they would find work for you or maybe not. If they didn't, you had to walk out of the mine and [in Consol No. 63 at Monongah] that was a fifteen-mile walk—and it wasn't easy walking along track that was never cleaned up. Yeah, I've worked in all kinds of conditions—loaded coal in water up to my knees. I'm lucky though; I never once had a serious injury. Got black lung and have to take medicine for it regular every day."[2]

Such are the tales of miners who survived their underground careers. For many centuries people have ventured below the surface for their initiation to the rites of the netherworld; sons often trained by their fathers, as I was. What I faced then was less arduous than the rigors endured by my predecessors. In the dozen years between my initiation and that of neighbor Paul Boydoh, many changes had come about: the reward for loading a ton of coal had increased nearly four times over; we had safer, more illuminating, battery-powered lamps instead of open-flame, flickering carbide flares on our caps. But much was the same: no safety legislation of note had been enacted; although the annual death toll was down somewhat, 1,266 coal miners died violent deaths in mines in 1941; and American mining authorities still did not recognize black lung disease. Not only were men like Boydoh and my father exposed to the disabling dust, but the malady's existence was denied. Compared with 1941 the work today is less demanding; new safety regulations exist, and the annual killing has dropped below 100 a year. Still, the lot of today's miner is by no means peaches and cream.

But then it never was a choice kind of life. Mining has long been regarded as among the worst of occupations. Until the fifteenth or sixteenth century it was never done by paid laborers; rather, it was assigned to prisoners of war, slaves, and criminals. In Scotland during the seventeenth and eighteenth centuries coal miners were serfs, bought and sold as property that went along with the mine. "Even as adults it was impossible for them to obtain their freedom and they were advertised for sale regularly in Edinburgh newspapers," writes Tom Steel. "By the end of the eighteenth century, various Acts of Parliament had given miners their freedom; but the legislation was brought about by economic rather than human concern and women, together with children, continued to work long shifts. . . . [Wives], to earn eightpence a day, . . . hauled thirty-six hundred weight to the surface."[3]

For thousands of years, says Lewis Mumford, "mining was not regarded as a human art: it was a form of punishment: it combined the terrors of the dungeon with the physical exacerbation of the galley. The actual work of mining, precisely because it was meant to be burdensome, was not improved during the whole of antiquity, from the earliest traces of it down to the fall of the Roman Empire."[4]

Something about working underground suggests a Satanic aura. Why is hell *down there* in some variously defined world of fire and brimstone where torture and agony are standard fare? Why is heaven *up there* amid blue skies, openness, and light? The attribution of evil to underground darkness is no new development. From the earliest descent into the earth to mine it, coal has long been associated with negative stereotypes.

1

Notes on the History of an Industry

W HEN MANKIND first used coal as fuel is not clear. In the standard works on anthropology I consulted the authors say nothing about the use of coal by prehistoric people. Many discuss the discovery of fire and of early peoples' ingenuity in starting fire and utilizing it for cooking and for warmth, but they do not mention coal, perhaps because there were no tools hard enough to excavate it even from outcroppings.

Nevertheless, in traceable human society the use of coal has ancient roots; China is said to have been using it since 1000 B.C. (Marco Polo found it in common use there in the thirteenth century). From Graeco-Roman times, the philosopher Theophrastus reports that ironsmiths used coal in their forges in 371 B.C.[1] Roman-style tools have been discovered in ancient mines in England. During the ninth century coal mining was done on a small scale in England, but it became significant in the thirteenth century when Henry III granted the people of Newcastle the right to mine coal.[2] By the sixteenth century England was consuming so much coal that the foul-smelling smoke aroused popular opposition to its use. The well-to-do burned wood, which was becoming scarce from overcutting and therefore expensive, but the urban poor did not have that choice. An indication of the demand for coal at that time is found in the growing output of Tyneside mines between 1534 and 1634: it expanded by a factor of fourteen,

from 32,000 to 452,000 tons.[3] As coal became the predominant fuel of England and of Europe generally, the noxious fumes again drew opposition,
particularly in cities: Queen Elizabeth I banned its use in London when
Parliament was sitting.

With the demand for coal came in turn the expansion of mining in England and on the Continent, and then the vicious exploitation of miners,
even though they were no longer slaves. In the steam-driven economy of
the nineteenth century the call for coal became insatiable, with the result
that now women and small children were drawn into the industry and exploited mercilessly. The treatment of these powerless people was so brutal
that it is hard to believe it could have happened—but it did. In the 1840s a
formal investigation, originally motivated by a concern for the abuse of
children, suggested there were almost no limits to what owners were willing to demand and *get* from women and children in their mines. Said the
official report of the British Commissioner of Mines in 1842: "Statements
as to the early age at which Children commence work in the pits are confirmed by the most abundant evidence derived from examinations of the
children themselves, and it must be borne in mind that many of the
youngest of these Children have to carry coals on their backs, from the
workings to the surface, up steep ladders." The father of a six-year-old
daughter had difficulty in lifting a fifty-pound basket of coal onto the back
of his child—yet children only five years old were found to be dragging as
much as fifty pounds of coal in "pans" from the face to haulage ways.
Some, on hands and knees, pulled their burdens through passages that only
they could pass, since the clearance was only eighteen inches high. Women
hauled carts to which they were attached by a chain passing between their
legs. A thirty-seven-year-old mother said this was "hard work for a woman,"
adding that the "belt and chain is worst when we are in a family way."[4]

The same treatment of miners, including those of tender years, was common in Europe. No one more effectively described those atrocities than
Emile Zola in his striking novel *Germinal*. The terror comes through vividly
in Zola's picture of four miners at work where the coal seam was barely
twenty inches high,

and they were flattened between roof and wall, dragging themselves along by their knees and elbows. . . . they had to lie on one side with a twisted neck, arms above their heads, and wield their short-handled picks slant-ways. . . . At the top, the temperature went up to 95 degrees, air could not circulate, and [the miner] was stifled to death. . . . But it was the wet that really tortured him, for the rock, only a few centimeters above his face, incessantly dripped fast and heavy drops with maddening regularity always on the same spot. Try as he might to twist his neck and bend his head backwards, the drops splashed relentlessly on his face, pit-a-pat. In a quarter of an hour he was soaked through, what with his own sweat as well, and steaming like a wash tub.[5]

In time Americans would experience similar, although not often quite so gruesome, working conditions in their mines. But that was to come later than in Europe; North American native tribes are not recorded as having burned any coal, the only exception being the Hopis, who, before European arrival in the Southwest, used it to fire their pottery kilns.[6] Depite the abundance of coal under American soil, it remained undiscovered until the seventeenth century, when the French explorer priest Father Louis Hennepin uncovered a significant seam on a riverbank in what would become Illinois.[7] The pace of discovery was slow, and national production in the eighteenth century was modest; much of the coal used was imported from England and Nova Scotia. Although the Revolutionary War temporarily interrupted that trade, before nineteenth-century American coal mining reached its stride, imports from Britain and Canada resumed. Coal from these sources increased from 22,000 tons in 1821 to 103,000 tons in 1842.

Early American mining development was so uneven that coal was transported to and from some unlikely places. For example, in 1750 mines near Richmond were shipping coal to Philadelphia. But Virginia's Richmond mines, surface operations using slave labor, were outclassed by the rich seams of anthracite coal found some forty years later in eastern Pennsylvania. Such discoveries were usually fortuitous; among the truly historic coal beds found by sheer accident was the treasure of high-grade anthracite beneath Pennsylvania's Lehigh Valley, literally stumbled upon in 1791. The

finder was Phillip Ginter, a settler and hunter in that valley who later wrote
of his stroke of luck:

> One day, after a poor season, when we were on short allowance, I had
> unusually bad [hunting] luck, and was on my way home, empty-handed
> and disheartened, tired and wet with the rain that commenced falling,
> when I struck my foot against a stone and drove it before me. It was nearly
> dusk; but light enough remained to show me that it was black and shiney.
> I had heard of "Stone Coal" over in Wyomink county and had frequently
> pried into rocks in hopes of finding it. When I saw the black rock, I knew
> it must be stone coal and on looking around I discovered black dirt and a
> great many pieces of stone-coal under the roots of a tree that had been
> blown down. I took the pieces home with me and the next day carried
> them to Col. Jacob Weiss, at Fort Allen.
>
> A few weeks after this, Col. Weiss sent for me and offered to pay for my
> discovery if I would tell him where the coal was found. I accordingly of-
> fered to show him the place if he would get for me a small tract of land
> and water power for a saw-mill that I had in view. This he readily promised
> and afterward performed. The place was found, and a quarry opened in
> the coal mountain. In a few years the discovery made thousands of for-
> tunes; but I may say it ruined me, for my land was taken from me by a
> man who said he owned it before I did, and now I am still a poor man.[8]

The great anthracite bed in Mauch Chunk Mountain had high-grade coal
that at its deepest was seventy feet thick. The Lehigh Coal Mine Company
developed the find and took over the Philadelphia market.[9] At about the
same time, coal began arriving in Pennsylvania from a surprising source:
Rhode Island. Anthracite from a seam covering parts of Rhode Island and
Massachusetts became the American counterpart of "coals to Newcastle"
—going to Pittsburgh. Its quality was low and the vein so twisted that it
was difficult to extract economically; nevertheless, some coal was produced
in New England during most of the nineteenth century. Just to speculate:
how different might southern New England have been had its coal deposits
been more bountiful? How might it have looked if pocked with coal shafts,
tipples, slag heaps, and company town remnants? A coal-country ambiance
would have made for a physical, social, and economic scene significantly
different from its rural, mill-town, and suburban atmosphere.

Early nineteenth-century coal development owed much to the canals that were constructed throughout the Northeast at the time, greatly reducing the cost and increasing the speed of moving coal from mine to market. Land transport by wagon was slow and expensive; roads were bad, and horses or oxen moved at a modest speed. Canal travel was also fairly slow but inexpensive. Canals such as the Delaware and Hudson, running 108 miles from Philadelphia to New York, revolutionized coal transport, serving a rapidly expanding market. The Delaware and Hudson, at the height of its days of service in 1863, transported 1.5 million tons of coal, stimulated by the demand of the Civil War.

Yet even as the canals were becoming important channels of commerce, they were already being challenged by the new steam locomotive. Railroads offered irresistible competition for moving most bulk goods. Not hampered by freezing during the season of heaviest coal demand, and swifter than the slow-plodding animals that towed the canal boats, trains soon took most of the coal trade. In fact, the expansion of railroads and the growth of coal production went hand in hand. When railroads came on the scene in the 1830s they used wood to fire their steam locomotives; even the first trains to move coal were actually fired with wood. But the pound-for-pound superiority of coal over wood soon converted trains into burners as well as shippers of coal (which also had the advantage of not spraying sparks over the countryside and starting forest fires). Steamships, then also in development, became heavy coal consumers, and in time steam-rollers, steam shovels, farm equipment, textile mills, and other steam-powered machinery came on the market, all boosting coal demand.

Coal production grew as industrial expansion accelerated in the American version of the Industrial Revolution of the nineteenth century. First, blacksmiths relied on anthracite's high heat and long-burning qualities. Then commercial smelting of ore into iron used increasing amounts of coal, and in time soft coal was converted into coke, which produced the high heat necessary for making steel. For a time hard coal took over the home-heating market, where its low ash and long-lasting characteristic made it popular. Expanding demand encouraged investors to enter the race to produce more coal—and the investment paid off handsomely. The period 1821 to 1842 illustrates that expansion. Imported coal, as previously noted, increased by a factor of five during those twenty-one years; the quantity of coal supplied to the northeastern market by Virginia grew from 40,000 to 68,750 tons; and anthracite boomed from 1,000 to 1,100,000 tons.[10] Indeed, takeoff in coal output during the nineteenth century was dramatic. Little coal was mined in America at the end of the eighteenth—only 108,000 tons in 1800—but in 1835 production exceeded 1 million tons and reached 4 million tons in 1850. By the end of the century annual tonnage amounted to 111 million.[11] Even so, coal mining in the 1800s barely scratched the surface of the huge country's reserves.

In the twentieth century the demand for coal, whipped on by world wars and industrial growth, resulted in the opening of thousands of isolated mines around the country.[12] In the Appalachian and midwestern fields countless small-time local entrepreneurs invested in scattered coal ventures, especially as rail lines extended into the mountains. Some of them made fortunes, some went broke. But eventually, most of the families that got accustomed to wealth and enjoyed European-style mansions (like those of the Watson family, originators of the Consolidation Coal Company, sheltered behind high brick and iron fences on Fairmont Avenue in Fairmont, West Virginia) had to readjust to lesser styles of living as the industry fell on hard times following 1929. In the early 1930s there were hundreds of closed mines, and the Fairmont mansions stood empty as an unemployed miner's lunch bucket.[13] Most of the surviving moguls lost out to or were squeezed out by absentee corporations whose directors foresaw a coming boom in coal and made ready to take advantage of it by buying up land and mineral rights for future exploitation, acquiring these means to riches for bargain prices from unsuspecting farmers in the hills of Kentucky and West Virginia particularly.[14] Then came the corporate takeovers as ownership and control passed to corporate officers located far from the coalfields in remote Philadelphia, Boston, New York, and London.

But it was not in these eastern and central states alone that coal awaited exploitation. Commercially viable deposits of coal are buried in twenty-six of the fifty states. Of the vast bulk of the nearly one billion tons of coal now produced annually in this country, however, only a minuscule proportion is anthracite, hard coal, from eastern Pennsylvania. Most of the rest is bituminous and comes from eleven states spanning three fields: Appalachian (including western Pennsylvania, West Virginia, eastern Kentucky, extreme western Virginia, central Tennessee, and northern Alabama), midwestern (from western Kentucky, Illinois, and Indiana), and Rocky Mountain (primarily Wyoming, Montana, and New Mexico).

The three regions produce distinctly different types of coal. The coal of Appalachia is high-quality bituminous with low to medium sulfur content; most of it goes to furnaces that generate electricity and some to industries such as chemicals and steel. Midwestern coal has a high sulfur content and is primarily burned to make electricity. Rocky Mountain coal is lower grade than eastern coal (meaning it produces less heat per unit burned) but competitive in price—even though transportation to major markets is expensive—for two reasons: its very low sulfur content makes unnecessary the expensive smokestack scrubbing that rids emissions of pollution, and the fact that it lies in veins close to the surface but as much as 200 feet thick, making extraction by surface mining unprecedentedly cheap. An important development in the coal industry of the last two decades has been the development of northern Wyoming's "ten-mile hole in the ground." The term is used by some geologists to describe these huge mines of northern Wyoming. Operators there justify strip-mining's damage to the environment by the vast quantity of coal which, owing to its depth, can be taken from a relatively small area—even though the land may be beyond restoration because of the low annual rainfall. Whatever the validity of that argument, the production of the Powder River Basin coalfield has altered the industry fundamentally as Wyoming has surged ahead to become the country's leading coal producing state; it passed West Virginia and Kentucky in 1990 and increases its lead every year (see figure 1).

It is significant that these strip-mining operations in the West are almost impossible for the United Mine Workers to organize. As a result, an increasing percentage of the nation's coal is mined by nonunion workers, thereby freeing the corporate coal directorate of one potential restraint on its independent power.

2

The Political Economy of Coal

In 1939, as a senior in high school, I confided in my diary my bright idea about writing a book on coal mines: "I spontaneously got an idea for a book while cleaning the front room today." The next entry shows that the thought was still percolating: "I am still thinking over that notion of a book on the mines." That said, I never seriously entertained the venture again for the next forty years. What gave rise originally to the juvenile dream I have no recollection. I certainly knew very little about the coal industry then, and a large part of what I thought I knew was wrong, for like most coal-country people I entertained a lot of patently false beliefs about the industry and its role in the complex social-economic-political system of the country.

Innocently ignorant of the way the leaders of the industry managed to influence what we thought, I didn't know that over a thousand men a year were being killed in American mines. I wasn't aware of efforts to pass federal mine safety legislation to stop the slaughter; had I been told that industrial leaders could suppress potential regulation by controlling the legislative agenda—and doing so in back rooms, unreported by the press—I would have been very skeptical. That the industry used its political power to influence the marketplace and manipulate capital investment, environmental degradation, tax policy, wages and working conditions, employment opportunities, and much more never darkened my naive thoughts. Instead my mind was filled with simplified versions of the blessings of "free enterprise."

Not for the next forty years or more would I realize the ugly truth about black lung, the disease that killed coal miners by the thousand annually. I am embarrassed to confess that as late as the 1960s I still believed that black lung disease did not affect bituminous miners, having been fed the line that only the abrasive grit of anthracite damaged the lungs. I remember seeing a miner grab a handful of coal dust and stuff it in his mouth to illustrate its harmlessness; it did not occur to me that ingesting dust was not the same as breathing it. In the 1940s and for decades thereafter I would remain oblivious to what was going on in Britain to cope with black lung—a successful campaign to eliminate a scourge that the American industry preposterously refused to concede even existed.

That West Virginia lacked sufficient income to provide public services I obviously knew, and especially that funds for education were woefully inadequate, having been among the thousands of high school students who went on strike in the spring of 1938 when the governor ordered a closing of schools a month early because the state treasury had run dry. For students with college aspirations the county board of education set up some special consolidated high schools to provide a useless extra month of classes at a fee of $10, as I recall—a sum that many could ill afford but paid in order not to jeopardize the validity of high school diplomas. This shifting of school financing to hard-pressed, low-income families was something we recognized, of course, but nearly fifty years would pass before it was documented that a major reason for the grievous shortfall in state revenue was the refusal of absentee coal corporations to pay an equitable tax on the property and mineral rights they owned. And I would have had to be pretty dense to have been unaware of the highly regressive Depression-era sales tax levied at a time when I was a drugstore clerk and had to listen to endless condemnation of politicians who dared to impose taxes on food and medicine that the poor had to spend a disproportionate percentage of their income to purchase. Yet I do not remember the complainers fulminating about the coal companies that successfully corrupted the politics of coal

states (especially West Virginia and Kentucky) to make corporate tax evasion as dexterous and nonrevealing a trick as the one Sally Rand did in those
days with her fan of feathers.

I had a lot to learn before I rolled a clean sheet of paper into the typewriter
and put "1" on the first page of the "book on the mines." That education
was chiefly a gradual discovery that the coal industry can be understood
only by looking at the political economy of the fuel that turned on the
Industrial Revolution in America and keeps generating indispensable electricity for a plugged-in society.

Before considering the institutional context of the industry, however, I
turn first to the essential human factor in the productive chain: the coal
miner's place in the competitive complex. Miners are not helpless figures
in the formation of energy policies, but in comparison with the other major
actors in the drama they are puppets on strings controlled by other actors.
Excerpts from my diaries for 1938 through 1940 show how a proud, independent, and hard-working coal miner—my father—was harassed by forces
he could neither control nor even significantly influence without severe
consequences not only for himself but for every member of his family.

Beleaguered Miner, 1938–40

The late 1930s were a difficult time for the coal industry: the economy had
not yet escaped the grip of the Depression; unemployment was still high;
and the war stimulus lay in the future. Mines in West Virginia almost never
had the demand to justify a full week's work. My father usually got no more
than one or two days a week, and a three-day week was good news. Everyone was acutely aware of whether the mines were scheduled to open the
next day. My diary often recorded, "Dad's going to work tomorrow," an unusual family concern for the typical self-centered teenager. I sometimes
walked (or hitchhiked) to pick up his semimonthly pay envelope for him,
and I noted in my daily jottings such sums as $30 and $33. He was a hard
worker, undaunted by the demands of loading coal; he met the stipulation
laid down by a character in a James Still novel: "Hain't nothing wrong with
hard work, if they's enough of it."[1] He accepted the discipline of the mine

and supplemented his meager income by gardening and keeping livestock whenever possible.

Yet he never stopped searching for his ticket out of the mine; in that he was like many miners who were ever looking for other ways to earn a decent living, but there were few alternatives that paid a living wage. One of his favorite dreams of escape was to build and operate a roller-skating rink to take advantage of what was then becoming a popular pastime. He was encouraged in this escape fantasy by a brother-in-law who specialized in spinning dreams and was a master at stretching facts to fit illusions and leaving a false impression of anticipated glory where none was warranted. A charmer and deceiver, he led Dad into a venture that left nothing to show for the planning, physical labor, and fruitless fund-raising efforts. Not surprisingly, money to keep the dream afloat was not forthcoming, and the partially built structure passed into the hands of the creditor who had supplied building materials—but not before a lot of hard labor had gone into the construction. I was among the construction crew and had been delighted at the prospect of earning 60¢ an hour, but the ill-fated venture went insolvent before my first payday came around.

I had given up a job at the drugstore in Worthington—where we lived at the time—in order to join the construction gang. It wasn't much of a sacrifice—the pay there was 10¢ an hour, and I quit despite the generous offer to raise it to 11¢—but from the time I was thirteen years old until I was nearly seventeen I had worked daily in that store. I swept up and stoked the potbellied stove mornings before I went to school, waited on trade afternoons and evenings until the druggist returned from dinner, cleaned up the place, shelved inventory, and made ice cream in summer. I earned about $2.00 a week, which made little contribution to the family—although I do remember putting part of my income in the spot behind the right-hand door of the kitchen cabinet where the family's small-change exchequer was kept. In 1938 we lacked the funds to buy our annual automobile license plates, and according to my diary I helped finance the license renewal. (That was partly self-serving, however, for in West Virginia then one could legally drive at age fifteen, and I loved cars and did my bit toward subverting an excellent interurban rapid transit trolley line by driving wherever I could, spending 19¢ a gallon for gasoline.)

But giving up any job was risky, since other jobs were scarce or nonexistent, and when in the early summer the skating rink went bust, I took a job that paid me nothing in cash: I signed on to dig ditches for the Worthington water department (it was not a company town) in order to pay off a water bill some months in arrears. I worked under the supervision of a retired Scotsman who taught me how to create a straight ditch for laying pipe. That was before the day of backhoes; ditches came to be when someone applied a long-handled shovel and swung a big pickaxe. At least it was good training for loading coal. And it helped make ends meet, which was a matter of great concern, for my diary says Dad expressed fear that we might lose the car and the refrigerator because we were behind on payments for both of them.

In June of 1938 came the ominous rumor that 347 (rumors are always so misleadingly precise!) men were to be laid off at Carolina mine, and we were all apprehensive that Dad would be among the unfortunate ones because of the supposed rule that the company laid off first those who did not rent company houses. That fear stirred our investigation of housing in Monongah, three miles to the north of Worthington. Anything was preferable to returning to Hutchinson where, before the Worthington years, we had lived in a small, isolated, company store-only community that Mother hated with a passion, for as a boss's daughter she felt middle class and above living in a working-class town. She liked Worthington—a town on the West Fork River where about four hundred people lived in twin rows of houses strung along the valley between a mountain and the river—but she raised no objection to the move; holding a job, after all, was paramount. Nobody doubted that Consol's rule slated nonrenters as first-to-be-fired; the rumor had the force of "law" because it was believable and therefore believed. I do not recall that anyone was dismissed for that reason, but after-the-fact memory is more rational than on-the-spot fear. Discipline comes not only with clearly stipulated edicts but also with beliefs about what those with authority have up their powerful but arbitrary sleeves.

Moreover, there was something to be said for Monongah with its two thousand residents scattered over hill and valley on two sides of the West Fork River and some non-company-owned businesses: bank, movie theater, small restaurants, drugstore, auto repair shop. The high school for the region was there, and several churches. It was a company town, yes, but not a typical one-company-dominated community. Accordingly, we found a vacant house there, and in August 1938 we moved—again.

During the summer if there was arable land available, Dad would find it, whether on a remote mountainside where a coal company owned land but paid no attention to it or nearer home and open to be rented for a small sum. In the summer of 1939 Dad and I set out two hundred tomato plants and eighty cabbages, planted bushels of seed potatoes, row after row of pole beans, and half an acre of sweet corn, plus cucumbers, beets, and carrots. My diary notes frequent trips into the woods to cut saplings for tomato stakes and beanpoles, and I learned to use strips of bark to tie up my loads for shouldering them back to the patch. I also reported, in years when we had gardens near the river, that I hauled endless buckets of water to relieve summer drought—and in retrospect I marvel that the sulfur-laden water pumped into the river from the mines didn't kill the plants we were trying to save.

In lean times we had help from our extended family in keeping the pantry shelves from becoming empty. Our tomato and cabbage plants, for example, often came from an uncle who had a greenhouse that I (a little bit, anyhow) had helped him build. One year a strike continued for six weeks, and the larder ran very low. (Looking back, I see now why my mother at times left the supper table in tears; I didn't realize in my youthful ignorance that it must have been the strain brought on by a simple lack of food to go around and questions about tomorrow's supplies.) The day before that prolonged strike ended, my mother's uncle, who ran a grocery store in Fairmont, turned up at our door with baskets of groceries. I was impressed and wrote, "A lot of food. Boy! Do we need it." Grandfather Lockard, who had a gristmill, contributed bags of cornmeal for making cornbread and other good things, and he gave us bushels of apples from his orchard and succulent blackberries from his cultivated vines. He lived some seventy-five miles south of us, so we converted our 1926 Oldsmobile two-door sedan into a truck by removing the rear seat cushions and placing stiff cardboard around the back. (The Olds was also our coal truck: we used that dependable piece of vitally important machinery to haul burlap bags of coal from the Carolina tracks and slate dump; never once did we buy coal for heating purposes during the Depression years.)

We also went to the open fields and woodlands for nuts and berries, available in quantity to all takers. Dad would wake me before sunrise, and we would go out early enough to pick our load before the August sun got too hot. Often we would get ten or more gallons of blackberries to be canned in quart jars for winter pies, or made into jam and jelly. The processing was as big an undertaking as the picking, and Dad would stay on the job until the last jar was sealed and shelved. He kept on helping Mother with this chore long after I had left home for the army. In fact, during the war he worked nine-hour days, six days a week, and still found time to get to the berry patch and then help preserve what he had brought home.

The Work Ethic

Indeed, my father's commitment to work was so complete that it was a defining characteristic of his life. He was in some ways a workaholic—although the term suggests such a helpless addiction to work that enjoying relaxation is impossible, and that didn't describe his way of life; he could relax and enjoy himself. During vacations I have played croquet with him for hours, even when we should have been driven indoors by day-long drizzle. He was also a reader—of novels, history, newspapers, and magazines. He could relax when tired, but tiredness was insufficient reason for him to cease his labors. When, after nine hours in the mine, he was spending his evenings digging a cellar and carting away the dirt in a wheelbarrow, he wrote in his diary "It's got to be done."

It is an interesting question why so many men of his generation were so committed to hard labor. I think in my father's case it may have been his sense of having ability that he never found a chance to exploit. Certainly he had the intelligence to perform more intellectually demanding jobs than loading coal, but he had chosen to leave school after the eighth grade, despite his father's urging him to get more education. "Dad wanted me to stay in school," he once told me, "but I wanted to go to work—and I'm still working."

I believe it was this feeling that he had not taken advantage of his potential ability that led him to emphasize education—not in a preachy or commanding manner but with a quiet attitude that "this is the normal thing for an intelligent young person to do, getting an education." When he and I talked about my going to work in the mines, there was never even any discussion of why I was doing it—to finance my transfer from a state teachers college to West Virginia University. I was the first in my family on either side to go to college anywhere, except for a half-brother, my father's son from an earlier marriage. He had never lived with my family, however, and if any outside stimulus led him toward higher education, it came not from his father but from an aunt who raised him after his mother died in his infancy. As for me, when I try to answer the frequent question "How come you decided to go to college, given your background?" (implicitly insulting as it is), I include my mother's influence too. She was highly conscious of her heritage of respectability, for like her mother before her she felt she was above the common run of coal-camp people. If my father was subtle and quiet about education and getting on in the world, my mother was volubly outspoken about "moving on up," and school achievement was a means to that end.

Consequently, when I finished high school in 1939, I was highly aware of our financial situation, for money was the key to the door of my future. I wanted to go to West Virginia University, but because it was twenty-five miles from Monongah, I would have had to live away from home, and I could not afford that. Next best was Fairmont State Teachers College, a traditional normal school on its way to becoming a four-year liberal arts school. FSTC was only six miles away, within easy hitchhiking distance, meaning that I could live at home and save money. Tuition was only $30 a semester, and I thought I could manage that—I so thought, that is, before the dreadful summer of 1939, when jobs were few. I sought work everywhere I could imagine or anyone suggested. I got sore feet one day tramping to nineteen places—and being rejected in nineteen places. I went to a

coal mine, a hospital, restaurants, supermarkets, and department stores—
and for a while I thought I'd been hired by the Monongah company store—
but all to no avail.

Then, unexpectedly, the brother of a friend took a franchise on a gas
station and offered me the job of running it during the daytime with pay
on a commission basis: a small percentage on each gallon of gas and quart
of oil sold, and the whole take for tire repair. It sounded dubious, but I was
in no position to be choosy, so in mid-June I started "work" nine to twelve
hours a day. There wasn't much work involved, since few cars went by; jobs
were so scarce that no one could afford to go anywhere. I got a lot of reading done, finishing several Charles Dickens novels by mid-summer, but the
gravity of the situation soon became apparent: at the end of the first week
I had earned a total of $4.35, and after a month I had $14.65 in the bank. I re-
proached myself for having wasted 20¢ on a movie; I liked the movie (*Stand
Up and Fight*) but regretted the loss of revenue. My diary entry reports the
extravagance: "Every cent I make MUST go toward school; I want to be a
LAWYER!" I was accustomed to being parsimonious. In late spring our senior class trip had been downgraded from a bus ride to Washington, D.C.,
to a truck jaunt to nearby Cooper's Rock for an afternoon picnic, and I
came close to missing even that until someone allowed me to owe the 40¢
the trip cost. But now every penny counted in a quite concrete way.

How concretely it mattered became clear in September. In late August
the gas station owner gave up the venture—joining that long line of disappointed coal miners and other aspirants to independence via business
franchise—and I had a bank account of little more than $20. Despite a brief
stint as a door-to-door book salesman, the day when I would have to face
the bursar with less than $30 in my hand was growing near. All summer I
had counted on the possibility that I would get a part-time job under the
National Youth Administration, a New Deal agency that aided students
through a work program; I had consulted the dean of men at the college
in July, and he had encouraged me about my prospects for an NYA place.
Then came a letter from the dean on September 6 with matriculation less
than a week away. The mimeographed form letter was abrupt:

Mr. Duane Lockard
Monongah, W. Va.
Dear Sir:

We regret very much our inability to offer you anything in the line of work-aid allotment at the beginning of the school year. Our government allotment is limited to ten per cent of our enrollment. . . and we have had about four times the number of applicants we could accept.

We hope that you will see your way clear to enroll even without the benefit of an allotment. Some vacancies will occur from time to time and at the end of the semester. . . . As the year goes on we usually manage to find some place for the majority of those who enroll and ask assistance.

Cordially yours,
John W. Pence
Dean of Men

To say I was disappointed puts it mildly. True, there was a postscript: "I have been interested in your application. If there are withdrawals, you are among the first we shall call." But how could I enroll without the tuition fee? Urging me to do so when I manifestly couldn't seemed to rub salt in the wound. I read the letter over and over through welling tears as I sat alone in our beat-up 1928 Dodge, cussing all concerned a blue streak. It seemed my hopes were dashed, and I would have to adjust to failure. Then I said, "God damn them all, I am going to get in somehow!" So on the appointed day, wearing new pants I had had to buy to replace a split pair—and costing about $5.00 of my sparse savings—I proceeded down the line of tables, selecting courses and registering successfully until I came to the outstretched hand of the bursar.

"That's $30, please," she said gently.

"All I've got is $15," I answered, offering my half fare.

Though embarrassed to hold up the line for folks with cash in hand, I gave no ground. When she suggested I talk with Dean Pence about our little impasse, I hurriedly agreed. He explained the harsh realities of athletics and college administration: priorities put athletes in front, and I was no athlete. That was not what he said, of course, but we both knew what he meant when he spoke of places usually opening up in late November—

that is, when football season ended. Pending that, he said, he would allow me to matriculate for half the amount due. I still recall the broad smile he always seemed to wear, and I remember that day with fondness for him; he did all he could, and it worked. As it turned out, resignations did come, and in January I got a job shelving books in the college library. Later I cleaned a chemistry lab and became assistant to a historian. Thus the government's NYA let me begin college, and the GI Bill paid my way through my Ph.D.— a good investment, I have always thought.

The two years at Fairmont State were a lean season; NYA jobs paid little, and my father couldn't help much, because he worked on the average only every other day, so other work was necessary to cover tuition and minimal expenses. I did odd jobs such as cutting Christmas trees on an uncle's land; I kept a steady fire under the superintendent of the Carolina mine— first for an outside job and then, when I was old enough, for inside work. But the mines weren't hiring at that time, and since the local economy was attached to the coal umbilical cord, local businesses faltered too when the demand for coal was weak. And that played into the hands of unscrupulous merchants who took advantage of the overstocked labor market.

One of those leeches was named Brooks, though his employees called him a wide range of more vivid names, and he ran an all-night Fairmont eatery called Brooks' Grill. He exploited his help ruthlessly, and he could not only get away with it; he could count on a measure of gratitude from young men and women glad to have any job and be earning even a Brooks-style wage when others were still searching for work. In his ruthlessness he was a case study in extremes. His waiters worked eighty-four hours a week and were paid $11.50, less than 14¢ an hour. It looked a little better if, as he claimed, he was paying us $15 a week but deducting $3.50 for our meals (and as growing boys we got our money's worth—if we could convince "Cookie" Wilson to make whatever we called for on the pretense that a customer was ordering a big midnight meal). Even so, that put our pay at less than 18¢ an hour. Nor did we make up the deduction in tips—they were in fact rare; I once experienced unexpected generosity when I got a 50¢ tip for serving a family dinner to three generations and felt uncommonly well treated by grandpa.

In my diary I summed up that job by saying I was tired of the sevens: seven days a week, from seven P.M. to seven A.M., with seven hours of sleep if it wasn't so hot you couldn't sleep. But we were young and could skip sleep; we found that in the wintertime we could work overnight, attend classes in the day, then go to a dance in the evening, all without ever going to bed at all. During the summer of 1940 Brooks promoted me to night manager with a bountiful increase of a dollar a week. Then I learned one of his lessons on honesty: if the cash next morning was less than the tape showed, the difference was withdrawn from the manager's pay, but if it was more, Brooks took it as profit. The flaw in this rule came out the night Brooks took over the register during a busy after-movie rush and gave my friend change for a twenty when he'd been given a ten. When my friend looked in his wallet while getting ready for bed, he realized what had happened, so he got dressed and returned the extra ten to me. Brooks never admitted making the error, but if my friend had not noticed or had been greedy, I would have lost most of a week's wage.

In truth Brooks was the typical exploiter of labor. To keep from reverting to the overalls and carpenter tools from which he had raised himself and to continue in symbolic white shirt and tie, he used people. To pay off his mortgages he had to show a profit. We laughed at the sight of old Brooks almost in tears when he saw spoiled steak that obviously had to be thrown away, but that was the reason he had to get the first two days' hard work out of apprentice waiters without paying them a penny: if you don't cut corners on the innocent, the knowing will cut corners on you. But the going labor market was not as bad as Brooks tried to make it; after leaving his sweatshop I went to work weekends in the new A&P supermarket down the street. I was paid 25¢ an hour for bagging groceries and never ate another meal in Brooks' Grill.

If I seem bitter about Brooks and his ilk, that is because I am. Yet what he did in taking advantage of us was less heinous than what generations of mine bosses did, either on their own initiative or at the behest of higher management. For as a flood of evidence demonstrates, (see chapter 4), more than 100,000 miners' lives have been sacrificed on the altar of "profit before humanity."

Whose Profit? Whose Loss?

I illustrate my argument by using a nonhuman example: mine mules and horses. I can recall no instance of conversation with miners about them that did not evoke some note of sympathy for these animals, denied fresh air and green grass for months or years on end, whether at work hauling coal or in their underground stables. Stories abound that these ancient nags, when their usefulness was past, were freed in green pastures; where they frolicked like colts. It was not sympathy that finally set them free from their haulage yokes, however, but the greater cost-effectiveness of motors, conveyer belts, and rubber-tired buggies.

Similarly, I suppose no mine bosses take explosions or roof collapses lightly; if nothing else, they were—and are—expensive in dollars as well as lives. Even injuries can be costly—by one company's reckoning, injuries ended up costing more than fatalities.[2] But they gambled with the lives and limbs of miners, the human equivalent of those mine mules. No one intended to kill anyone else; no one desired a loss of millions in equipment or from long periods of nonproduction. Still, the poker hand dealt the operator led him to risk losing his shirt in a disaster, for the percentage move dictated that he take the chance his "reasonably safe" mine would survive without trouble, rather than pay out large sums to insure *against* trouble. As long as the law didn't require safety measures, American mine owners played percentage poker—treating lives as relatively low-cost poker chips and making a bundle in the process.

The aptness of the gambling analogy is suggested by something that occurred during the early stages of my research for this book. A Princeton colleague invited me to participate in an "alumni college" in which faculty spoke on current work that might interest returning alumni. I talked about the tragic massacre of American miners in contrast to the much lower rate of killing in British and European mines at that time (the early 1980s), and I used the most common measure of industrial endangerment: the death and injury rates per million man-hours of labor. I observed that not only were the American rates much higher than the British but that the American industry was not closing the gap. In the discussion period one alumnus (from the coal industry, I suspected, because he quoted pertinent statistics) said it was misleading to use the rate per million man-hours; I should instead be measuring the rate per million tons of coal produced, and on that basis he cited data to show an improvement in the American record in recent years. (He didn't say the British rate calculated his way had actually gone up slightly in the same period, reflecting lower productivity in British mines despite the low number of accidents, but he could have, had he known that fact.)

Which, then, is the appropriate measure of the incidence of accidents in mining? That depends on what you are trying to examine: the productivity of mines or the exposure of miners to danger. The per-million-tons figure measures the amount of coal mined against the number of accidents, and nowhere else in the world do miners produce as much coal per working miner as in American mines. As shown in the next chapter, 60 percent of American mining is done on the surface, where falling roofs and explosions do not threaten workers; our underground mining too has greatly increased in productivity, thus reducing the per-million-ton rate sharply. That does not mean American mines are safer, only that they are more productive—a very different matter as seen by workers as opposed to statisticians.

The implications of using the productivity index can be seen in the inferences drawn by a historian in discussing accident rates for a Virginia coal company whose data he examined: between "1919 and 1924, the Stonega Company averaged 4.09 men killed per million tons of coal mined." He notes that this figure was higher than that for the American bituminous industry as a whole (3.45) but lower than the British average of 4.57.[3] Measured by man-hours of exposure to danger, however, the British preoccupation with safety paid off in fewer miners dead and wounded, even if less coal was produced per accident (chapter 4 provides data comparing U.S. and U.K. rates).

Defenders of the coal industry emphasize that competitiveness in the fuel market has forced coal operators to take desperate steps just to remain alive and functioning. Competition, they say, sets the parameters of initiative in the industry. A major portion of that competition is between fuels, mainly coal and oil and, to a lesser degree, natural gas. Petroleum was found in Titusville, Pennsylvania, in 1859; it first substituted for whale oil in lamps, and in fact, its use was limited until gasoline engines were developed. At the beginning of the twentieth century, coal was still king of fuels, accounting for 70 percent of the energy used in the United States, but its share dropped steadily thereafter. Coal was efficient (22 million Btu per ton), but oil (roughly 20 million Btu in four barrels) was cheap, abundant, easily transported, and readily adaptable (as was natural gas). Hence, petroleum products' percentage of the market grew as coal lost ground—and their competitive position was enhanced by political clout. In 1926 oil interests persuaded Congress to give them a lucrative tax break known as a depletion allowance, which permitted oil companies to subtract 27.5 percent of their gross revenues from their taxable income. The ostensible reason for this gratuitous treatment was that no one could predict when the oil in a working well would be exhausted. Once in place, this subsidy was almost beyond challenge, as the politicians of Texas, Oklahoma, and other big oil states successfully fought off enemies for four decades. Oil speculators became millionaires, and they had the power to advance oil at the expense of coal, which had a depletion allowance of only 10 percent.[4] In the years just after World War II, oil severely undercut coal sales, which became a major excuse for the coal industry not to spend money on safety provisions.

Competition also came from within coal's own ranks.[5] When demand ran high, the opportunity to invest in small mines with relatively modest capital outlays meant that low-priced coal flooded the market. One would not expect what were called doghole mines—which operate on a shoestring, often with family members as miners—to be able to compete with large corporate operations, but they did and still do. That comes in part because they are not reached by the United Mine Workers of America (UMWA) and therefore pay minimal wages, make no contributions to health and retirement funds, and often operate in primitive fashion; they lack modern safety equipment and are dependent on hard labor, much of it from laid-off experienced miners forced to work for low wages. They have been assisted by provisions of the safety laws that exempted mines with fewer than fifteen employees, an exemption larger outfits opposed as unsafe, whereas small operators claimed that being forced to buy expensive equipment would drive them out of business—which, indeed, was precisely the idea behind large corporate and UMWA opposition to the small-mine safety exemptions. Thus, although these mines are vulnerable to fluctuations in demand and often pay little on investment, they still get by—in exceptional cases even making the investors rich.

The union itself contributed to the difficulties of coal operators—by insisting on higher pay, better working conditions, and health, hospital, and retirement benefits, among other contractual demands. Since strikes, both authorized and wildcat, disrupt operations and are costly, the potential influence of union activity has greatly disconcerted corporate mine management; historically and contemporaneously, coal operators have resisted unionization with everything from infiltration by Pinkerton and Baldwin-Felts detectives and gun thugs to right-to-work legislation and judicial contempt of court fines and injunctions.

Similarly, coal operators have felt pressed by government interference with their independence.through safety regulations and, particularly in the 1930s, prounionization requirements. Operators have resisted government interference in labor matters since 1902, when Theodore Roosevelt first used the presidential office's popularity and visibility to try to settle a strike. Coal companies bitterly resented the seizure of the mines in 1947, especially when they were faced with a *fait accompli* in the Krug-Lewis agreement (see chapter 4), which established the welfare and retirement fund. Similarly, they have resisted—frequently with considerable success—government regulations to curb pollution and prevent environmental damage from strip-mining (see the discussion of the externalities concept in chapter 7).

The difficult competitive position of the large corporate mining concerns forced them into mechanization because labor costs were so large a factor in the price of coal. Small mines were even more labor-intensive, but they could cut corners because they could avoid the direct and indirect costs that unionization involved, including the royalty per ton that union mines had to contribute to the miners' health and retirement fund. UMWA president John L. Lewis fully recognized the imperatives of the large producers and collaborated with them in trying to stabilize the industry. The intervention of the union in the intra-industry conflict—involving the use of union funds to sustain some operators and undercut others—was an important aspect of industry strife in the 1940s particularly. The union's agreement to forgo strikes in exchange for wage increases and to accept mechanization no doubt strengthened key elements of the industry and aided the miners whose jobs survived the productivity boosts from mechanization. But it was disastrous for the large majority of mine workers, who lost not only their jobs but in some instances their right to medical care, even when they were desperately ill with black lung. After 1970, when the demand for steam coal to generate ever larger quantities of electricity revived the industry, most miners still got little sympathy or aid from their union. But for the leading coal outfits it was a time of profits and promise—and no better indication of that could be found than the fact that oil companies began to buy coal properties to cash in on the bonanza.

The foregoing sketch identifies some of the forces at work in the economy and political system which materially affect the lives of all concerned with coal: the management and stockholders of coal companies, miners and ex-miners and their families, consumers of energy—and indeed all people inside and outside the United States who are affected by pollution of the world's atmosphere.

3

The Productivity Revolution

MY FIRST NIGHTS with a shovel in hand were highly educational. And as weeks turned into months I kept on learning and widening my awareness of the abundant mysteries of the underground world. I had long known, for example, of the difference between "machine coal" and "pick coal"; I knew the union contract called for a bonus of a few cents more per ton for pick coal, which involved a lot more time and work because it had to be dug out entirely by hand. I am certain, however, that I had no conception of the danger of "stumping out," the final stage of what is known as "room-and-pillar" mining. By observation I began to grasp a salient fact about the relationship between mine managers and miners: one was there to drive the other to take chances with life and limb in order to maximize output per unit of compensation. Nothing better illustrated that truth than the room-and-pillar mining method.

Room-and-Pillar Mining

Like nearly all mines in the United States in the 1940s, Carolina mine used the room-and-pillar technique, a very wasteful system that left behind as much coal as it took, but it was simple and inexpensive (to the operators, that is; not necessarily to the miners) and dangerous (to the miners, that is;

not the operators). Essentially, unmined coal was used as a prop to hold up
mined-out sections, and then part of the prop would be removed, permitting the vacated space to be filled by the sinking of the whole overburden
right up to the surface. (This subsidence of the terrain sometimes caused
buildings and streets to fall into the cracks in the earth, but that part of
the story can be deferred to chapter 7.)

The room-and-pillar method mined out the coal in squares about a hundred feet on a side with the corridors around these squares emptied of coal
to the outer edge of the company's ownership of mineral rights. Then
working backward from the outermost borders of the mine, miners would
take out square by square as much of the remaining coal as could be
"robbed," in their language. Pressure on the remaining coal would be re-
lieved by permitting the roof of these undermined squares to fall in. Two
sets of miners reduced the blocks on the outer sides, entry by entry, till
nearly the whole block was removed, putting enormous pressure on the remaining "stump," as it was called. The final step in the process was the
tricky one. Many a miner died "stumping out" that last coal prop.

Pulling a stump was not only dangerous; it was also arduous, for nearly
everything had to be done by hand. Electrical cutting machines could not
be used under so unpredictable a top, that meant the undermining had to
be done in the old-fashioned manner, using a pick to cut away the layers
of coal. As the undermining progressed, the pressure on the remaining
supporting wall increased, and the coal would begin to act strange. At
one point when I was working with my pick, several pieces of coal suddenly shot out into my face and cut a notch on my nose, leaving a scar that
lingered for decades before the bits of coal dust under the skin finally disappeared.

During my first week in the mine I experienced the ultimate phase of
room-and-pillar mining—blowing the stump: that is, dynamiting the final
block of coal. As the coal around me made noises like strings of small fire-
crackers popping off, I cranked away at a hand drill (made like an old-
fashioned brace and bit, but about five feet long). When the hole was
deep enough, Dad put in a stick of powder and detonated it. Everything
seemed to be falling; huge hardwood posts eight to ten inches in diameter

broke like toothpicks under the crushing weight of the mountain as it settled in to fill the empty space.

It is testimony to the danger of stumping out that seasoned veterans as
well as novices have died in the process. Keith Dix reports that among the
540 fatalities caused by roof falls between 1898 and 1907 in West Virginia,
61 percent of the victims had "two or more years of underground experience," and one in every five had been a miner for ten or more years. Characteristically timid state officials blamed the miners themselves for the
carnage: "Strange as it may seem, quite a number of those injured are old
experienced men" who, they added, "seem to take greater risks and continue to do so, notwithstanding the object lessons that are given to them
when other men are injured or killed under similar conditions."[1] These
state officials conform to tradition by blaming victims for their own disasters, suggesting that experienced miners had a choice about whether to
be exposed to the dangers of stumping out. No matter how long you have
worked in mines, a weakened roof is dangerous to all beneath it. It was not
a matter of bosses leaving men the choice of whether or not to risk stumping out their own pillars. Accusing experienced miners of carelessness for
letting a roof fall on them is equivalent to blaming farmers for crop failure in a summer-long drought: rain comes or doesn't; the roof holds up—
or comes down.

In the 1940s the rate for coal loaded in the stumping-out process was 96
cents a ton, 21.5 cents more than for machine-cut coal. The bonus payment
was more than justified by the extra work and considerable risk involved,
yet the miner stood to lose money because there usually was not enough
pick coal to permit him to equal what he would have earned in the same
amount of time with regular coal. Given the fact that it also required high
skill—managing a controlled accident, in effect—it merited more total
compensation, not less. The miner, after all, was risking being buried alive
or crushed to death while trying to get as much coal as possible out of the
seam before the earth reclaimed the void in the mountain.

So it was too with cleaning up after a slate fall. The work was unusually
hard because the slate was extremely heavy, loading it into cars was often
possible only after breaking up huge pieces that defied your tools and

bent the tip of your pick; and one could never be sure that loose pieces one was pulling down would not start a new avalanche. And it was poorly compensated—at the day-labor rate.

My father was a man of caution generally, but in nothing was he more careful than with a dangerous roof, stopping work often to tap it with his pick; he was able to tell from the sound whether disaster was imminent. To me it all sounded the same, but to the veteran the sounds of the coal "working" overhead were as clear as the lightning that heralds coming thunder, telling the experienced ear when the time had come to get out of the area. On one occasion when the two of us were shoveling away, Dad asked for quiet and tapped the top with a pick, read the message, and shouted, "Grab your bucket and run!" We did and with not much time to spare, for the roof soon came crashing down over everything—car, tracks, and tools but, thanks to his warning, not the miners.

On such occasions Dad must have thought of the time in the early 1930s when he was told to clear a space near a haulage passageway while the boss went elsewhere. (As a rule miners are supposed to work in pairs, but in this instance he was alone.) He was shoveling away coal debris at the edge of the track when suddenly everything broke loose and the top caved in, covering him entirely. Fortunately, he was pushed into the coal dust; he was able to breathe, but he lost consciousness, and when rescuers finally came for him, they walked over the slate and coal covering him and for a time couldn't even locate him. Several of his spinal vertebrae were cracked, and one knee was badly twisted. I remember vividly when he was brought home. One of the mine superintendent's sons, a huge man, picked Dad up from the front seat of a car as if he were a child and carried him into our house. I was about ten at the time and was desperately frightened.

In time he more or less recovered from his injuries, though the knee would trouble him for the rest of his life. But he was never one to complain or even to mention his close call. A rare reference in his diary years later speaks only of a cane his father had made for him "when I hurt my knee."

Another legacy of that accident was the mass of cuts the coal sliced in his back and upper arms, leaving them marked with countless blue scars from the coal dust that the company doctor did not bother to clean out of the wounds. They resembled the work of a tattoo artist who had doodled aimlessly on a human scratch pad. Bodies thus decorated were a common sight in the bathhouse.

In my day as a miner, machines were increasingly replacing hand labor. Some mechanization had been on the scene for a long time, of course, but many innovations got nowhere. As far back as the 1870s a puncher tool, powered by steam, came on the market—essentially a mechanical pick, capable of hammering into the seam of coal at a rate of more than a hundred times a minute—but it did not prove particularly helpful and was not used very long. In the late 1880s electricity was brought into the mines, and that made the cutting machine possible. By 1900 nearly a quarter of all bituminous coal was undercut mechanically, and twenty years later almost two-thirds.

The next major development was the mechanical loader, which made its debut in the early 1920s. In 1925 in partly experimental use in ninety-five mines, 340 of the new machines loaded 6 million tons of coal, but that was only 1 percent of the year's output.[2] The early models were called duck-billed loaders because of their vague resemblance to the scooping curve of a duck's bill. After coal had been undercut by machine and shot down with powder, the loader was shoved up against the pile of coal, and a pair of arms, working something like the blades of an egg beater, scooped up coal and passed it back on a conveyor belt to a "buggy" (more properly known as a shuttle car), which moved it to a mine car to be transported outside.[3] The duckbill made a lot of dust and a great noise, but it got out coal more rapidly than humans could possibly do, and in time it replaced manual loaders by the tens of thousands. By 1947 almost two-thirds of all coal was machine-loaded.

Not long thereafter the duckbill was in turn challenged by a new and expensive piece of machinery called the continuous miner. The new system had many advantages, particularly its high productivity. It simplified mining by eliminating several previously necessary steps. No longer was a cutter needed, and dynamite was eliminated. Barring breakdowns, a crew of three could equal the output of some seventy handloaders. The continuous miner has a revolving drum two feet in diameter and of varying width depending on the coal being worked. The drum has dozens of sharp teeth that bite into the coal directly and throw it onto a conveyer belt, which directs it to a shuttle car.

Working behind the continuous miner is a roof bolter, who shores up the top as the coal is removed. The roof bolt, which came on the scene in the 1940s, gradually replaced the timbers that had served to support the roof. It involves a platelike base attached to a four- to five-foot shaft, which is power-driven into the top; the pressure of the surrounding coal or slate secures the bolt in place and holds up the roof. Bolts are particularly suited for use with the continuous miner because unlike posts they are not subject to being knocked over by the huge machine as it maneuvers in close quarters.[4]

Like earlier versions of mechanical loaders, the continuous miner throws up clouds of coal dust, making it hard to see and hard to breathe. The voluminous dust also settles on the working area, creating an explosion hazard when electrical sparks may ignite escaping methane gas.

Longwall Mining

Continuous miners are still widely used in U.S. mines, but the prince of present and future high productivity is the longwall miner.[5] The longwall process, an alternative to the room-and-pillar method, involves mining coal on a lengthy front instead of running tunnels into the coal and then having to remove the pillars that separate them. Longwall mining was practiced in Europe long before mechanical longwall machines were developed. In fact, when I visited a coal mine in England in 1943, I saw longwall miners at work, lying on their sides to dig with their picks and then kneeling to shovel coal onto conveyer belts. The area behind the miners was held up with piles of debris and cribbing (timbers placed crisscross within squares from floor to roof so that they can sustain enormous loads).

Europeans had an incentive to adopt the technique because they were running out of accessible coal, and longwall got nearly all the coal from a seam. Given the abundance of coal in America, there was little incentive to invest huge sums in longwall equipment. In the 1970s, however, the lively competition of mammoth surface-mining machines and the improvement of longwall technology changed the situation. The incredible productivity of longwall devices, even though one of them cost as much as $5 million, provided a way to compete with strip-mining and with other fuels. The high cost of the equipment creates incentive to keep it in operation as much as possible; operators are willing to pay overtime for Saturday and Sunday production, although the union remains reluctant to permit Sunday shifts.

Longwall mining machinery is fascinating; nothing else compares with its scope of operation. No longer are there tunnels or conventional entryways; the operation takes place on a mile-long front. Two large wheels cut coal from the face and move it onto a conveyer belt. Those wheels, called shearers, have teeth of tungsten-hardened steel that chop coal along the face, and when it has finished running the mile (or more) in one direction, it can be reversed to make a cut in the opposite direction. In the process it scoops out more coal in eight hours than a whole mineful of handloaders could dig in days gone by.

In Consolidation Coal's Loveridge mine in 1989 I saw a longwall setup that whirls across a block of coal 7,000 feet wide with a depth of 750 feet. The sides of the operating front are maintained by a continuous miner, which daily removes coal to facilitate the longwall operation. Behind the machine, huge hydraulic jacks in a row along the whole working face protect the workers and the machinery from roof falls. When the mechanism has cut a swath of coal, the jacks (made of steel and strong enough to hold the top in place) are moved forward the distance of the cut, providing continuous protection. Behind the advancing jacks the top is allowed to fall, thus reducing the pressure on the roof at the working face.

The longwall uses a nine-member crew—small in proportion to the coal it produces—consisting of two shear operators, one headgate operator, three shield (hydraulic jack) operators, two mechanics, and a foreman. Breakdowns are common—and costly—in so complicated and sophisticated a piece of machinery: hence the two mechanics assigned to each crew. The record high production for a longwall operation, as of 1989, was 20,384 tons in one twenty-four-hour, three-shift workday.[6] One measure of the productivity of these monsters is that in 1989 a third of all coal taken underground was mined by the one hundred longwall machines then in operation.[7] Another indication of the impact of the new technology is that in 1989 the Consolidation Coal Company produced 55 million tons of coal with 9,500 employees, whereas fifteen years earlier 23,000 employees were required to produce the same amount of coal.[8]

At the Loveridge mine the record production of a longwall operation was 18,460 tons in three shifts (that is, twenty-seven miners) in twenty-four hours; by contrast, *four* regular continuous miner crews of eight miners each mined 5,308 tons. Another way of visualizing the output of longwall technology is to note that it would take 1,150 handloaders, doing sixteen tons each, to shovel that much coal in a three-shift day—and at far greater risk to life and limb. With respect to safety it is interesting to observe that the daily reports of the Loveridge longwall bosses regularly listed delays in machine operation for safety meetings and visits by fire bosses, who check the workplaces for gas or other hazards. I was struck too by the fact that the safety supervisor called a halt to operations until everyone present, including the visitors, was wearing protective ear covering.[9]

The longwall system does have its problems, however. One is that the very rapid removal of so much coal increases the chance that a large amount of methane may be released at the same time. Most coal-bearing strata contain methane to some extent, waiting to be released, and longwall's speed raises the possibility of a dangerous concentration of the gas. That makes adequate ventilation imperative to mix methane with fresh air and render it nonflammable. The rapid removal of coal with whirling shearers also means the dust levels are high, bringing the danger of black lung disease and reducing workers' ability to see clearly for work and safety. That calls for spraying water on the working face to minimize the dust in the air. Also longwall raises special problems of subsidence because it allows large areas of the top to collapse a short time after coal removal, and without pillars to hold the earth in place for a time, subsidence of the "big rock," as miners call the overburden, can be swift and devastating.

A smaller version of this technique is the shortwall system. Again, without the familiar tunnels of room-and-pillar operations, mining proceeds on a broad front, although the working face is likely to be 150 feet instead of a mile. The shortwall machine does not have the capacity to run backward but must retrace its steps when it finishes a swath. And the coal is taken from the face by a continuous miner protected by the heavy hydraulic shields that cover the roof across the whole active coal block. As in longwall mining, the roof behind the jacks is allowed to fall to reduce pressure. Shortwall mining has several advantages. Compared to longwall it is inexpensive to install and operate; it gets a very high percentage of the coal in the seam; and the machinery is mobile and can readily be relocated. It is safer than room-and-pillar mining, partly because of the relatively long front on which it functions and also because of the protection of hydraulic shields over the heads of the workers.

Still another method of mining is the auger system, especially suited to mining coal too deep for economical removal of the overburden (as in surface mining) and too shallow for efficient underground mining. A huge auger with a bit about five feet in diameter (depending on the seam being worked) drills horizontally into the coal from a hillside, as deep as 200 feet, and brings the coal out in the same way that a wood auger or a metal drill brings out wood or metal shavings. This is an inexpensive system that does not need a large work force, but it is wasteful because it leaves behind the coal not touched by the circle of the auger. Moreover, it creates an unsightly mess, and restoring the terrain to its original condition is somewhere between difficult and impossible.

Strip-Mining

Of all the technical innovations in mining of this century, none has been more drastic in its impact on the environment than the earth movers and power shovels of strip-mining. The first coal mining in this country was done in "open pit" style, also then called quarrying. But deep mining became the standard method, and strip-mining on a large scale had to await the development of machinery that could move deep layers of rock and dirt overburden, and the huge scooping shovel that could lift unbelievable quantities of coal in every bite. There was no reporting of the amounts of surface-mined coal prior to 1915, but it was less than 1 percent of total production. In fact, little coal was mined this way before World War II, and as recently as 1950 less than a quarter of it came from stripping. Then surface mining became more pervasive: by 1975 half the coal was removed by that method, and since 1985 more than 60 percent has been stripped.

Why has strip-mining become the dominant mode of production during the last quarter-century? The answer is simple: it is far less costly than underground mining. The financial returns from the development of surface coal reserves are so bountiful that makers of earth-moving machinery and coal-loading behemoths have invested huge amounts of capital in their development. In strip-mining the first job is to remove the stone and soil above the coal, and manufacturers developed a device capable of picking up 200 cubic yards of dirt and rock in a single bite. This is called a bucket-wheel excavator, and it can move 24,000 cubic meters of overburden in a single eight-hour shift—equivalent to excavating a football field to a depth of 15 feet. The equipment for scooping out and transporting the coal is capable of equally heroic performance: the shovel bucket can hold 22 cubic yards of coal, which it loads into trucks that carry 110 tons or more per load.[10]

This productivity makes strip-mining highly profitable, especially the since high cost of equipment is offset by the relatively low cost of labor. Hourly wages are high for operators of the specialized machinery, but especially where coal lies in very thick seams (up to two hundred feet thick in the Wyoming-Montana Powder River Basin), the productivity of these mines is far beyond anything ever achieved in underground mining. Even the less startling rates of output in eastern mountains and midwestern flatlands still greatly surpass underground production rates.

The opening of deep surface-mining pits in the upper plains states, particularly Wyoming, has moved the difference between surface and underground mining output to unprecedented levels. In 1988, for example, the Burlington and Northern Railroad moved 129 million tons of coal from the Powder River Basin; that compares with total U.S. production that year of approximately 900 million tons. The mines of Wyoming are centered in Campbell County, where enormous amounts of coal are moved daily. To begin with, this is not the small territory an easterner thinks of as a typical county. Campbell County, with 4,796 square miles, equals the land area of Connecticut, and it produces about as much coal as the whole state of West Virginia, which is five times its size. Moving such a quantity of coal is no simple matter, and it has given rise to innovations in railroad transport from the mine to point of use—mostly for generating electricity. Producing as much as 300,000 tons of coal daily, Campbell County operations alone require trains over a mile long and consisting of as many as 110 to 115 coal cars that remain coupled together permanently and move as a continuous unit, lining up for loading and then traveling to the market site and back again to the tipple for reloading.[11]

Surface mining has the decided advantage of being generally safer than underground mining. There are accidents with heavy equipment, of course, but the surface miner does not face the threat of fire, poison gas, explosions, roof falls, or the dust-impaired vision that often leads to grave injuries when miners working in very close quarters get caught by lumbering machines. Dust does endanger surface miners but is not as serious a problem as it is underground. Overall, the fatality rate in surface mining has leveled off, despite its increasing percentage of total coal production. One cannot conclude, however, that the surface mine is free of dangers to workers; in fact with underground fatality rate declining, surface fatality rates are now similar.

Strip-mining contributes significantly to the environmental problems associated with coal. Water pollution and stream silting are common to stripping operations. Water that runs off stripping sites pours large doses of sulfuric acid and other noxious minerals into rivers, lakes, and sometimes reservoirs. Soil around open mines is often devoid of vegetation because the spoil that is dumped from the mine results in serious erosion. Also, stripping machinery, especially in eastern mountainous regions, peels off the overburden and sends it cascading down the mountainside, covering whatever is in its path—gardens, cemeteries, barns, fences, livestock, houses. Often the operator cannot be held to account for the damage done, because some long-gone ancestor of the victim signed away the property's mineral rights, and mineral rights implied a right to remove whatever lay between the sky and the coal—and to disclaim responsibility for what happens when the spoil obeys the laws of gravity.

But not all landowners accept the strippers' invasions. One famous resister was the Widow Combs of Knott County, Kentucky; when the bulldozers arrived to strip her land, she simply lay down in front of them. She went to jail for a day but saved her land. Another Kentuckian, a man in his eighties, got his gun and threatened the machine operators: "I told 'em, 'somebody's going to get hot steel in 'em if you come here again.'" He was arrested later—after standing off seventeen state policemen.[12]

State laws generally require that strippers restore land to its original contour and vegetation as far as feasible; since 1977 federal law has made the same demand. But enacting such a rule is one thing, and getting it enforced is another. In the mountainous East heavy rains wash away new vegetation before it takes sufficiently deep root in the steep terrain. In the West conversely, reclamation is difficult because of drought. In the Wyoming and Montana strip-mining areas the average annual rainfall of about fifteen inches makes revegetation chancy at best. Environmentalists worry that reclamation in both East and West is difficult and perhaps even impossible; certainly it is often very expensive, and in many cases restoration has not been achieved—some say in about one-fourth of the sites that have been surface-mined.[13]

Strip-mining is controversial, and efforts to regulate the damage it does invite the same kind of evasion of enforcement that has characterized underground mining with regard to safety matters. Inspectors have often been hampered in performance of their duty by political superiors who are more concerned about excessive restraint on operators than they are about the safety of miners or injury to the terrain (see chapter 4).

For example, the Surface Mining Control and Reclamation Act of 1977 supposedly forbids granting permits for new mines when the operator in question has outstanding violations on environmental or other grounds. The prohibition was generally ignored until a computer system was inaugurated in 1984 to check the records of strippers. When coal companies challenged the computer system, the secretary of the interior sided with the companies, to the dismay of environmentalists.[14] Inspectors from the

Office of Surface Mining, Reclamation, and Enforcement claimed in 1992 that ranking officials in the Interior Department had pressed them to curtail their reporting of violations, reduce penalties, divert prosecutions, and omit inspections. In one illustrative instance the federal inspectors cited a Tennessee company that had been charged with pollution of streams and had been ordered to stop work until the violation was corrected. The company failed to comply with the law, but within three days it was back in operation. Meanwhile, the outflow from the mine killed fish in streams and eliminated vegetation from streambanks; while environmentalists complained, strippers went about business as usual.[15]

Fig. 2. Annual coal output and number of miners, 1930–90

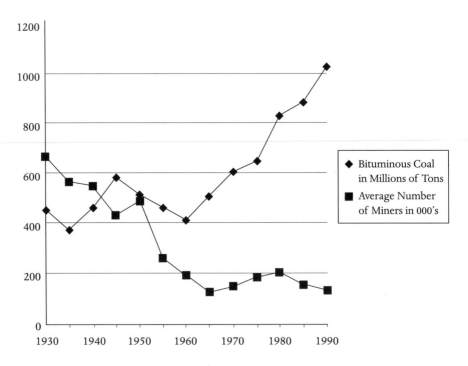

Source: Historical and Statistical Abstracts, selected years.

The combination of strip-mining with new underground production modes—the continuous miner, long- and shortwall systems—has resulted in levels of productivity hitherto unimaginable and steadily boosted the output per miner. Production boomed during and just after World War II, and in 1950 a half-million miners turned out 500 million tons. During the 1950s and 1960s the number of miners decreased, and in the 1960s the amount produced began to grow rapidly; by 1992 it took only 134,000 miners to dig nearly a billion tons. Thus, while the number of miners fell by almost three-fourths between 1945 and 1990, coal output rose from 577 million to more than a billion tons. This revolutionary development is starkly illustrated by the graph in figure 2: The production curve takes a sharp upward turn as the manpower line plummets.

Table 1. Consumption of bituminous coal and lignite, 1970–93
(in million tons)

Purpose	1970	1980	1990	1993
Electrical production	320	569	774	814
Industrial uses	184	126	76	75

Source: Statistical Abstract of the U.S., 1995, table 1200.

Table 2. Coal production increases 1970–93

Year	Daily Average per Worker (tons)	Index of Output (1987 = 100)
1970	18.84	
1975		57.8
1980	16.32	61.9
1985	23.13	85.2
1990	32.90	118.4
1993	37.71	

Source: Statistical Abstract of the United States, 1995, tables 1200, 669.

The demand for coal has expanded mainly because the ever increasing amount of electricity used by Americans has resulted in increased coal consumption, despite steady decline of industrial use of coal (see table 1). Computing the average number of tons of coal produced daily per worker (table 2) shows how rapidly productivity has advanced since 1970, having doubled by 1993. Moreover, the output index for coal mining has more than doubled; it was third highest among the seventy-one occupations covered in the Census Bureau's *Statistical Abstract of the United States* for 1995, exceeded only slightly by railway transportation and gas/electricity.

In short, as the production of coal escalates in response to insatiable demand for electricity, the work force employed dribbles away, from over 600,000 in 1930, to 135,000 in 1993, leaving it to the erstwhile miners to absorb the shock of ending a way of life that was hard and dangerous but proud and financially rewarding.

4

Health and Safety

AFTER SPENDING the summer of 1941 as a novice coal loader, I left in September to begin my third year of college, transferring to West Virginia University in Morgantown (tuition, $45 a semester), which I could now afford. Thanks to my summer job, living in a rented room away from home was also manageable. But December 7 put the world in a new perspective, and being an airplane buff, I signed up as an aviation cadet of the U.S. Army Air Corps. While my name worked its way up the waiting list, I left the university and returned to Fairmont State in order to take the second phase of the Civilian Pilot Training Program; I had completed the first stage the spring before. I dearly loved flying, and the prospect of doing aerobatics in the (comparatively) powerful Waco biplane was exciting.

I studied aerodynamics and meteorology and three other courses at FSTC and commuted (by thumb) to the airport twenty miles away in Bridgeport for flight training. I also worked weekends at Carolina mine, mainly doing maintenance work; mines were hiring freely now because of the tremendous demand for coal to fuel the arsenal of democracy. I did many different jobs—track laying, timber setting, rock-dusting (discussed below), slate fall cleanup, and haulage work—much of which was put off to weekends in order to keep production workers unencumbered by maintenance tasks. The haulage work involved gathering coal cars loaded but left behind when Friday's shift ended. One day when I was acting as a "snapper" (brakeman, in railroader's terms) for a twenty-ton electrical haulage motor, I had to throw any open rail switches along the way to keep the motor and cars from leaving the main line. The low, rectangular motor was pulling about twenty cars, each loaded with three tons of coal. The motorman shouted to me to run ahead of the "trip," as it was called, and throw a switch so as to keep us off a sidetrack loaded with empties. I had to run fast, because the trip was moving down grade at a rapid pace.

The lamps on our caps and the dust-caked light on the motor were not nearly enough to illuminate the path beside the track, which was littered with chunks of coal that had fallen from passing cars or worked loose from the roof or rib. As I ran I stepped sideways on a piece of coal and my left ankle turned, throwing me sharply to my left—across the tracks in front of the oncoming motor. The motorman, seeing my light swing in an arc, knew I had fallen and hit his brakes, but the load was too heavy and the trip moving too fast for brakes to have much effect. With, you may be assured, great speed, I scrambled to avoid the threatening wheels and missed by inches becoming a statistic in the casualty list labeled "haulage accidents, fatal." I had sprained my ankle but was otherwise unharmed and spent the rest of the day helping untangle the loaded from the empty cars.

I find it interesting that there is no reference to this close call in my diary. Was it because I felt silly for having childishly stumbled on a piece of coal? Or could I, with brash youthful assurance, have thought it too unimportant to mention? I know it was not a figment of my imagination because I remember telling my father about it. And he recalled it in a letter he wrote me two years later when I was in England: commenting on Consolidation's sale of the Carolina mine to Bethlehem Steel, he noted that among other safety changes, the new owners had walled up haulage ways with cinder blocks to reduce the trackside hazard that had nearly caught me.

Significantly, Bethlehem Steel's mining branch is a so-called "captive" company, meaning that it produces coal solely for its owner's use (in fabricating steel), and the accident records of conventional and captive mines show the latter to be the safer of the two. For example, in 1973 Bethlehem had the second best record of the top twenty coal producers, whereas Consolidation Coal ranked nineteenth.[1] (In later years Consol did work its way up to seventh of the twenty.) And in 1978–79 the disabling accident rate of all captive mines was one-third to one-half that of the conventional mines.[2]

Further corroboration of this difference was cited by Congressman Ken Hechler in debate on the floor of the U.S. House of Representatives in 1974. He commented that the coal operations of U.S. Steel and Bethlehem Steel had the lowest fatality records among all coal companies for the period 1968 to 1971 with an average of 0.36 deaths per million man-hours worked, whereas the five worst of the top ten producers (all conventional companies) an averaged 1.02 deaths. Ranking tenth was Consolidation Coal with 1.52, or more than four times the rate of the two captive companies. In the number of nonfatal injuries per million man-hours, U.S. Steel and Bethlehem ranked first and third, with an average of 7.5; the lowest-ranking five companies had an average of 57.5 injuries—a startling difference. Consolidation scored better on injuries than fatalities, ranking third at 18.7, still more than twice the captive mines' rates. Said Congressman Hechler, "The good safety record of the captive mines stems from the fact that they have a strong commitment to safety—which is exhibited in their steel operations as well—and they are free from the competitive pricing pressures of the marketplace which push other deep mine companies to cut corners on safety."[3]

The Safety Record: U.S. versus U.K.

Still, any way you look at it, the record of American coal mine safety is dismal. Since records on injuries began to be reported in the 1880s, more than 100,000 coal miners have been killed on the job, and millions have suffered serious injury. In the first three decades of this century an average of 2,210 miners were killed each year. Part of the reason for this toll of death underground is that coal mining is inherently dangerous. If the roof doesn't fall and crush you, you are endangered by clumsy machinery swinging around in restricted space in poor light and obscuring clouds of coal dust. And if that doesn't get you, there is danger lurking in high-voltage cables and in escaping gases that are poisonous or explosive. It is therefore not sur-

prising that historically coal mining has been the worst of American industries in its rate of accidental death and injury. Even in the years just after
the (long-delayed) 1969 safety legislation was enacted, miners suffered an
incidence of death and injury four times higher than that of other workers: in 1973 miners had 40.92 disabling injuries per million man-hours
worked, whereas the average for all industries combined was 10.55. In the
steel, chemical, textile, electrical equipment, aerospace, and automobile
manufacturing industries, the rate averaged 3.19 disabling injuries—in even
starker contrast with the 40.92 rate for miners.[4]

Thanks in part to the 1969 safety legislation and in part to the shift of production from underground to surface operations, coal mining, though still
one of the accident-prone industries of the nation, is no longer its worst.
As of 1993 coal mining was fourth among ten major categories of work,
ranked according to their incidence of nonfatal occupational injuries. Manufacturing led the list with 12.1 injuries per 100 full-time employees;
construction (11.5), and agriculture, forestry, and fishing (11.2) followed, pre-
ceding coal mining at a rate of 10.3.[5]

Despite this improvement, when the American safety record is compared
with those of foreign nations, the contrast is sharply evident: American
miners have been at far greater risk than their foreign counterparts, at least
for those countries for which data are available. The International Labour
Office, which formerly provided statistics of coal mine accidents in the leading coal-producing countries of the world, no longer does so, but the last
published information (1973) shows that of ten nations the two with the
worst records were Canada and the United States. Canada's average annual
fatal accident rate was 2.20 per 1,000 workers in underground mining for
the years 1963–72; the U.S. record was 1.67. At the other end of the scale with
the fewest fatalities were Poland and Great Britain, with 0.47 and 0.44 per
1,000 respectively.[6]

Although the accident record of American mines has improved since the
1970s, the relative failure to take precautions that could have saved lives can
be seen in a comparison between the rates for death and serious injury of
American and British coal mining. From 1970 to 1993 the fatality rate per
million man-hours worked in U.S. mines declined from 1.02 to 0.2, but the

British achievement is far more remarkable. In the first place, British miners were at far less risk in 1970, when the rate of fatalities was 0.18 per million man-hours worked; by 1988–89 the rate had declined substantially, to 0.06—less than one-third of the 1990 U.S. rate (see table 3).

How can these striking differences be explained? How is it that American miners in 1990, two decades after the 1969 act, were still three times as likely to die a violent death on the job as British miners? Is the American mine fraught with dangers that other mines do not have? Quite to the con-

Table 3 U.S. and British coal mine accident rates

	United States					Britain	
	1970	1980	1985	1990	1993	1970–71	1988–89
Number of injuries							
Fatal	260	133	68	42	47	92	18
Nonfatal[a]	34,515	18,689	9,073	12,240	8,375	599	684
Rate per million man-hours							
Fatal[b]	1.02	0.3	0.2	0.2	0.2	0.18	0.06
Nonfatal	41	45	27	41	36	1.19	2.11
Fatalities per 1,000 employed							
	1.72	0.55	0.35	0.40	0.35	0.30	0.017

Sources: Statistical Abstract of the United States, 1972, 1984, 1988, 1992, 1995; National Coal Board, *Reports and Accounts, 1971–72* (London: Her Majesty's Stationery Office), 1: 7, and British Coal Corporation, *Reports and Accounts, 1988–89* (London: Her Majesty's Stationery Office), 17.

[a] Britain divides its nonfatal accidents into "serious reportable injuries" and "other injuries." Figures for the first category are given here, but because it is less inclusive than the U.S. classification "nonfatal" (which involves accidents that result in one or more days' loss of work), the data for nonfatal injuries are not comparable; comparisons over time within each nation are valid, however.
[b] British fatality rates are calculated as deaths per 100,000 "manshifts"; for purposes of comparison they are adjusted here to the U.S. rates per million man-hours.

trary, in their physical character American mines are inherently *safer* than European mines: they are generally speaking less gassy and not nearly so deep, and their coal seams are thicker, less steeply pitched, and generally more accessible. The deeper European mines have heavier pressure on roofs, which are therefore more dangerous. Furthermore, surface mining accounts for a much larger percentage of American than European and especially British output (since 1980 some 60 percent of American coal is surface-mined, whereas an average of only 15 percent of British coal has come from what they call "opencast" mines) and is therefore less likely to involve fatal accidents, partly because it is free of one of underground mining's worst threats: the falling roof.

In the early 1980s I asked an experienced and much respected British coal mining official, John Brass, about this difference between U.S. and U.K. mines and their respective safety records and this was his reply:

> British mines are inherently more dangerous than yours and therefore our safety standards have to be all the higher. . . . Our rock-dusting standards are very high and rigidly enforced [to reduce the explosiveness of coal dust]. I believe our standards of electrical safety are higher than in the U.S. Indeed, most American machinery—if not all—that has been installed over here has had to be redesigned [for] electrical [safety].
>
> It sounds as though I'm being beastly and critical of your mining people and I would hate to be so, because we have a lot to learn from them in some matters while still trying to retain our safety standards. We have learned by experience, much of which has been bitter, and I am quite sure that it is the inherently greater danger in our mines that makes us more careful and creates our higher standards.[7]

No doubt the dangerous conditions of British mines do help explain the need for extra safety precautions, but that does not explain the social, economic, and political motivations for stringent rules enforced strictly enough to improve vastly the survival chances of the British miner. Why are those motivations missing in the United States, where mine conditions would presumably have made it possible to raise safety standards to levels comparable to those of British mining? It is not easy to identify the cultural variations that lead one nation to adopt strict policies that save lives and another to develop practices that for more than a century sacrificed lives by tens of thousands. For many decades British coal production has been an economically marginal operation; during World War I the industry thrived on the heavy wartime demand, but in the 1920s and during the Depression it fell on hard times. Indeed, it was the nonprofitability of British coal that made it politically feasible to nationalize the coal industry following World War II. One commentator on British coal experience attributes "an almost indecent haste" to mine owners as they welcomed the postwar Labour government's bid to nationalize. They were apparently eager to receive a generous compensation for run-down properties subject to strict regulation and no longer profitable.[8]

Nor has the industry been profitable under nationalization. Loaded with debt from the original takeover, the nationalized mines also faced high production costs because old mines were worked out and had to be replaced with less accessible new operations. Accordingly, coal production declined from 200 million tons in 1947 to 103 in 1988–89. The number of collieries in the same period was slashed from 958 to 86, and in late 1992 the British Coal Corporation announced plans to reduce the number of active mines to 19, employing only 13,000 miners—a striking contrast to the million men who worked in Britain's mines in the 1920s, and the 700,000 employed when nationalization began.[9]

In general, nationalization may be a contributing factor to better safety records. Mines in nearly all of Europe have long been nationally owned, and their safety standards have traditionally been far higher than those of the privately owned American and Canadian mines. The fact that government itself is responsible for making and enforcing its own rules rather than having to deal with independently powerful coal businesses may have permitted higher safety standards, because bureaucracy and socialized control may be more responsive than corporate versus government contesting over safety.

Yet even if the socialized system is a factor, a comparison of British and American safety records reveals the difference in rates *before* nationalization. British figures show that in the 1920s miners had four times better survival chances than Americans. The U.S. Coal Commission's report of 1925 gives comparative data for coal mine fatalities that puts the American miner at the bottom of the heap. In Great Britain the number of miners killed per 1,000 employed was 1.13; in France and Belgium the rates were 1.22 and 1.56 respectively. In Germany the rate was 3.11, and for the United States it was an astonishing 4.08 dead per 1,000 employed.[10] John Brophy, when he was president of U.S. District 2 of the United Mine Workers of America, made a similar point: that in 1921 the U.S. ten-year average of mine fatalities was 2,466 a year, "more than double the number in Great Britain and Ireland, where the number of miners was 50 percent greater."[11] The 1920s conditions had not improved in 1940, according to the report of a congressional subcommittee. At a hearing on May 16, 1940, Representative Kent Keller said that American miners were being killed "three men to every one killed in England." He added for emphasis, "Get that."[12]

The postnationalization decline in British accident rates continued after the introduction of what amounted to incentive piece-rate pay scales in the 1970s. It is widely believed (although hard to prove) that piece-rate compensation invites high accident rates because workers cut corners with safety rules to maximize their pay. Whatever the relationship between injuries sustained when workers are paid by hourly rates as opposed to production incentives, the fatal injury rate in Britain continued to decline in the nationalization period (down by 67 percent from 1970–71 to 1988–89). In the two decades after the enactment of the 1969 Federal Coal Mine Health and Safety Act in the United States, the fatality rate went down by 80 percent, but even then the U.S. rate was worse than the 1970 U.K. rate (compare the data in table 3). In neither country did nonfatal injuries decline greatly in the decades after 1970, although there is ground for suspicion about the reliability of the U.S. data: the annual variations are high enough to suggest indifferent reporting.

Why then the U.K.-U.S. difference, whether pre- or post-nationalization in Britain? One can only speculate, but it appears that the American miner has simply been considered more expendable than his British counterpart. If so, why? One possible reason is the composition of the American mine work force. American miners in the late nineteenth century were mainly drawn from three groups (see chapter 5), mountaineers, immigrants, and blacks, and all three were looked down upon to some degree by most other Americans.

The expendability of people was nothing new in American experience. General Grant had made it his major strategy in winning the Civil War, taking advantage of his numerical superiority by throwing human waves against entrenched troops until numbers prevailed. A nonmilitary parallel applied in the mines: there was a seemingly inexhaustible supply of recruits from the Appalachian mountain country, the South, and abroad; and though they died by the thousands every year, replacements always seemed ready to fill the diminished ranks. Why was the same not true of the British? They had after all been willing to expend lives to an unprecedented degree in the bloody campaign on the Somme in 1916. It is said that British generals learned military strategy from their study of the U.S. Civil War—if so, they learned the lesson too well—but it does not appear that those in charge of British coal mines copied the American example. The British were willing enough to sacrifice their conquered colonial masses, but they did not put their mine workers to similar tests of survival. It is possible that the lack of an inexhaustible supply of recruits made English mining authorities more careful to husband the native supply, since mass immigration from abroad was by law unavailable in Great Britain.

If one compares American and British miners as to their pay and their safety precautions, the Americans got the money and the British got safety. That may be a result of American wealth as compared with British relative poverty in the aftermath of two world wars. The United Mine Workers of America emphasized the pay envelope and neglected safety except to talk about it strategically, whereas the National Union of Miners sought pay increases but had to settle for safety. Great Britain could not afford wages like those in America but found safety less expensive; American companies could afford both but chose to put off spending for safety until political developments in the 1970s compelled some action—at last.

Given a greater apparent commitment to safety in the United Kingdom, what procedures brought safer conditions? One important difference in safety measures taken was the extent of safety training required in European and British mines. Traditionally, very little training in safety has been offered or mandated for new miners in the United States, except perhaps some first aid lessons and practice. In my own case, the company taught me nothing about safety, and formal training was never even mentioned. My father tutored me extensively on safety in all its aspects, but when on occasion I worked with other experienced miners, I cannot recall that the subject was ever raised in conversation.

Little more safety training was provided to a new miner who began his own brief career in 1974. Meade Arble, in *The Long Tunnel: A Coal Miner's Journal,* says that three days of classes were supposedly required, but as he describes them, a good part of the time was taken up with stale jokes from an inspector, first aid instruction for emergencies, and information from the company's paymaster on pay scales and deductions; scheduled training inside the mine was canceled. Following that skimpy preparation and a first work shift with a timbering crew, he was assigned to the four-man crew of a continuous miner consisting of a machine operator, a buggy (shuttle car) driver, a roof bolter, and a helper. Arble was the helper, and his duties included keeping the 12,000-volt wires out of the path of the machine and the buggy. It was difficult to see what he was doing, since the dust was so thick it obscured the light of the buggy driver a few feet away, and he exhausted himself shoveling coal in knee-deep water. "For the last few hours I stumbled around half blind. Sweat poured down my face. My knees were like hamburger from coal inside my knee pads. My fingers were stiff and swollen from being caught between a couple of props. I couldn't feel the burning gashes down my back [from scraping against the low top]. My body had finally turned off the pain, and it took every ounce of will for me to drag the cables around. At the end, I really didn't care if they exploded or not."[13]

By contrast, training at that time (1970s) in England consisted of forty weeks of classroom and inside instruction with strict limitations on what a novice miner was permitted to do. In Germany, apprenticeship lasted three years with even more rigorous formal training and close supervision until the novice became a full-fledged miner.

A year's apprenticeship is now required in the United States, and a new miner wears a yellow hat designating him or her as a "greenie" until certification is achieved.

Explosions: Monongah, 1907

Another thing that has changed in coal mine safety is a decrease in—though not the elimination of—coal dust and gas explosions, major fires, and suffocations. In the decade following the enactment of the 1969 Coal Mine Health and Safety Act the number of "disasters" (defined as accidents in which five or more workers lost their lives) was reduced to three from ten (killing 258 miners) in the previous decade.

That does not mean that the worst of those threats, the explosion, is no longer a danger. A reminder of the unhappy history of explosions can be found in the events that caught a small Nova Scotia town in 1992: on May 9 a mine called the safest in Canada blew up, taking the lives of twenty-six miners. Only seven months earlier, Canadian authorities had claimed that the mine at Westray was disasterproof. But apparently methane gas (which is highly flammable and commonly found, sometimes in commercially profitable concentrations, in the same rock strata as coal) had escaped faster than sensors could give warning. An official of a town near Westray told a newsman that when he was a boy delivering newspapers in 1952, an explosion had killed nineteen men in the community of Macgregor, and "they told us something like that would never happen again. But really things are no different than they were 40 years ago."[14] Well, things *are* different in that explosions are less frequent, but the way to prevent them has yet to be found.

Once it was said that no one really knew why coal mines exploded. Expensive and destructive as explosions were, coal operators accepted them as a necessary risk, one of the costs of running a mine. Union leaders too took this fatalistic view. For example, W. A. "Tony" Boyle, then president of the UMWA, said in 1968 that explosions had to be expected. Standing at the site of the catastrophe in Farmington, West Virginia, which claimed the lives of seventy-eight miners, he declared, "As long as we mine coal there is always this inherent danger of explosion. . . . This is one of the better companies as far as cooperation and safety is concerned." The company Boyle found so cooperative was Consolidation Coal, and he knew or should have known that federal safety inspectors had reported dozens of violations of the safety code in the Farmington mine over the previous two years. And

Boyle certainly must have known that in 1954 and in 1965 explosions in the very same mine—Consol No. 9—had taken the lives of another twenty miners.

The pretense of ignorance of the causes of explosions was not limited to owners and union leaders; public officials uttered the same nonsense. At the Farmington disaster site U.S. Undersecretary of the Interior J. Cordell Moore said, "Unfortunately we don't understand why these things happen, but they do happen." Governor Hulett C. Smith of West Virginia added his note of fatalism: "We must recognize that this is a hazardous business, and what has happened here is one of the hazards of being a miner."[15] One could search a long time and not find better reasons why the coal mine death rate in America is so different from those of other civilized societies. What corporations can get away with, *free of criticism,* they will take advantage of, QED.

The truth is that the primary cause of most mine explosions has long been known: coal dust in suspension is explosive and needs only a small fire to ignite it; escaping methane gas can start that fire, being ignited easily by sparks from an electrical wire, by a match lighting tobacco, or by flame from an improperly set dynamite charge. The likeliest cause of a coal dust explosion under present-day circumstances is methane combined with electrical sparks. (Several earlier hazards have been eliminated: smoking or even the possession of tobacco inside a mine carries a fine of $250; modern mining methods no longer require the use of dynamite; and battery-powered lamps have replaced open-flame lights—candles or oil-fired and, later, carbide headlamps—which are no longer permitted.)

It is also known that the explosiveness of coal dust can be reduced significantly if it is covered and mixed with a layer of what miners call rock dust, which is spread by a blower that sprays all surfaces with a protective coating of this finely milled limestone. In the United States, 65 percent rock dust to 35 percent coal dust is deemed adequate, except for return air passages, where a ratio of 80 to 20 percent is required. European mining regulations generally stipulate a 75 to 25 percent ratio for all passages.

In 1942 I spent a weekend rock-dusting a section of Carolina mine that had just begun to use a new mechanical duckbilled loader. It was hard work lifting eighty-pound bags of pulverized limestone over my head, emptying them into a hopper at the top of the machine, and then spraying the whole area with a generous coating of white powder that turned pitch blackness into a snow scene (one had to be sure the wind was at one's back, or the dust was suffocating). The other member of the team and I talked at lunchtime with the repair crew of the mechanical loader and learned that during the week the new duckbill had been working in the 17 Right section, though no rock-dusting had been done there at all; consequently, there was a thick layer of raw coal dust over the whole section. Toward the end of my work shift our boss, Bill, came and asked us to stay on and to finish rock-dusting 17 Right; he explained that the state inspector was coming Monday, and the area had to be properly treated before his arrival. It turned out to take five more hours of work to finish the job—at doubletime pay, since it was Sunday. "And why not do it, at $1.80 an hour?" I wrote in my diary when I got home at eight o'clock Sunday evening. The diary makes no reference to two facts to which I was oblivious: that working in a sea of coal dust was dangerous, and that the purpose of inspections was defeated if the company could cover its infractions of the safety code by being forewarned of the inspector's arrival.

Mine explosions are dramatic events made to order for news media. Today, television portrays the anguished families waiting at the mine portals for a miracle they do not really expect. In the pre-TV era newspapers sent crowds of cameramen and reporters to photograph and describe the scene and sell newspapers. Media coverage both then and now has political significance, for public attention is convertible into the coinage of political favor on the part of officials who want to appear responsive to public concern.

A crowd of newshawks gathered in a small West Virginia town on the afternoon of December 6, 1907, as quickly as existing transportation could get them to the site of what turned out to be the worst coal mine disaster in the history of American mining.

The town was Monongah, the final hometown of my youth, and I vividly recall hearing old folks tell tales of 1907. Stories ranged from the macabre to the bizarre. One elderly Scotsman attributed his avoidance of death to the virtues of whiskey; he had been on a bender the night before and was too hung over to go to work next day. Memories differed, but they all spoke of the rumbling thunder from underground which, like all coaltown people, they recognized immediately and with horror. Streets sagged as mine tunnels collapsed; buildings shook and windows rattled or shattered; fire and smoke belched from both portals of the mine—the No. 6 opening upstream on the West Fork River that divides the town, and the No. 8 entry downstream. The wives and relatives of Monongah's miners headed for one or the other of the pit mouths, calling in "a dozen different languages or dialects and in the common language of terror. Hundreds of men and boys went to work those mines this morning. Only four dazed survivors have emerged. Where are the rest?"[16]

The rest were dead—or soon would be, for there were no recorded survivors. How many died? To this day no one knows or will ever know. The official count is 361, but it is a certainty that far more than that actually perished—some estimates say at least 550. No records were then kept of who was in the mine; in fact, anyone could wander in, as a hopeful insurance agent in search of clients is thought to have done on the day of the explosion. One would have supposed that the names of those working that day would be readily available from their families, but many of the victims had no families to report their absence because they were immigrants from Europe who had left their families behind. Miners often took their sons to work with them without reporting it to anyone, child labor laws then being more commonly flouted than observed.[17] And since mining was done on a contract basis, a miner in charge of a working place could hire a helper on his own without making any official record of it. Furthermore, the violence of the blast was such that many bodies were totally destroyed, leaving nothing to be identified. And because some sections of the mine were never dug out, oldtimers believed that undiscovered bodies were still interred there. Grandfather Walter helped bring out the remains of victims, and he believed there were more bodies in those never excavated sections.

I asked our neighbor Paul Boydoh to tell me about the woman who had hauled tons of coal home in a demented search for her husband, who had been killed in the Monongah explosion. Boydoh obliged:

Her name was Sophie Dabio. She lost her mind, and she would go in search of her husband, and she would fill a feed sack with coal and haul it home every day. She'd go over to the tipple and take coal off the cars over there. She thought her husband was still living and was mad at her about something, and she would carry that coal—it was almost two miles. And she would get up to the grave where her husband was buried over here in the park, and she would cuss him, saying I have to carry this here coal while you lazy devil you lay in the dirt. I don't know how many tons of coal she had when she died—they gave it to some institution. I forget how many hundreds of tons of coal it was. It was piled—aw, it was an awful pile of coal. She lived pretty old; she went half the time barefoot— she went winter and summer every day, didn't make no difference. She would make four or five trips a day, every day till she died.[18]

Those whose bodies were identified were mainly from foreign countries; only 23 percent were American born. (No two listings of survivors are identical, so the statistics have to be taken with a grain of salt.) Italians were the largest ethnic group, by some listings 171, more than twice the 85 (74 white and 11 black) U.S. natives. Hungarians and Austrians combined (52) and Russians (31, mostly from what would later be Poland) were the next most numerous groups. Still others were from Greece, Turkey, Latvia, Lithuania, Ireland, and Scotland. Most of these newcomers did not speak English, and when time came to fix blame for the explosion, some natives asserted that the cause was "the large number of aliens. . . . These men are for the most part illiterate, and of a lower standard of intelligence than their counterparts of some years ago."[19]

Of course, no one came forth with any specific evidence that connected the non-English-speaking miners with the Monongah tragedy. Trying to find the actual triggering incident was largely guesswork. Some believed it was the result of a runaway haulage motor crash. Others suspected escaping methane, although fire bosses had found no evidence of gas on their morning rounds. Also cited as a possible cause was excessive coal dust, common especially in winter months (when production rose); a team of French mine experts called it the root cause.[20]

Whatever the cause, the calamity left 250 widows and 1,000 fatherless

children, plus 63 more when pregnant mothers gave birth. To aid these survivors, a panel of dignitaries was selected to solicit and distribute relief
funds. They set a goal of $175,000 but failed to meet it and scaled back pay-
ments accordingly, allotting $200 to each widow and $155 per child.[21] The
owners of the mine, the Fairmont Coal Company, contributed to the relief
fund but in its testimony before a coroner's jury denied any corporate responsibility for the explosion. In responding to the Austrian ambassador,
who wrote to complain about the inadequate compensation paid to the survivors of Austrian miners, the company's attorney took the same position:
"The company has never contributed anything to persons here or abroad
otherwise than as a gratuity or donation. The company never for a moment
considered that it was legally liable. . . . I think the $2,000 distributed prin-
cipally among 41 children and 20 widows would be quite a Christmas
present."[22]

Safety and the Law: Centralia, 1947

The coroner's jury concluded that it could not identify the event that
caused the explosion and urged Congress to appoint an investigatory panel
to study the causes and prevention of coal mine explosions. Congress at
the time was disinclined to involve the federal government in the affairs of
private business, but public concern about mine disasters was so aroused
that lawmakers could not very well ignore the problem. The Monongah
disaster was only the most conspicuous of the mine explosions hitting the
headlines at that time. In the same month, December 1907, three others
caught the public's attention: two in Pennsylvania and one in Alabama,
killing a total of 329. In 1908 three more explosions took the lives of 280
miners in Wyoming, Pennsylvania, and West Virginia, And in the next two
years another five explosions and a massive mine fire claimed 631 lives. In
fact, during the first decade of the new century an astonishing 20,763 coal
miners died on the job.

On July 1, 1910, Congress finally acted—reluctantly and minimally: it created the Bureau of Mines in the Department of the Interior, with instructions to investigate mining methods, "especially with respect to the safety

of miners, and the appliances best adapted to prevent accidents, the possible improvements of conditions under which mining operations are carried on." But the new agency was specifically told that it did not have the "right or authority" to undertake "the inspection or supervision of mines in any state." The legislation provided no enforcement power whatever; bureau representatives could enter a mine only by specific permission of the owner, and even then, they could not publicize their findings. All the act did was to create a small-scale research program.

After three more decades of death and destruction—and much agitation for safety legislation staunchly resisted by coal operators and their allies in Washington—Congress again took minimal steps to support safety. The Bureau of Mines was granted authority to inspect mines and publicize its findings and recommendations, but it still had no enforcement power, and there were no stated safety standards for the bureau to use as enforcement criteria. Further, the bureau was specifically instructed to cooperate with the states and not to usurp state regulatory power.

Specific federal standards for safety enforcement came into being through a back door. In 1946 and 1947, battles over wages and working conditions that had been deferred during the war finally resulted in strikes, pitting UMW leader John L. Lewis against the unyielding operators. The deadlocked negotiations ended in a government seizure of the mines under the supervision of Secretary of the Interior Julius A. Krug. The famous Krug-Lewis agreement that settled the strike (temporarily) in May 1946 was noted for the historic establishment of a miners' health and welfare fund, but also important—if less recognized at the time—was the agreement to formulate a code of safety standards, the first such national regulations ever established. Yet although the Federal Mine Safety Code provided a set of guidelines for Bureau of Mines inspectors, compliance remained voluntary on the part of the operators.

Behind the decades of controversy about federal versus state regulation of mine safety was the dispute over federalism. Historically, federalism has been an important aspect of American political life; originally it was a compromise that allowed central authority and local counterforce to coexist. In time, of course, it became the focal point of the conflict over slavery:

whether local (that is, state) independence meant discretionary power to have and solely to control slavery. And after the Civil War, jurisdiction over the civil rights of the descendants of slaves became the core of political controversy between state and federal authorities.

As in civil rights matters, states defended their control over coal mine safety, and keeping national power from entering the field became a key political objective; at the state level, coal operators' political power over state and local officials could minimize governmental interference. This went hand in hand with a laissez-faire economic policy; at the time of the Monongah disaster a Parkersburg, West Virginia, newspaper editorial took a very negative view of governmental attempts to promote mine safety, saying that a "legislature is about as well fitted to cope with a mine as a muskrat with a stone dam. Why don't expert miners do it?"[23]

In keeping with the spirit of federalism, Congress in 1947 tried to play up the potential role of state agencies by promoting cooperation between state and federal mine regulators, requesting that states and coal companies report on the extent of their compliance with Bureau of Mines recommendations. Reports came in from seventeen states and partial responses from two others; seven coal states did not respond at all. Operators had a 33 percent compliance rate. The law lapsed after one year, another expert congressional attempt to appear to be doing "something" while actually doing nothing.

During the year that Congress was playing show-and-tell, there was further evidence—as if any were needed—of how limited was the capacity of the states to make mining safe. It cost 111 lives in the Centralia, Illinois, mine explosion to demonstrate that inadequacy. In this case study in nonaction, miners had pleaded for years that the mine had dangerous amounts of coal dust not adequately countered with rock-dusting. Their complaints went to the federal and state mining agencies, to the company, and to the union, but nothing came of their warnings and pleas. Illinois law provided authority to force compliance with regulations, but authority to act is not the same thing as the will to act, and bureaucratic lethargy and political compromise can thwart even persistent efforts to get steps taken for safety.

In the Centralia episode not only had the miners' safety committee begged for action, but one state inspector had reported countless violations and had in fact done so for five consecutive years before the inevitable disaster. His carefully spelled-out citations of violations went through the standard channels and were duly stamped as received, then filed away and forgotten. Even direct orders to the mine owners to correct unsafe conditions were contemptuously ignored. And the new U.S. Bureau of Mines safety code, put into effect nine months before the fatal day, resulted in a report citing fifty-seven violations, but the actual condition that caused the explosion was not among them. John L. Lewis put on a dramatic pose to denounce "criminal negligence," but the United Mine Workers representative who was supposed to speak for the union on a state safety board had ignored pleas from local union members and filed them away, as had his state bureaucratic counterparts.

To cap this parade of irresponsible negligence, Governor Dwight Green compromised the state's role in safety regulation when, under his authority, state inspectors were ordered to solicit campaign money from coal mine owners. John Bartlow Martin, author of an insightful study of the Centralia disaster, points out that the Illinois Department of Mines and Minerals was a political agency. Inspectors, as political appointees, were expected to act accordingly or face being fired.[24] The ultimate irony of the whole affair was that although the coal company was found to have committed two violations of the state safety code, it was fined a total of $1,000—less than $10 for each life lost.

Four years after the Centralia disaster Illinois experienced another explosion, in West Frankfort, this one costing 119 lives. Once again dead miners became effective lobbyists; the drama of death created an atmosphere that Congress responded to with legislation. As usual there was some doubt about the intent of Congress: did it mean to create a mine safety code or just pretend to do so? In the opinion of President Harry Truman, the 1952 Federal Coal Mine Safety Act was deficient, and although he felt compelled to sign it as better than nothing, he laid out his criticisms. One key defect was that the law excluded from its provisions all mines employing fewer than fifteen miners. This exclusion was significant because small mines are less safe than larger ones. Often marginal operations run on small capital investment, they are likely to lack necessary safety equipment and to save money by using outdated materials such as "PrimaCord," a dangerous and outlawed explosive. Although prohibited for years, it had apparently been in common use in a small mine in eastern Kentucky when it blew up in 1970, killing thirty-eight men. [25]

President Truman also objected to the continued primary reliance on the states for accident prevention, despite the fact that it was the failure of state regulation that had prompted the legislation originally. Further, the law allowed long delays before operators were required to make changes in electrical and ventilation equipment. Finally, the president complained that complex administrative procedures would make enforcement difficult. But the law did at least make compliance—at least for larger mines—mandatory, not voluntary. Inspectors were authorized to close mines if conditions presented a serious likelihood of a major accident. Lesser dangers would be reported, and if operators did not correct the hazards within a "reasonable" time, then the mine could be closed until they did.

Despite the new law, during the next eight years the slaughter continued: 3,179 more miners were killed; an average of more than one coal miner a day became a statistic for the record and a tragedy for a whole family. Once again pressure mounted for Congress to close loopholes in the law. And predictably, Congress went into its legislative tango—one step forward, one backward, one to one side, one to the other. Representatives and senators resorted to a bag of parliamentary tricks to stall action. Bills would pass one house but die on the agenda of the other; various delaying tactics killed bills quietly by binding them up in the inevitable end-of-session logjam; bills were shanghaied in committees or kept off action calendars by unanimous consent rules, filibusters (threatened as well as undertaken), and backroom deals. Finally, in 1966 Congress passed a minimal revision of the law: it now covered also the small mines (called Title 1 mines) employing fourteen or fewer miners, and it gave the Bureau of Mines authority to issue "reinspection closing orders" as a means of coping with certain types of repeated violations. A gaping hole remained, however: the law applied only to ten percent of all mining accidents—those involving major disasters such as explosions, but not the day-to-day incidents that caused 90 percent of the fatalities. Those accidents remained the province of the ineffectual state regulatory agencies.[26]

Farmington, 1968, and the Act of 1969

Then came the Farmington disaster of November 20, 1968.

This West Virginia mine, Consolidation Coal's No.9, had a history of accidents. It had blown up in 1954, killing sixteen men, and in the two years before the 1968 catastrophe safety inspectors had cited numerous violations involving inadequate rock-dusting. It was also a gassy mine; one geological map of the surrounding area showed 151 natural gas wells. The special vigilance required by the gassy conditions was not forthcoming, and a fire in one section of the mine on that fateful day led to a ferocious explosion that took the lives of seventy-eight miners—the worst casualty count since the Centralia and West Frankfort disasters. The mine itself was destroyed, and the resulting fire was so enveloping that all hope of recovering the bodies of the victims was abandoned; the mine was sealed in an attempt to smother the flames.

The mine's portals were tightly sealed but the issue of coal miners' health and safety was blown wide open. A month after the Farmington carnage the Department of the Interior convened a conference on mine safety which Secretary of the Interior Stewart Udall opened with these words: "The tragedy that occurred at Farmington, W. Va., last month is the catalyst that has brought us together. What we say and do here, however, must be in a larger context than that of a coal mine disaster. Our deliberations must embrace all of the measures and all of the responsibilities that have to be adopted. . . if we hope ever to banish death and disease from our coal mines. And this we must do. For let me assure you, the people of this country no longer will accept the disgraceful health and safety record that has characterized this major industry."[27] President Richard Nixon, in his message to Congress calling for passage of the federal Coal Mine Health and

Safety Act, added these words: "Death in the mines can be as sudden as an explosion or a collapse of a roof or ribs, or it comes insidiously from pneumoconiosis, or black lung disease."[28]

In the course of a year's controversy over the new legislation, several major points of contention divided pro and anti forces. One was the previously debated issue of classifying mines by size. Defenders of small mines argued that the cost of expensive equipment would doom the owners and drive them out of business. Advocates of the large mining interests said the exclusion of small mines would give them an unfair competitive advantage. The United Mine Workers sided with the large operators, partly because they found small mines hard to organize. Whatever the opposing sides' motivations, the record unmistakably shows small mines to be more dangerous than large ones. Ten years after the enactment of the 1969 law—despite the inclusion of small mines under its provisions—their accident rate ran several times that of large ones: in 1978–79 those with fifty or fewer employees accounted for 15 percent of all work hours in coal mining but sustained 43 percent of all fatalities; employees of the largest mines (with 151 or more workers) accounted for 66 percent of all mine work hours and suffered 40 percent of the fatalities.[29]

Another contentious issue was again a matter of classification, between gassy and nongassy mines. Those with low levels of detected gas should be classified, according to one group, as nongassy and not be required to provide the expensive equipment that was deemed necessary for gassier mines where even a slight spark could ignite the prevalent methane. Defenders of the classification argued that nongassy mines (which tended to be small mines also) had good safety records and that making them buy expensive but allegedly unneeded gear would drive them out of the industry. Their opponents held that there were no truly nongassy mines, that all mines were potentially gassy, since methane is often located in the same strata as coal. The latter argument prevailed, and all mines were required to provide spark-free wiring and equipment.

The issue of black lung disease also generated dispute: how to prevent it and whether to compensate those who were disabled by it. Awareness of black lung, an ancient curse for miners, dates back as far as the seventeenth century. It has commonly been called "miners' asthma," a term derived from a medical report dating from 1837. In Great Britain, unlike the United States, black lung was studied seriously in the 1930s and made a compensable industrial disease in 1943. Published research was readily available to members of the American medical establishment, but they took little notice of it (perhaps because they were busy at the time fighting "socialized medicine"). A few doctors did begin research on their own, but small heed was given to their calls for action to deal with the cause of the disease—coal dust.[30] Sufferers from the disease in its more advanced stages often guessed correctly that dust and the foul air of inadequately ventilated mines were at the root of their acute shortness of breath. Again and again they brought the issue to the conventions of the UMW—only to have their resolutions rejected without a hearing. A victim of the disease interviewed by Barbara Ellen Smith said that he was delighted when a scientist of the U.S. Public Health Service reported having found black lung, a "new" occupational disease that soft coal miners suffered from: "All down through the years we'd been told dust had no effect"[31] But he knew it did, and he was, of course, right.

It was not recognized as an occupational disease in the United States generally, whatever a Public Health Service staffer may have found. In the late 1950s Alabama and Pennsylvania gave limited recognition to the disease with inadequate compensatory programs; other states and the United States Congress did nothing. State worker's compensation laws did recognize silicosis but compensated victims only when they could prove that hard substances had impaired their lungs—which bituminous miners could not do, since soft coal dust works in a different way, causing a fatal lung fibrosis. In West Virginia, even when the compensation-awarding committee acted favorably (which was rare), the disabled miner was paid a flat sum of $1,000 for the first stage and $2,000 for the second stage of the disease. That would have meant little to black lung victims like those described by a miner's wife in recounting early mass meetings of the forming Black Lung Association (BLA): "You go to these rallies, there'd be these old men there . . . couldn't get no breath at all. You'd think they'd go up to the ceiling trying to get air. Before they'd get done telling you how dirty they'd been done, they'd be crying. Couldn't work. Don't get no pension. Didn't have nothing to live on. Now that gets to you. It still makes me mad when I think about it."[32]

In England those who contracted black lung had three sources of support: the medical profession, the miners' union, and the coal companies (after nationalization, the National Coal Board), whereas in the United States these three elements opposed miners' efforts to win recognition that the disease was real and not imagination, and to get worker's compensation when they became totally disabled. The American medical profession bitterly opposed the black lung program and claimed that there was no scientific evidence to support the existence of the disease; they were affronted that these laymen, untutored in medical matters, dared to dispute the professionals' diagnosis. And the companies leaned on the doctors in their campaign against recognition of the disease. In West Virginia in 1969, when the BLA was conducting a wildcat strike to insist on black lung legislation, the West Virginia Coal Association denounced the few doctors who supported the miners—claiming that the strikers showed a "total disregard for proven medical facts"—and described the proposed legislation as "galloping socialism." The cruelest blow of all was the steadfast opposition of the United Mine Workers hierarchy. The irascible Tony Boyle did all in his considerable power to kill the BLA's project, ordering an end to the strike and insisting that local unions cease financial support of the movement. Both orders were ignored. The accusation that the BLA was the dreaded "dual unionism" (two unions competing in the same industry) got nowhere. To prove the baselessness of the charge, the sufferers early in the game urged national union support for a national black lung law—only to have Boyle propose virtually impossible state-by-state drives. And even when the BLA did try to get action in one state, West Virginia, their staunchest opponent was Tony Boyle.

There were three of medical men who supported the BLA wholeheartedly and imaginatively: Drs. I. E. Buff, Donald Rasmussen, and Hawey Wells. They spoke to countless assemblages of miners and their wives, explaining the medical facts of the ailment and rallying the crowd to political action. They indulged in some theatrics, such as displaying a blackened human lung that Dr. Buff kept in a plastic bag. And Dr. Wells would show the gathering a portion of an autopsied black lung, saying, "Here is a slice of one of your brother's lungs." Brit Hume, in his book *Death and the Mines,* comments, "The miners loved it and roared their approval, particularly when one of the doctors would ask, 'Where has your union been all this time?'"[33]

Another of the small band of cooperating physicians was Dr. Lorin Kerr of the Welfare and Retirement Fund, who had researched black lung long before the BLA existed. At the 1968 convention of the UMWA he gave an illuminating speech, pointing out that this disease, different from silicosis, affected a large percentage of American miners; in fact, fund data showed that there were four times as many deaths from chronic lung diseases among miners as in a sample of all American males of comparable age. Kerr was denounced by the medical fraternity, and ultimately told by the union leadership to stop speaking.[34]

For me, black lung hit close to home: my father suffered painfully from it but died (in 1965) before much attention was given to it. Thus, although his health worried him considerably, he never knew what was wrong. The words "black lung" never appear in his diary, but there are hundreds of references to chronic and unshakable colds and wracking coughs that kept him from sleeping. I vividly recall visiting him in winter, when dry, cold air left him gasping for breath if he did anything as demanding as crossing the street. He kept going to the company doctors about his problem, partly because he feared it might be tuberculosis, which had killed his first wife. The doctors would take X-rays of his chest and assure him that nothing was wrong. On one occasion they sent the pictures to the state health department, which reported that his lungs were congested. But his company doctor dismissed this as insignificant and gave him, along with some pills that I suspect were placebos, the same advice he usually dispensed: "Take it easy!" As advice to a coal loader, that is so ridiculous it is almost funny.

Dad wrote about bronchial trouble as early as 1950, once saying, "I stopped in at the Dr.'s office on my way home from work to find out about the X-ray, and he said it was clear, nothing at all wrong. I was mighty glad to hear it too for I was a bit worried." But that he clearly had black lung was certified posthumously, making my mother eligible, as his survivor, for a modest monthly benefit check. The company doctors whom he saw were not necessarily under a directive to play down respiratory troubles among miners, but they might as well have been for all the help they gave. Not that there was then, any more than now, a cure for black lung, but the American medical community was remiss in not even taking the disease seriously.

Meanwhile, by contrast, the British medical establishment, coal companies (and, later, the National Coal Board), and National Union of Miners had systematically investigated the ailment and initiated a program of regular black lung examinations for all miners, switching anyone who showed positive signs to less dusty workplaces. Thus they learned how many were contracting the disease, devised a system for minimizing the damage by early discovery, and sought to control dust at the working face—all this while the American coal establishment was denying steadfastly that the scourge existed. When the Black Lung Association made demands first in West Virginia and later at the federal level, the coal operators kicked and screamed bankruptcy. And when it came to paying compensation to black lung sufferers, the companies managed to shift the burden to government. Their resistance to corrective measures left America far behind the British, with the result that we have to guess at how many miners contracted the disease; the best estimate is about 350,000, but no one really knows (half a million miners or their widows have been compensated under the federal program). It killed and still kills thousands annually, and for countless others it is among the contributory causes of death.

There remains much to be learned about black lung, and researchers so far cannot say why some 30 percent of those exposed to dust get the disease while others do not. The lungs of those affected by it are clogged at first by fine particles of coal, and later a massive fibrosis of lung tissue so impairs the capacity to take in oxygen that victims must struggle for every breath. Thus weakened, they are susceptible to death from heart or other problems, or ultimately die from inability to breathe. And as the British showed beyond all doubt, only one thing could reduce the incidence of the disease: a drastic reduction of coal dust in the mine atmosphere.

Accordingly the drafters of the 1969 act specified a limit on the amount of allowable dust. At first it was set at 4.5 milligrams per cubic meter of air, to be reduced to 3 milligrams after six months and 2 milligrams after three years. Opponents argued that this was too restrictive, not technically feasible, and—even if possible—unnecessary. They also emphasized that the limit in England at the time was 5 milligrams. The advocates of tougher standards responded that whatever the current British requirement, research in that country had shown the efficacy of a 2-milligram limit in reducing black lung, and ultimately that lesser limit went into the law. A massive campaign of fraud in reporting on dust, however (described below), compromised enforcement of the rule.

Whether to pay compensation to miners disabled by pneumoconiosis was debated at length, and the focal point of the controversy was the issue of making a special case of these particular victims of an industrial disease. If black lung sufferers were to be beneficiaries of a federal (as opposed to state) compensation program, then why not those with other industrial disabilities? In other words, would the bill invite the transfer of worker's compensation programs from the state to the federal level? The reasoning of opponents of a federal program of compensation followed the line of traditional debates over federalism: keep the function at the state level and it may be controllable; transfer it to Washington and who knows what extravagance may emerge from the political process? Proponents pointed out that the states had been remiss about including black lung disability as grounds for compensation: at that time only three states had such provisions in their laws. And even there the sums awarded were woefully inadequate, insufficient to cover, for example, the cost of supplying oxygen tanks, which even in the 1960s could amount to $180 a month. At the root of the problem was the lack of recognition of black lung as a compensable disease under state laws. Victims seeking pensions were sometimes compelled to claim that they had silicosis—which was difficult and expensive to prove to medical panels, since they did not have it. Dependence on state laws posed another difficulty at a time when mine workers' ranks were being cut from 600,000 to 135,000: those laid off were scattering across the country in early retirement or in search of jobs. That often put ex-miners in states without a coal industry, and these states were disinclined to make aid available to victims of a disease contracted elsewhere.

Although the compensation feature was finally adopted, the law attempted to shift the financial burden from the federal budget to the states and (unsuccessfully) to the coal industry itself—but members of Congress had to vote on the bill without knowing who would ultimately bear the cost of the program.

Given the history of the American coal industry, it is not surprising that coal operators took a verbal beating in the course of public discussion prior to enactment of the Coal Mine Health and Safety Act of 1969; during congressional debate, likewise, coal industry leaders were repeatedly accused of showing a callous disregard for the well-being of miners. Of course, company officials were sensitive about such allegations; Stephen F. Dunn, president of the National Coal Association, told the Senate Committee on Labor and Public Welfare that the coal industry "does not believe profits should be put ahead of the health and safety of mineworkers." Traditionally, however, mine operators had explained their lack of funds to pay for health and safety measures by citing their competition with alternative fuels, particularly oil. That line of defense made the comment to Congress by John Corcoran, chairman of the National Coal Association, sound somewhat hollow: "There can be no question that the health and safety of employees in the coal industry must be given first priority."[35] To advocates of safety legislation the evidence seemed directly the opposite: coal operators had forcefully resisted safety regulations for a century. Safety reformers saw confirmation of their skepticism in a letter sent by Dunn to every member of the House of Representatives. Dunn warned that passage of the bill would force the closure of many mines and result in a "nationwide power and steel shortage." Claiming that the bill required operators to do the impossible in six months, Dunn added, "The coal industry will not close its mines—it sincerely hopes Congress will not do so."[36] In fact, the number of operating mines declined insignificantly during the year after passage of the act and then increased by about a thousand in the next five years. And far from causing power and steel shortages, the act did not curtail the supply of coal, which not only remained abundant but expanded from 1970 onward.

There was more than crying wolf going on in Washington. In the words of then Representative Ken Hechler of West Virginia, there were crowds of pleaders for the "economic health of the coal industry: you can see them running around Capitol Hill. They have been here doing some very effective lobbying every time this Congress has considered coal mine legislation. The coal operators are shedding tears that this bill might force the closing of mines. They threaten power blackouts. . . . Mr. Chairman," Hechler continued in the rolling cadence of congressional rhetoric, "we have heard this cry, this threat, this form of insensitive and implacable opposition for a long time. When are we going to place the priority where it belongs—on the value of human life? When are we going to declare that the threat to close down a mine is not nearly as serious as the threat of closing down a man? . . . The coal industry has fought every step of the way against measures to protect health and safety, and I am sorry to say that the union leadership has been insensitive to the needs of the men. There is no profit incentive in health and safety, and there is plenty of profit incentive in high production, high wages, high coal dust levels which produce a high rate of industrial murder."[37]

Not many members of Congress engage in such open and frank criticisms of coal managers (and Hechler eventually paid for his temerity when strip-mining and other coal interests combined to defeat his reelection in 1978), and fewer still attack the leaders of the United Mine Workers of America. In fact, some members who had coal mines in their districts or states were so accustomed to praising the UMWA leadership that despite its lackluster performance in the campaign for the 1969 law, they commended the union for its assistance in putting the legislation under way. Some even went out of their way to congratulate Tony Boyle for his contributions to the cause of safety. Others pointedly did not, however, since Boyle was increasingly coming under fire for various indiscretions; the union faced internal problems; and already the conflict was brewing that would cost Boyle his sinecure and land him in prison for the remainder of his life. (Indeed, the Boyle-inspired murder of rival UMWA leader Jock Yablonski took place one day after President Nixon signed the 1969 statute.)

Once again it was the irrepressible Ken Hechler who voiced a complaint that many of his colleagues shared but dared not articulate. Not only did Boyle fail to take the initiative in the health and safety struggle, but "furthermore," said Hechler in the course of House debate,

even after the Farmington disaster, the top leadership of the United Mine
Workers of America bluntly stated that in their judgment it would not
be possible to enact any health and safety legislation for the miner this
year. Later they took the same timid approach toward the enactment of
compensation for victims of black lung. . . . It took the pressure of the
legacy of Joseph A. Yablonski to awaken the leadership . . . to their legislative responsibilities to the miners. The leadership began to wake up
and become more active. . . . the real question is whether President W. A.
Boyle and the leadership of the union intend to insist on the strict enforcement of this law for the benefit of coal miners or whether they will
in a self-satisfied fashion lapse back into their cozy relationship with the
coal operators."[38]

Safety Enforcement

Hechler was prescient in identifying the cardinal issue for the next phase of
miner health and safety: enforcement. Would the new rules save lives or
lead to more business as usual? The 1969 act established full enforcement
authority in unmistakable terms. Inspectors finding a dangerous condition
could order the closing of a mine until it was corrected. Workers idled by
the closure would get a full day's pay for the first day and four hours' pay
for each additional day. New requirements covered ventilation, roof support, electrical equipment, gas detection, noise abatement, and a special
health program for control of black lung through X-rays and medical examinations. It amounted to a new beginning for the protection of the
American miner. To what extent has it worked?

The rate of fatal accidents did decline gradually and irregularly, in the
decades following the passage of the bill. But there was not even a gradual decline in the number of nonfatal accidents; in fact, an increase in disabling accidents developed between 1976 and 1980 and again between 1985
and 1989. The numbers are not trivial. In 1970 just under 12,000 injuries
occurred, and in no fewer than eight of the next twenty years there were
even more; in 1980 the figure reached 19,000.

There are many reasons why the law may not have met the high hopes of its original promoters. One was the failure of the administrative system to act with vigor and firmness sufficient to persuade operators that the law had to be obeyed—or else. The first ominous note was sounded when President Nixon delayed for seven months in hiring a new director of the Bureau of Mines. The previous director, a holdover from the Johnson administration, had mining experience but was apparently too much on the miners' side to be acceptable to Nixon's pro-business views. His successor, Elbert F. Osborn, had no experience in coal mines or familiarity with the 1969 law; he was a geologist who taught at Pennsylvania State University, where he had also been director of research. He cannot have been helped much by the White House decision to make the assistant director position a political patronage appointment. That job went to Edward D. Failor, sometime lobbyist in Iowa, who he had also worked as an aide to several Republican candidates and was a fund raiser for election campaigns. He had no experience in coal mining, yet he was given the power to determine the size of penalties for violations of the safety rules, and that turned out to be a very significant power indeed.

Since there was a major hassle over the bureau's program to reduce the "burden" on operators, it is a telling fact that Failor arrived with a White House mandate to restrain regulatory enthusiasm. And he fulfilled the mandate, after a fashion, by drastically reducing the amounts of fines. Consider, for example, the case of the vanishing penalty. The family of a miner who had been killed in an accident brought suit against the United States Steel Corporation on the ground that the carelessness of the company and its supervisory personnel had caused the miner's death. The fine, first set at $7,500, was reduced to $300. Not all reductions were so huge, but the list of significantly reduced fines is a very long one. In the first four years after the 1969 act took effect, coal companies were fined $243,225 but had to pay only $70,092 for 648 violations.[39] For violations of safety regulations coal companies paid an average of about 30 percent of the assessed fine; for health infractions they were levied a scant 1 percent of the original (table 4 shows examples for individual companies).

Table 4. Reduction in assessed fines, 1970–73

Company	Fines Assessed	Number of Cases	Fines Paid	Payment as % of Assessment
Consolidation	$15,030	11	$1,965	13%
Jones-Laughlin	$8,100	19	$1,305	16%
Pittson	$11,390	48	$3,350	29%
Eastern Assoc.	$23,685	39	$5,683	24%
Mathies Coal	$16,500	85	$4,935	30%

Source: Don Stillman, "The Assessment Scandal . . ." *United Mine Worker's Journal,* 1–15 July 1974, 8.

As indicated by these drastic reductions, enforcement of the new law was a problem. Not only were penalties reduced, but the movement of cases from the docket by cutting levies to as little as $15 was heralded as a sign of administrative efficiency.[40] The Nixon administration even brought in a public relations firm to preach safety to miners while refusing to appoint enough mine inspectors to find safety violations; such disasters as the one at Hurricane Creek in 1970 may have been caused in good part by the inadequacy of inspections.[41]

Apprehensive about the performance of the Bureau of Mines in enforcing the law, concerned members of Congress asked the General Accounting Office to investigate the administration of the new set of rules. The GAO, whatever its name may suggest, is not an accounting agency but an investigatory body responsible to Congress and headed by the comptroller general. Its inquiry into the bureau's effort to carry out the health and safety statute produced some devastating findings: during 1970 bureau inspectors made fewer than one-third of the required safety inspections and only 1 percent of the health inspections. The GAO also found that 90 percent of all mine accidents were due to inadequate safety practices of coal operators. When the bureau did cite operators for violations, reinspection found that the same types of violations continued because, the GAO reported, "the [Interior] Department's policies for enforcing health and safety standards have been, at times extremely lenient, confusing, and inequitable."[42] The report also stated that coal mine operators had not carried out required samplings and inspections and had not submitted plans for roof control, ventilation, and emergencies caused by fan failures. These and many other shortcomings were cited, including a lag in appointing inspectors, which would continue to be a problem for years to come. In specific response to a request to ascertain whether the law was causing a reduction in coal output, the GAO's finding was inconclusive, but in overall tonnage produced there was an increase from 560.5 million tons in 1969 to 590 million in 1970.[43]

Two years later the GAO made another investigation of the performance of the Bureau of Mines, this one at the request of Congressman Ken Hechler, the nonstop gadfly critic of the coal industry. It was not a full-scale inquiry but one based on data obtained from bureau "records or from officials at the headquarters office . . . not verified by GAO."[44] The report said that the number of inspections had increased considerably since 1970 and that the number of miners killed had declined slightly (from 144 in 1971 to 122 in 1972). Orders to withdraw miners from unsafe mines, however, had declined in 1972 as compared with 1971, and, significantly, nonfatal accidents were up in 1972. Bureau officials attributed this increase to better reporting of accidents—but if so, what must the previous statistics have actually been?

In general, the findings in the follow-up investigation indicated better administration of the law and improved safety conditions, but the improvement was modest at best. The difference between health and safety standards in American mines and in European mines was still enormous and reflected little credit on either American coal companies or the bureaucrats charged with protecting workers from mining hazards. Despite the new law, disasters continued to plague the industry. In 1970, 38 died in the Hurricane Creek mine explosion, caused in the opinion of many experts by grossly inadequate inspection on the part of both state and federal inspectors. In 1972 a fire killed 9 in Blacksville, West Virginia, and an explosion took 5 lives at Itman, West Virginia. And at the Scotia mine in Letcher County, Kentucky, two explosions in March 1976 "murdered" (one might say) 26 men—three of them inspectors for the federal Mine Enforcement and Safety Administration (MESA), the enforcement arm of the Bureau of Mines. Following "inspections" that overlooked excessive methane gas, inadequate ventilation, and a dangerously short-circuiting compressor, MESA seemed incapable of learning from the first of the two explosions and sent three of its own employees to their deaths while trying to restore the mine to operational status.[45]

In the late 1970s and early 1980s disasters continued—not the least of them was the move by the Carter administration to deregulate many industries, including coal. A reduced budget for inspections was furthered by President Ronald Reaqan's freeze on hiring inspectors, calculated to reduce the staff by 10 percent by the end of the fiscal year. As Congressman Carl Perkins of Kentucky said, the mine inspectors were "not doing their job," partly because a reduction in their number had lowered morale, and one reason for that was "the Government [having] cut back their budget."[46]

Not surprisingly, cutbacks were followed by an increase in the number of miners killed on the job. The 1981 toll of 153 dead was the highest since 1975. In the winter of 1981–82 a series of disasters and individual fatalities caught public attention: in a five-day period just before Christmas three mine disasters claimed 24 lives in obscure Appalachian towns in West Virginia, Kentucky, and Tennessee; 14 miners died in the first twenty days of 1982, and the explosion in a small Kentucky mine that killed 7 on January 20 marked the fourth disaster in Appalachia in less than seven weeks.[47] A major disaster followed in December 1984 in Wilberg mine, Utah, killing 27 in a fire: 21 men, 1 woman miner, and 5 mine managers present to observe an attempt to set a twenty-four-hour record-high production.[48]

The history of the enforcement of the 1969 act was so unsatisfactory that more and more people involved with the industry began to call for remedial action. J. Davitt McAteer, an attorney who headed the Occupational Safety and Health Law Center in Washington pointed out to a Senate committee in 1987 that since the passage of the 1969 act 2,029 fatal accidents had occurred in coal mines, thirty of them involving multiple fatalities.[49] The committee chairman, Edward M. Kennedy, said, "We know how to prevent many of the unnecessary deaths in the mines. What we seem to have lost is the will to do what good judgment and the law require. It makes me angry every time I hear about a miner killed because someone would not do his job." Senator Orrin G. Hatch, ranking Republican on the committee, called the Labor Department's Mine Safety and Health Administration (MSHA) "an agency in trouble," with a "disturbing pattern of misconduct, mismanagement and serious abuse." Herschel Potter, then recently retired safety enforcement chief of MSHA, responded that he and other officials of the agency had been ordered to "water down" rule changes "to match less stringent industry recommendations."[50]

It was not just inspectors, bureaucrats, and their political superiors who played fast and loose with the law and with the health and the safety of miners in the decades after 1969; no less involved were the companies that ran the mines. Of all the acts of flagrant disregard for the spirit as well as the letter of the law, perhaps the most cynical and calculated show of contempt was the massive fraud of coal dust samples. The 1969 act required coal companies to take regular air samples at the working face of mines in order to enforce the specified limits on the amounts of coal dust in the air breathed by miners. Not long after the law took effect some operators began falsifying the samples of air they submitted to the Bureau of Mines in order to avoid the expense of remedial measures—despite the risk of large fines. One dodge was to take the sample at some less dusty spot away from where coal was actually being mined, or even outside the mine entirely. Companies resorted to vacuum cleaners to remove dust from the sampling devices worn on the belts of randomly chosen miners—not an isolated practice but widespread across the country. Lynn Martin, secretary of labor during the Bush administration, told a congressional committee in April 1991 that mine operators apparently could not be trusted to police themselves: 500 companies (including major ones) were being charged with fraudulent submission of samples, and she was proposing $7 million in fines.[51] The nation's largest producer, Peabody Coal, admitted its guilt and agreed to pay $500,000 in fines for its deliberate tampering with samples from its mines in West Virginia, Kentucky, and Illinois.[52] In all, 4,700 false reports were identified, and they came from 847 mines. The fraud was so extensive that even a coal consulting firm, Triangle Research of Grundy, Virginia, was among those pleading guilty, admitting that its employees "would . . . send on behalf of the coal company a dust sample that had been taken at some place other than the mine site."[53] Gross disregard for the health of miners was demonstrated by the company that was ordered to transfer a miner suspected of getting pneumoconiosis to a less dusty area: management did transfer him but then falsified the dust content of the air in the new location.

Lynn Martin summed up the situation when she told the House Subcommittee on Health and Safety that she was "appalled by the flagrant disregard for a law designed to protect coal miners against disabling lung disease. We are talking about tampering with people's lives."[54] That has been the theme of this chapter—the wasting of the lives of coal miners. It has been and doubtless will continue to be a social problem of the first magnitude. At best, coal mining is a dangerous pursuit, but its hazards are made all the more threatening by the callous attitude of American coal operators.[55]

5

The Miners' Way of Life

Long before I ever saw the inside of a mine my life was significantly shaped by the fact that my father, attracted during World War I to the high wages coal miners were earning, in 1917 left his job as a barber in Shinnston, West Virginia, to load coal in nearby Owings, where in time he met and married one of the mine superintendent's daughters. In deciding to go underground, where his tender hands would bleed from blisters rubbed raw by his pick and shovel, he inadvertently decided much about my life too: that I would be born in a company house in a company town where dust from the tipple covered everything; that I would be tended to by a company doctor and educated in company-built schools. Life in a company town meant that a public library was an institution I would know only long after I had left home. It meant that the high school I attended did not offer physics, modern languages, or mathematics beyond plane geometry.

It also meant that the job insecurity of a coal miner was visited on each member of the family. In moving from Shinnston to Owings and then from town to town, my father set my family work obligations: to raise food crops, carry water, gather berries and nuts, spend Saturday mornings picking up coal from the slate dump and along railraod tracks to keep the house warm in winter. When available work narrowed to one or two days a week, or a mine shut down and the town turned belly up like a fish dead in the water, then all family ties were stretched, tensions became exacerbated, and opportunities had to go by the board. That nearly happened to my college career, when my father did well just to feed the family and manage to pay off some part of overdue house rent, and $30 for tuition seemed not ludicrously cheap but impossible to find—particularly during the Depression, when all high school graduates were competing for very few jobs.

By that time in my young life I knew well the problems of moving from town to town as mines closed or work grew slack: I had attended schools in seven different towns and had lived in nine communities, five of them company towns. On one occasion Dad grew weary of the pursuit of coal employment and took a job in a steel mill in Wierton, West Virginia; we stayed there three unhappy years. My mother hated company towns, my father disliked living in city apartments. We returned to a coal mine town, Hutchinson, West Virginia, in 1931, but after three years we packed up our abused furniture again and moved to Worthington to escape company town life.

Company Towns

There was nothing was quite like life in the no longer existing company town. The company held all the cards: it owned everything, it controlled everything, it kept discipline through a combination of paternalism and domination. If you had no economic ties to the company you were not welcome; there was no chamber of commerce to encourage you to set up an auto repair shop, a pharmacy, a grocery store or branch bank. Outside competition was not only not encouraged; in most instances it was forbidden— and that was easy, since the coal companies owned all the land. It also owned the houses that miners and their families occupied, the streets, schoolhouses, water systems, church buildings, recreational facilities (movies, pool halls, soda fountains, playgrounds and baseball fields, if any), doctor's office, the one and only company store, of course, and—not least—the constabulary and, by influence, the local government.

In keeping with the fiefdom motif, companies had their own monetary system, issuing their own "scrip." Some would advance scrip in anticipation of earnings, thus putting miners in debt (as the song says, "I owe my soul to the company store"), but the Consolidation Coal Company in my day granted scrip only if the income had already been earned. I always found it galling to have the company store clerk telephone the paymaster's office and ask clearance for my requested scrip—as if one could not be trusted to be truthful about money. Scrip was good at face value only in the company store; noncompany businesses elsewhere discounted it by as much as 15 percent. Either way, since prices were higher in company stores, scrip's value was inevitably less than that of coin of the realm. My family saved cash to buy a few things that they especially wanted to get from the A&P store, where quality was better and prices lower. One of those products was Eight O'Clock coffee, and I remember once when I was about eleven years old being sent to the next town with the family's only dollar bill in my pocket. It was about a two-mile ride on my worn-out, $3.00 bicycle, and the dollar bill somehow worked loose and was lost before I reached the store. I carefully retraced my steps, but someone must already have discovered my treasure, and it was nowhere to be found. I don't think I have ever felt more guilty about any misdeed of my life than I did over the loss of that bag of coffee and the change I would have taken home after paying 19¢, as I remember it, to the A&P clerk.

Company towns, given the geology and geography of coal seams, were usually isolated and remote, and before owning an automobile was common nearly all miners lived in company housing near the mine. That isolation facilitated control over the town by excluding outside troublemakers and alternative employment; it allowed management to impose discipline through eviction from the community as a penalty for breaking the rules—such as prohibitions against joining a union or trying to promote one. But the totalitarian note suggested by the armed patrols that often maintained owner-operator rule was not the whole story. In towns so small and isolated a sense of community did often exist. There were anticommunitarian differences among social groups, too—sometimes consciously stirred up for management control through intergroup conflict—but everybody could know almost everybody else in a town of a few hundred, and sharing and mutual help in times of family stress were common. When tragedy hit, helping was traditional and abundant; when strikes or layoffs reduced families to penury, sharing was standard, for most of these families came from areas of Appalachia, the deep South, and Europe where traditional community ties were strong.

Sympathy and understanding could be shown even by bosses, who often found themselves caught between the miners with their demonstrable hardships and company executives with their eye, (as the current cliché goes) on the bottom line. In James Still's remarkable 1940 novel *River of Earth,* the superintendent of the coal town, "Blackjack," is a sympathetic and understanding character who tries to make life tolerable for the family forced to leave subsistence farming for mining. Similarly, in Helen Hiscoe's account of her experience as the young wife of a newly licensed doctor in a southern West Virginia town she calls "Coal Mountain," the "super" of the mine is a perfect example of the mixture of patron and disciplinarian. Trying to be both puts him in such a difficult position that in frustration he gives up and retires.[1]

Company paternalism, though born of a desire to keep miners busy and their minds off the idea of unionism, had benevolent consequences when it resulted in providing recreational facilities, churches, schools, improvements in housing and sanitation, and opportunities for a social life in general. Company-sponsored baseball leagues became commonplace in eastern coalfields, and movie theaters proliferated in the camps.[2] All this slowed down and then nearly stopped after the industry hit the wall in the latter half of the 1920s. With coal prices down and demand slow, the need to recruit and hold miners was replaced by the necessity to cut back, and by my day on the scene, when the beehive-shaped coke ovens were idle (except those commandeered by Italian American housewives, who used them to bake wonderful bread), the ballfield next to the ovens was overgrown with weeds and littered with debris. About the only recreational activity still sponsored by Consol that I can remember was organizing first-aid squads whose members, dressed in white slacks, sought prizes of honor and perhaps a little cash by competing to see who could be speediest in providing first aid to injured miners.

All things considered, even in its better days the company town was, to put it mildly, not an ideal place to live; my mother was right in wanting to move away whenever feasible. This is not to say there was nothing good about life there. Most company towns were out in the country, surrounded by mountains. If you could get to a place where no mines poured sulfur into streams, fish were abundant, and the woods still had wild game for the hunter and trapper. There was land available for gardens; the woods had nut trees and wild berry bushes open to all. Like many young families, ours accommodated to circumstances, enjoyed life as much as possible, and didn't gripe unduly about our conditions. And it is true that many families saw nothing much wrong with outdoor privies if the company's men came around to clean them regularly; a lot of these people had come from the back country where privies were nearly universally suffered in peace. But once you have enjoyed the privilege of going to the bathroom in comfort when it is zero outdoors, you happily relinquish the pleasures of a frigid two-holer. My family, moving in and out of company towns, alternated between the two forms of sanitation and used the last outdoor one in 1944. But their desire to be rid of the old way was intense, and for hundreds and thousands of families who eventually bought and rebuilt their company houses, indoor plumbing was among their first alterations.

The universality of this reaction is, I think, the answer to the argument of the leading historian of the company town, Crandall Shifflett, who in trying to present a balanced picture of company towns takes pains to quote oldtimers who harbor some nostalgia for the better side of the old home place. He takes a condescending view of the 1947 *Medical Survey of the Bituminous-Coal Industry,* known as the Boone Report (for the admiral who was dispatched to coal country by the Interior Department, which was temporarily running the industry during a government seizure to keep coal coming during a strike). The report made much of the "average" coal camp's "monotonous rows of houses and privies . . . close to a foul creek." No doubt Shifflett is right about the difference in outlook between middle-class naval officers and the miners, often rural southerners "who had migrated from conditions inferior to those they found in the company towns."[3] But it does not follow from that difference in understanding that rural migrants did not know filth when they saw it; they understood discomfort as well and acted to eliminate both as soon as they could—that is, when their houses were no longer company owned.

Another constant problem for the coal-town housewife was the ubiquitous, windblown dust from the tipple where coal was dumped, sorted, and cleaned; from coal trains, and trucks, and the ash of ever-burning slag heaps; from innumerable chimneys both industrial and residential. Newcomers to coal-mining areas are often impressed by the speed with which coal dust accumulates. The battle against dirt was unending. No miner's wife would think of hanging out the wash without first thoroughly wiping the clothesline to prevent dirt stripes on laundry. In the Pennsylvania coalfields "window curtains have to be washed continually; bureau drawers must have their contents covered; silver and brass tarnish overnight; and each spring ushers in an orgy of cleaning wallpaper, rugs, and upholstery. Even the daisies in the fields have dirty faces."[4]

The lack of running water was a special burden for the housewife, but not for her alone. Coal miners took their after-work bath in a washtub if companies did not provide bathhouses with showers, and fewer than half of them did in the 1940s. And bathing after work was no casual undertaking; dirt sticks to sweat-soaked skin, and you get clean only after serious scrubbing with lots of soap and water. It was a common chore of the children to supply water for family needs; I recall that it was my job every Sunday evening to lug endless buckets of water from the street hydrant that served a dozen houses. This was preparation for Monday—traditional laundry day—and it took a lot of water plus backbreaking labor over a washboard to free workclothes of grease, sweat, and coal dust. Then it fell to children to use leftover wash water to scrub porches and wooden walkways. Once, while reminiscing about the old days with a friend from southern West Virginia, I mentioned my Sunday evening chore, and he exclaimed, "That was my chore too. Had to make dozens of trips to the 'crick' every Sunday."

Among other childhood tasks was summertime gardening. No matter how strong the inclination to play baseball, the garden took priority, because it was a vital factor in coal-town life. Each family tended a small backyard garden, and often they planted separate patches on company-owned but otherwise unused hillsides, to supply not only fresh summer vegetables but equally important preserved food for winter use. When work was slack or a strike occurred, not having the basement shelves full of packed Mason jars could spell hunger. One well-remembered canned item was vegetables for winter soup: into half-gallon jars went tomatoes, green beans, carrots, peppers, corn, and onions; with a bit of meat that combination made a nourishing and tasty meal, especially when supplemented with cornbread made from meal ground at Grandfather Lockard's gristmill.

The miner's garden was a natural for yesterday's coal workers, who came from rural and farming backgrounds where growing their own food was a family custom. In the towns I knew, many families of Italian heritage would use West Virginia's steep hillsides as their Italian forebears had made vineyards on steep terrain—by terracing. With their special tools and their ways of growing and preserving tomatoes they introduced their neighbors to new foods as well as new ways of agriculture. Appalachian natives who had been subsistence farmers traditionally were accustomed to growing their food, as were the blacks from the South, about half of whom had been sharecroppers before they became miners.[5] Among all three groups the garden was an undertaking of the whole family; fathers worked there before going to the mine in the morning and on Sundays; sons too young to go into the mine worked in the garden, and wives and daughters took their turns as well.

The coal town with all its defects is now history. Some may find a romantic aura about good times they experienced there; others have grimmer memories. The 1947 Boone Report stressed that living conditions were worse in coal towns than around the country generally, and that coal miners and their families had been denied the benefits of scientific findings about sound shelter and safe sanitation: in "Coalvale, U.S.A." the "decrepit houses," and "disease breeding privies that were the despair of earnest reformers earlier in the present century have persistently survived. That they are anachronistic in a day that boasts innumerable testimonials to the march of science tends to intensify the reality of the deficiencies. That they exist in shocking contrast to modern, sanitary, well-maintained communities stigmatizes not only the backward coal-mine operators but the whole industry."[6]

Today's miners have living conditions far different from those of 1947. While the term "coal camp" aptly described the impermanent atmosphere of Great-Grandfather's company town, there are not many such tumble-down rowhouses leaning over debris-filled gutters today. In 1922 more than half of all miners—in Appalachia, three-quarters—lived in company houses; very few miners do so today—less than 1 percent in 1980 when President Jimmy Carter's Coal Commission reported its findings.[7] Thousands of erstwhile company houses have been bought by the miners themselves and remodeled and upgraded. The owner-occupants have an incentive to make their dwellings permanent and attractive—a motivation lacking among renter-miners of the coal camps of the past. (Interestingly, though, in the expanding western coal operations some companies have again begun building housing for their miners—for the same reason that eastern companies did at the beginning of this century: to attract and hold miners where housing is scarce.)

Home ownership is now as common as it was rare in the past: about two-thirds of miner housing today is owner-occupied. It is true that many houses are mobile homes; indeed, two of three new homes are on wheels, and they often seem rather haphazardly tacked onto steep hillsides. Still, they are convenient, relatively low in cost, and often situated in attractive woodland. And even where land for housing is scarce, space for parking trailers can be rented.

To anyone familiar with the open mountains and valleys of Appalachia it may seem strange that space for housing development is hard to find, but an enormous amount of that open territory is owned and awaiting mineral exploitation by coal companies that are not interested in releasing it. For example, 48 percent of Harlan County, Kentucky, and at least half the land in twenty-seven West Virginia counties is owned by corporations; 33 percent of all privately owned land in West Virginia is in the hands of twelve corporations. The 1980 coal commission noted further that companies buy mineral rights to land in addition to what they own, thus further limiting opportunities for housing development. The commission cited a study estimating that besides direct ownership of land, companies "controlled leases on an additional 4 million acres" in West Virginia and were increasing such leaseholdings by half a million acres each year. Said one miner: "There's just not that much land to build on. You get down too low and you're gonna get flooded, too high and you can't get to it in the wintertime."[8]

Another striking difference between then and now is the distance between the mine and home. Before automobiles were virtually universal, miners generally lived within easy walking distance of their mines, or drove at most a few miles (public transportation in the coalfields then, as now, was rare). Carpools were used only when absolutely necessary—such as during the war, when gasoline was rationed—partly because coal loaders did not work on an hourly basis but were free to leave when the day's coal was "cleaned up." A loader's shift might end one or two hours before hourly workers had put in their time, and getting home early was a prized aspect of being a handloader. Or, if a buddy became sick or was injured, a loader would have to finish loading the day's coal alone. Then having his own car could save him a walk home if his fellow carpoolers had "run off" without him.

Today, however, coal miners tend to commute even longer distances in general than do other workers: their average driving time between home and mine now is twenty-nine minutes, compared with a nationwide average of twenty minutes. Coal miners in one survey were found to travel an average of 26 miles to work, twice as far as other rural workers and three times as far as urban workers, who averaged 8.4 miles. The longest average time in commuting by miners is found in central Appalachia (thirty-two minutes), where commuting time is exaggerated by the poor condition of roads, due in large measure to the havoc wrought on highways by extremely heavy coal trucks.[9]

Today's miners, then, are no longer isolated, out-of-the-mainstream workers; they are more independent than their predecessors. They are also better educated; many have had some years of post-high school education, and it is not uncommon to find miners who have had jobs such as teaching before turning to the better-paying mine work. They are in the mainstream in other ways, such as their choice of recreation. In the old days one would never expect to find them on a golf course, but the *United Mine Workers Journal* reported a few years ago on coal miners who set out for the links on their days off.[10] They also take their families to lakes and rivers for vacations—often with a boat trailing behind the pickup or recreational van. Miners still tend to high absenteeism on the opening day of deer season and the first day of trout fishing, but gone are the times when gun, rod, and beer were their only forms of recreation.

Women Miners

Among other significant changes was the coming of women to mining in the mid-1970s. Although in World War II and the years immediately thereafter women increasingly did jobs once reserved for men only—working in steel mills and construction, driving buses—they had been absolutely barred from coal mines except for a few small family operations. That was chiefly due to the superstitious fear that a woman inside a mine spelled danger; they were often refused permission even to visit a mine because of it. No doubt there were also economic reasons for excluding women because they were potential competitors for jobs. There was also a strong belief in the obligation of men to "protect" women from danger. Whatever its source, the prohibition had been around for a long time. In Great Britain in the 1840s, for example, when a special panel investigated the treatment of small children in coal mines, it was the abuse of women in the mines that caught public attention sufficiently to produce protective legislation: in 1842 women were barred by law from working inside mines in Great Britain. Hundreds continued to work at the "pit brow" (outside the mine itself) until 1972, when the last female surface coal workers were made "redundant," in the terminology of British labor relations.[11]

In the United States women's coal mining experience was nearly the opposite. Discrimination against women in employment became unlawful under the 1964 Civil Rights Act, partly because women struggled politically to win equal treatment in the job market and partly because opponents of the bill in the Senate hoped that adding women's rights would overload the bill and kill it. But the strategy backfired, and when the act took effect, an arduous campaign began, largely in the courts, to force recalcitrant employers to comply with the law of nondiscriminatory hiring. The first suits against coal companies were won in 1973, and within four years nearly a thousand women had become miners. In 1979 there were 2,600, earning higher wages than most men or women could earn in other nonprofessional occupations.

Women miners faced special problems, however. Not least was sexual harassment from both bosses and fellow workers. More lawsuits brought successful challenges against the harassment (such as the childish drilling of a peephole between men and women's bathhouses and foremen's demands for sexual favors as a condition for fair working arrangements that men were given routinely). And although bosses claimed that they were physically unable to do the heavy work, women proved themselves strong enough and able through training to master the tools and mechanical skills of contemporary mining.[12]

Soon another facet of coal mining began to take its toll among women miners. They lost fingers in accidents, and one had an arm severed (it was successfully reattached).[13] Then came the inevitable—the first woman miner to die on the job was crushed under an eighteen-foot section of the top that fell on her while she was working as a roof bolter. Marilyn McCusker, age thirty-five, had been among the hundreds of women who sued coal companies for denying them employment; in 1977 she had won a cash settlement of $30,000 and a job at the Rushton mine in central Pennsylvania. She had been working there for two years at the time of the accident. She was proud of being a miner and enjoyed the work and especially the more than $9.00 an hour she earned (in contrast to the $85 a week she had previously been paid in a nursing home). "She loved it from the very first day," said her husband. "It's dirty and dark and rats running around all over the place. All her life, though, basically she'd never had a good day's pay. She was just doing menial work. When she came home the first day, she was smiling from ear to ear. She just loved it."[14]

The ultimate and decisive form of discriminatory treatment of female miners has been their loss of jobs through cutbacks: observers of the current scene assert that being last to come on the job, women have lost jobs faster than men. In light of the fact that blacks and women have both been disproportionately overrepresented in the discharged ranks, however, it does not appear to be merely a question of seniority, since African Americans have been miners in considerable numbers for almost a century. That the UMWA contract does not have an airtight seniority clause—allowing management to dismiss anyone they dislike—may help to account for the decline in blacks and woman. Further, some miners claim that companies put blacks, women, and malcontents to work on mined-out sections which soon close down, offering a covering excuse for planned dismissals.

Appalachian Miners

The negative attitude toward women miners is a recent link in the chain of prejudice that newcomers to the industry have faced. Local residents in coal country, both farmers and townsfolk, took a dim view of the hill people who came in to work the early mines; those Appalachian miners likewise derided the European immigrants and southern blacks who followed. One of Marilyn McCusker's supervisors asserted that women were incapable of mine work not for lack of physical power but because of plain unwillingness to work. Equally derogatory and unwarranted remarks were made about the previous groups: each in turn was claimed to be inherently stupid and unable to learn.

The earliest and most numerous contingent of the coal work force in the first half of the present century, when the demand for coal swelled the mining population to an unprecedented and since unequaled extent, were mountaineers—or, derogatively, hillbillies. In the opinion of many observers, these people were a sad sample of humanity. Arnold Toynbee, the British historian, called them illiterate barbarians who practiced witchcraft, who were poverty-stricken, who lived in squalor and poor health; he said that as examples of people who once had been civilized but had slipped back into barbarism they were worse than peoples whose uncivilized ways were survivals of ancient barbarism, such as the Rifis, Albanians, Kurds, and Hairy Ainus.[15] That undoubtedly says more about Toynbee and his imperialistic dismissal of inferior colonial people than it does about the upland residents of Appalachia, but he was not alone in his views. The late Harry Caudill, who certainly had a sympathetic attitude toward the mountain people of whom he wrote in *Night Comes to the Cumberland,* also makes categorically derogatory remarks. He speaks of them as a population "born of embittered rejects and outcasts from the shores of Europe—as cynical, hardened and bitter a lot as can be imagined outside prison walls. They were free hands with the fists, knife and rifle, illiterate, uncouth and harddrinking."[16] No doubt many descendants of the frontiersmen had these dubious qualities, but that these were universal traits is just not true.

Another charge against mountain people was that they were given to

violence and murder. Caudill mentions two Kentucky lawyers of his acquaintance, one who defended a thousand mountaineers charged with
murder, and another who prosecuted six hundred homicide cases. Caudill
adds that it is "scarcely probable that the monstrous number of industrial
accidents in the Kentucky mines have greatly exceeded those of pistol,
knife, and whiskey."[17] Stories about lethal feuds among hill people are legion. Surely the Hatfield-McCoy story must be the most widespread legend
of interfamily dispute in American history. But unlike the Capulet-Montagu
affair, it is reported not sympathetically and poetically but derisively ("The
Hatfields and McCoys, they were reckless mountain boys"). Yet for all their
reported proneness to violence, hill people must surely be mild in disposi-
tion compared with the "civilized" ethnic purity zealots we remember in
Germany and Japan, or the Serbs in Bosnia. Even at their very worst, hillfolk in America are tame indeed compared with the sixteenth-century Spanish conquerors of Central and South America.

Anyone inclined to believe the Hatfield-McCoy fable should read Altina L.
Waller's little gem of historical research: *Feud: Hatfields, McCoys, and Social
Change in Appalachia, 1850–1900.* She blows away clouds of misrepresenta-
tion about this alleged hillbilly vindictiveness and moonshiner violence.
First, it was not a lengthy intertribal dispute of murder and mayhem and
hatred. It cost twelve lives, it is true, but it lasted twelve years, not generations. Nor was it based on the romantic attachment of a McCoy woman
and a Hatfield man; that affair was short-lived, sordid, and unrelated to the
underlying roots of the dispute. The men involved were far from being the
commonly described quick-tempered gunmen distrustful of society and
the courts; both families were given to a rural, peaceful kind of life and
inclined to use the courts to settle small disputes. Rather, the interfamily
controversy had aspects of the conflict between traditionalist (land- and
farming-oriented) and modernizer (coal, railroad, and timber development)
factions. The latter were egged on by corporate interests seeking to exploit
the mineral and timber riches of the southern West Virginia and eastern
Kentucky mountains along the Tug River. Political factions aligned with
these economic interests did much to perpetuate the feud, and tabloid-style
newspapers made up and published lurid fairytales about these "primitives"

whom they condemned as hell-raisers given to excessive drink—although when these same mountain people were brought into a new style of life as industrial wage earners, they became *more* given to whiskey and carousing than their hill country predecessors.

The case against the feudists is indeed unproved. The twelve-year conflict and its ensuing disorder involved a fundamental change in the region, culminating in a dispute that was symbolic of the changes: it was "one of a series of contests for hegemony over Appalachia's rich resources. After the fighting was over, the [area] . . . became one of the richest coal-producing hollows of the Tug Valley. A feeder railroad line ran along its narrow bottom and the water ran red with sludge from the mine, which produced fabulous profits for the developers, but only ugliness and poverty for the people who lived there."[18]

Also in diametric opposition to negative views of Appalachian people are the observations of Robert Coles, whose *Migrants, Sharecroppers, Mountaineers* lets hillfolk speak for themselves via his tape recorder and presents an abused but proud and responsible people who do not remotely resemble Toynbee's derelicts. When Coles refers to their poverty, their poor health, and their despair over their inability to earn enough to sustain their families, he is not critical but understanding. Their lack of economic prospects is not a personal shortcoming or lack of civilization but something they fear and regret and try to overcome, however much the social, political, and economic forces of Appalachia deprive them of security and minimal life comforts—such as enough to eat or medical attention. Here, for example, speaks a worried mother: "There's nothing I hate more than a child crying at you and crying at you for food, and you standing there and knowing you can't give them much of anything, for all their tears. It's unnatural. That's what I say; it's just unnatural for a mother to be standing in her own house, and her children near her, and they're hungry and there isn't food to feed them. It's just not right. It happens, though."[19]

Another of Coles's subjects thinks many of the hill people will have no choice but to leave their hills and hollows, however attached they are to their ancestral lands.[20] To remain means slow starvation for their children. "The trouble with our people is that they're willing to suffer; some of them don't know anything else. All their lives they've been in bad shape, barely getting by from one meal to the next, one day to the next. . . . They're proud they have those cabins in the hills." Raising gardens, hunting, and fishing may allow them to survive, he adds, but if survival is all that is involved, "then they're in for a lot of trouble."[21]

Nor are they in much doubt why they face such conditions. One after another of Coles's people talks of the role of coal companies in making misery in the mountains. Coal operators, outsiders who are not concerned with the fate of erstwhile miners and their families, are the *real* crooks, not just small-time crooks like the county politicians who do the companies' bidding. The people identify the companies as the reason jobs are lost by miners who are not only willing to work hard for a living but willing to do nearly any kind of work—a fact known to the coal overlords but of little concern to them. The local people know what strip-mining has done to the environment and to the mountain scenery, where hilltops have been butchered to get at underlying coal. They see the source of their problems in Pittsburgh (the Golden Triangle) and New York (Wall Street) and New England, where oil interests have come to dominate coal concerns and have promoted destructive but profitable strip mining. They also look back to the times when representatives of coal companies came to the mountains and bought up mineral rights to millions of acres of farmland— rights that entitled the holder to do anything deemed appropriate to get at the coal or other minerals in the ground. And as Caudill pointed out, these university-trained lawyers sat down in the kitchens of log cabins and bought from often barely literate or illiterate landholders mineral rights worth thousands of dollars for as little as 50¢ an acre.[22]

Mountain people also recognize the special role of county and state politicians in dominating the lives of those living up the hollows and along the creeks. It is no accident that politics in Appalachia is so riddled with corruption (several West Virginia governors have been found guilty of corrupt practices in the last couple of decades). Politics is a major source of employment in coal country, and to hold on to income it is necessary to hold on to power, and that requires cutting corners. One of Coles's former miners tells of a conversation with his wife's cousin, a landowner, insurance dealer, and county politician with whom the miner discussed the possibility of getting work with the county. "He asked me if I'd do a good day's work and if I'd mind my business and be loyal to the county, and not cause trouble to anyone, the county officials and all the others. I said all I wanted to do was work, and if I could work, I'd never stop being loyal to those who give me the work. So, I got the work. I drive the kids to school." Then he added that if there were factories in the area, the county politicians wouldn't be a "law unto themselves." But as circumstances stand, fearful residents are apprehensive about what the politicians can do to dissidents: removing them from welfare rolls, changing the school bus route so as to deny service to their children, cutting children's eligibility for free school lunches, or a hundred other things the "court house crowd can do to you."[23]

Much as in the earlier company town there is no competitive source of potential income to fall back on when coal employment wanes or disappears. So, with county patronage being the most significant economic factor in the region, the local population has no choice but to become beholden to the local politicians—and so grows the politicians' power and the invitation to corruption to hold that power. This is not to deny that corruption occurs in areas of more varied economic development, but corruption has a particularly powerful appeal when politics has a singular role in the local economy. The politics of West Virginia and Kentucky bear out this argument in striking fashion.

Immigrant Miners

With the burgeoning of industry late in the nineteenth and early in the twentieth century there was a tremendous demand for workers to operate steel mills, construct industrial and commercial buildings, manufacture great quantities of goods, and wrest from the earth the raw materials necessary for the economic expansion. Most new industrial growth required coal in one way or another, and to meet that demand, miners were among those recruited from beyond American shores, flooding into the coal camps that were being built.

From the 1880s onward new workers in general arrived by the millions. In the 1880s 5.2 million immigrants came, mostly from Europe; the number declined slightly in the 1890s, but in the first decade of the new century Ellis Island was a swinging gate for 8.8 million newcomers. During the 1920s laws restricted immigration, and in the 1930s the Depression slowed the wave: whereas from 1901 to 1910 the rate of immigration was 10.4 persons per thousand of the U.S. population, in the 1930s the rate was 0.4 per thousand.[24] But the slowdown came after the fundamental change in the nation's social mixture had already taken place. So too had the ethnic composition of the country's coal community been permanently changed; migrants, particularly from Italy and Poland, and their descendants were thereafter a large segment of Coalville's people.

Immigrants were often recruited specifically as strikebreakers, frequently without their knowing that a strike was taking place. Naturally, that made the foreign-born recruits unpopular with union men, but there were other sources of animosity: just the fact that immigrants were outsiders and "different" and did not, at least at first, understand or speak English made them objects of scorn. They were often given the most dangerous jobs, assigned the worst housing, and denied chances for advancement. Disliked as potential or actual strikebreakers by native-born whites, immigrants were also denounced as inciters of radicalism by coal operators who were quick to suspect anyone of harboring anti-operator views. When some turned out to be genuine radicals with Marxist leanings, coal company men leaped to the conclusion that immigrants were commonly inclined to be bomb-throwing anarchists.

It was true, however, that immigrant miners were often strong adherents to the cause of unionism, and many union leaders welcomed them into the union's ranks. Foreign-born miners often achieved leadership roles in the United Mine Workers, despite the lingering disdain for nonnative miners or those born of immigrant parents. Discriminatory thinking is not as prevalent as it was in the past, yet as late as 1972, it is said, when the leaders of the Miners for Democracy (MFD) caucused to select their candidate for president of the UMWA with the intention of choosing Mike Trbovich, they ended up picking Arnold Miller reportedly because they feared that Trbovich's "foreign" name might alienate native rank-and-file miners and cost the MFD votes—this despite the fact that Trbovich had been elected leader of the MFD when the movement was founded in April 1970. The comment of George Titler, vice-president of the UMWA, about the Jock Yablonski murder is equally revealing: "You don't know that foreign element of coal miners from Russia and Yugoslavia and the like up there in Pennsylvania. I don't mean there's anything wrong with being foreign, but they stick together behind their man. It's not like down in the [Kentucky and Tennessee] fields where everybody's an Anglo-Saxon."[25]

One Italian American who migrated from Italy to Monongah, West Virginia, in 1903 (but was not at work on the day in 1907 when Monongah's mine blew up) believed one reason for the union's ultimate success was that it granted equal rights to all, regardless of race, religion, or national background. "We had meetings with everybody," recalled Dan Colanero. "If you was Italian, you made your speech in Italian, then somebody explained to the others what you said. If you was Polish, the same thing. I say we're all here together; the only real Americans was the Indians." He went on to say, however, that the companies talked a lot about the "American Plan," which amounted to "an open shop policy, claiming that the union was the work of foreign agitators. . . . No Goddamn Dagoes was what they would say."[26]

Black Miners

I remember an occasion that illustrates the ability of African Americans to take the lead in social organizations, an opportunity rarely afforded them in either the UMWA or the ranks of coal management. There was a dispute in the Carolina union local about whether to join a wildcat strike (over some long-forgotten issue) in sympathy with other area locals and in defiance of the national union. I was taking a course in labor economics at the time, and I persuaded Dad to come with me to a meeting to decide whether to strike. The mob attending the meeting was too large to fit in the union hall, so the meeting was moved to an adjacent open field. The president of the local, an articulate black man, handled the debate fairly and effectively, despite the rancor and heated temper of the proceedings. There was reason to expect that words might be replaced by rougher means of dispute, so when the time came for the vote the president prudently asked those in favor of striking to step across the narrow creek that divided the field; those opposed were told to gather for the count on the near side. There was some good-humored comment on the president's move, but fist-shaking and shouted name-calling from a distance did not give way to the violence that might otherwise have occurred.

It was not uncommon for blacks to be elected to leadership positions in local unions. Many were potential leaders who, denied opportunities to advance in the union hierarchy at national and regional levels, were available as local officers. This paradox of ability being available because it was denied opportunity elsewhere parallels the black experience in coal mining history generally. There is an intriguing ambiguity about that experience: blacks were victims of racism in the coal industry as they have been in the society at large, yet racism has often been muted inside the mine because, many believe, people facing common danger tend to develop mutual protection attitudes that mitigate prejudice.

It is not the case, though, that all discrimination stopped at the pit mouth, however different race relations may have been underground. Blacks were not allowed to take better-paying jobs such as operating cutting machines. Many whites flatly refused to work with black motormen, and of course that refusal was accepted by white bosses as another of those "facts" of race relations that it seemed pointless to dispute. The easiest course was to allow discrimination to continue, since opposing it would invite organized opposition, whereas going along brought no particular trouble. This is, of course, the basis upon which Jim Crow thrived for over a century, and it applied to coal miners just as it did to other Americans. Thus whites refused to work for black bosses, and no one opposed the practice of excluding blacks from mining extension courses offered at West Virginia University just before World War I, classes intended to train workers to become mine foremen. As one commentator noted, supervisory jobs went "even" to immigrants rather than to "native Colored men." African Americans had to accept the less agreeable jobs such as mule driver, or the dangerous task of being a brakeman on a haulage motor. Outside the mine, few black miners got the less hazardous work. Jobs in coke yards, hot and disagreeable, were predominantly held by blacks; indeed, immigrant and native whites constituted less than one-fifth of the coke-yard work force in 1925.[27]

A current development that demonstrates continued discrimination is the gradual elimination of African Americans from the ranks of coal miners. As the number of miners employed in these times of unprecedented productivity declines steadily, blacks have been among the first replaced by machines. One labor historian predicts that longwall technology will make black miners—assuming a continuation of the downward trend in their employment during the period 1930 to 1970—statistically extinct by the end of the twentieth century.[28]

Other commentators see the situation differently, claiming that discrimination both inside and outside the mine is much less prevalent than in the society at large. For example, David Alan Corbin argues that not race but social class predominates in coal communities. Basing his findings on the experience of southern West Virginia, he contends that the rigid domination of miners by coal mine owners precluded the forming of a caste or racial hierarchy and led instead to a capitalist class system. Rather than opposing each other on the basis of ethnicity and race, miners joined in common and concerted opposition to the coal operators and their exploitation of working-class miners. Because they felt themselves to be exploited by the profit-hungry owners of mines, they became unified in their "class feeling and behavior."[29]

Corbin maintains that blacks who fled the South seeking liberation in large cities did not fit easily into the social order of metropolitan centers such as New York and Chicago and were subjected to extreme racial animosity and oppression. In city after city violent race riots erupted, and hundreds of blacks were killed, but in small communities like the coal towns of southern West Virginia, relative harmony prevailed between black and white.

There were a few violent incidents between the races, however, and in a 1916 case African Americans so feared the lynching of a black man arrested after he was charged with killing a white man in an election-day street fight that they assembled a black group to deliver the accused from jail. Shots were fired and the county sheriff was killed in the exchange. The area was thrown into confusion by the events, and many were apprehensive that anti-black violence might break out, since white reaction to this show of contempt for white "justice" was racist.

White outrage toward blacks in general was revealed in letters written at the time. A mine manager in Wyoming County, George Wolfe, wrote to the mine owner, Justus Collins: "It will never do to let a matter like this rest. It shows the sentiment of the negrows and that is that if you arrest some of their race, that it is proper for them to gather in a mob and kill white officers and turn the prisoners lose." Wolfe believed the unrest was rooted in the current political campaign for governor which, he thought, had "seriously effected some colored people. You cannot send for a nigar and sit him down in the executive mansion and plot with him to overthrwo the white people without evil results." Then, in what may have been a considerable exaggeration, he added, "The feeling on the Plant [around the mine?] is not good towards the negrow."[30]

Of course, the racist fulminations of one mine superintendent do not a culture make, but it sounds like the West Virginia I knew as a young man more than the class unity of the races perceived by Corbin. For, no mistake about it, West Virginia in the 1930s and 1940s, when I was beginning to become aware of such matters, was a racist society. I emerged slowly from my own racist cocoon; indeed, like Molière's *bourgeois gentilhomme,* who was surprised to learn that he had been speaking prose all his life, I am surprised in retrospect to discover how prejudiced I was. It was not because of any personal experience involving race—there were few African Americans in my towns, and none at all in neighborhoods where I lived—yet there it was.

I became aware of it slowly. I recall being taken aback by the druggist in whose store I worked as a teenager when he instructed me to try to sell anything possible to blacks, since they were gullible and would spend while their money lasted. I said nothing in response, being about thirteen at the time, but it stuck in my mind as something that didn't sound quite right. A year or two later another episode gave me to think: two young black men who worked at Carolina mine came to our house to buy a car Dad was selling, and they were so hat-in-hand, so deferential, that I was uncomfortable and embarrassed to realize that they thought we required such exaggerated politeness. And once I observed a company doctor who became outraged and abusive when a black miner did not show him respect by removing his hat and saying "Sir" in speaking to a white man. This struck me as absurd and quite unexpected, for although West Virginia had segregated schools (by law), segregated social gathering habits, and decidedly segregated occupational patterns (by rigid custom), it was not Mississippi: state law required little discrimination. But still, in the detested way of the North, it was segregated and oppressive, even if no signs designated separate water fountains for "white" and "colored."

Nevertheless, Corbin finds evidence of interracial harmony in the absence of race riots in the small towns of southern West Virginia. But that may have had more to do with the small black population there—small enough not to be threatening, not large enough to constitute a counterforce. Moreover, newcomers who arrived from the rural South found life in West Virginia familiar, less hostile and forbidding than large cities were to migrants there.

Corbin also cites a case in which four white miners were fired and blacklisted because they had struck over the hiring of a black motorman. One wonders if this was action to support hiring blacks for better jobs or disciplinary retribution for striking; certainly the hard evidence of the general failure of blacks to get more of the desirable jobs would suggest that a company crackdown on recalcitrant whites was more significant in its singularity than its frequency. Nor is Corbin convincing in his comment on housing integration. No doubt some company towns were integrated to a degree, but others were stiffly segregated. Bill Love, a friend of mine who was a miner in Wyoming County in southern West Virginia in the early 1950s, recalls that in his town the company bought nine houses from a timber firm which blacks alone occupied, some distance from houses reserved for whites. In my experience, too, the friendly contact between the races that Corbin describes was a near-impossibility, for physical separation kept black and white families from more than the barest knowledge of each other. And what housing segregation didn't accomplish, school segregation finished. We were races apart—and kept that way both by custom and by the intent of the dominant powers.

The "rules" tended to be arbitrary. Perhaps Bill Love sums them up best with his description of life in his boyhood town, where his father—migrating from sharecropping in North Carolina—spent fifty years mining coal and contracted a fatal case of black lung along the way. Bill remembers that blacks and whites worked side by side in the mine, but when the shift ended, they went to segregated showers before going to their segregated homes, and "we couldn't go to school side by side." And yet "I was raised up with some white boys, eight of them in a family that lived on a farm and had an old truck. They would ask us—me and another fellow— if we wanted to go to the movies with them on a Saturday night, and then we'd go off together in the truck. When we got to the movies, they'd go to one side and we'd go to the other. When the movie was over we all come home together—get in the truck and come home." To top off the crazy quilt of this-you-do and that-you-don't, Bill's father, a Pentecostal preacher, "had a little church and he had as many whites as blacks."[31]

The work of miners, the dangers they faced, their endurance of derogation and discrimination, their exploitation and susceptibility to being declared surplus goods—all this shaped the life-style of the mining community. So too, for both good and ill, did their labor union.

Nº 10.

Monongah Explosion

1. Street morgue following the Monongah explosion, 12 December 1907. The author's family home was one block beyond the steps seen at upper right. A State of West Virginia historical marker in Monongah commemorates the event: "Monongah Disaster: On the 6th of Dec., 1907[,] 361 coal miners, many of them from countries far across the sea, perished under these hills in the worst mining disaster of our nation. The four who escaped died of injuries." (Courtesy West Virginia and Regional History Collection, West Virginia University Libraries, Morgantown)

2. Author's parents, Clyde and Virgie Lockard, c. 1920, Owings, West Virginia. (Photographer unknown)

3. Typical company town, this one at the White Oak Company's Cranberry No. 3 Mine. (Courtesy West Virginia and Regional History Collection, West Virginia University Libraries, Morgantown)

4. Last mine car from No. 3 coal seam, Freeman, West Virginia, 1939 or 1940. Mulepower used to be the common means of moving coal inside mines. (From the collection of Allen Pack, Cannelton, West Virginia.)

5. Typical bathhouse locker room. Miners' clothes were suspended on chains and locked in place. (Courtesy West Virginia and Regional History Collection, West Virginia University Libraries, Morgantown)

6. Handloading underground. (Courtesy Eastern Regional Coal Archives, Craft Memorial Library, Bluefield, West Virginia.)

7. Fire boss using Davy lamp to check for presence of gas. (Courtesy West Virginia and Regional History Collection, West Virginia University Libraries, Morgantown)

CONSOLIDATION COAL COMPANY
Received payment in full for account noted on this statement.

AD 3B

FOR HALF MO. ENDING   MAY 31, 1942

86

WALTER DUANE LOCKARD

950   950

	@			RENT		
TONS	..			ELECTRIC LIGHTS		
	..			WATER		
	..			BACK RENT		
	..			HOSPITAL		
	..			DOCTOR	1 —	
HOURS	28 .. 1 —		28 00	INSURANCE	2 48	
	42 966		40 56	DEBIT BALANCE LAST HALF		
YARDAGE	..			LEASE BALANCE LAST HALF		
	..			STORE LEASE (NEW)		
	..			U. M. W. OF A.	2 —	
TRANSFERS				CASH HELD LAST PAY		
				U.S. BONDS		
GROSS EARNINGS						
	EXPLOSIVES					
	SMITHING					
	LAMPS		88			
TOTAL OCCUPATIONAL						
NET TAXABLE EARNINGS			67 68	TOTAL CHARGES	12 16	
S. S. TAX			68	DEBIT BALANCE NEXT HALF		
CHECKWEIGHMAN				LEASE BALANCE NEXT HALF		
BURIAL FUND			1 00	NET CHARGES		
METAL MONEY			5 —	BALANCE DUE YOU	55 52	
CENTRAL GARAGE						
SUPPLIES				BALANCE DUE COMPANY		
COAL SALES						
BOARD				CASH HELD FOR NEXT PAY		
CASH ADVANCE				NET AMOUNT		
BATH HOUSE						

8. Author's pay envelope, 31 May 1942, for two weekends' work. "Metal money" refers to scrip drawn before payday. Note the amounts withheld for burial fund, lamp, doctor, insurance, and union dues.

9. Preparatory plant where coal is cleaned and readied for shipment, Fairmont, West Virginia, 1947. (Courtesy West Virginia and Regional History Collection, West Virginia University Libraries, Morgantown)

10. Outside a mine at Mansfield, England; December 1943. Author (at right); in center, John Brass, superintendent of the mine.

6

Coal Miners and Their Union

IN THE COAL TOWNS of my youth the United Mine Workers of America
was an important presence with a decided impact on the life of the community. Local union halls were important centers of activity. In some places
they were imposing structures—at least by local standards (such as the large
brick meeting hall in Monongah). The union was an institution that made
significant decisions; it was a place where vital demands were lodged, re-
wards granted, favors done, disappointments and reversals suffered. As a
powerful influence, the union left no one without an opinion about it—
positive, negative or ambivalent. Mostly my father was in the last category;
he was not an organization man, never held or sought a union office or attended its meetings, and sometimes grumbled about the UMWA and its
national leadership, but he was generally in favor of union objectives.

His nonparticipation did not set him apart from most of his fellow miners, however, for nonparticipation is normal after all. People tend to be
socially inert; like an infantryman in combat who does not fire his weapon
because attracting attention is likely to invite retaliation and be regretted,
most civilians resist social involvement. It has often been shown that even
revolutions which in retrospect appear to have involved huge numbers actually engaged the full commitment of relatively few. Even when large
numbers do get into the act, social somnolence soon returns. This is in fact

a constant problem for organizers: it is rational to let others take chances and exert energy on behalf of a class whose members all will gain, whether or not they participate.

All labor-organizing history reflects this phenomenon—even the "coal wars" in southern West Virginia just after World War I, when miners so detested the actions of mine owners that thousands of them assembled in an army of sorts, "invaded" Logan County, and exchanged fire with a huge posse composed of Baldwin-Felts "detectives" and company-paid scabs in the famous confrontation at Blair Mountain. It seems to me that the proper inference to be drawn from these wars is that the circumstances must have been extraordinary to generate that much voluntary action and risk taking. One historian of American coal mining argues that a counterbalancing treatment of the data—emphasizing the number of miners who even in those conditions did nothing—is imperative to set the record straight. Contrary to the notion that from the 1880s to the 1930s coal miners constituted "a mass movement of class-conscious workers rising up as one against an oppressive and exploitive labor system," Crandall Shifflett's examination of events "reveals two things: long spasms of relative inactivity broken by briefer periods of intense industrial conflict; and a substantial, if indeterminate, number of miners who refused to join the union even during the age of notorious labor repression."[1]

I understand his desire to balance the exaggeration of enthusiastic writers, but the fact remains that the degree of participation was far beyond the ordinary. A balanced view of the action is one that perceives it neither as a universal joining of the movement nor as an extensive refusal to support the union cause. What is extraordinary is not that some stayed at home but that so many risked blacklisting and eviction and took up arms by the thousand against recognized (if corrupt) authority. Relative to the natural inertia of most people most of the time, surely the massiveness of the participation is the "historical" point to be made.

That my father was not an active unionist did not mean he was uninterested in union policies and actions; his diary reflects continuing awareness and concern. Few if any names of public figures appear more often in his diary than that of John L. Lewis—hardly surprising, since Lewis inevitably caught all miners' attention (and usually their approval) with his overblown rhetoric and the scorn he turned on the coal operators whom he accused of not caring what happened to miners. Coal miners had to accept the domination of their bosses and the owners in silence, but they resented it, and Lewis spoke for them in denouncing coal company hegemony in stinging language. President of the union for forty years, he was keenly aware of the miners' need to hear the oral flogging he gave the operators; he made it an important part of his leadership strategy.

And Lewis *was* the union for those forty years, a fact clearly evident in the diary my father kept during roughly the second half of Lewis's reign. Dad's comments revealed the success of Lewis's personal identification with the union through his histrionics and skilled public relations. Dad made frequent entries about paying his "John L. dues" and about his eligibility for and receipt of his "John L. checks"—retirement pension payments, which, he wrote later, "John L cut . . . by $25." He was often sarcastic about Lewis. In 1946 during a dispute involving the union, the operators, and the federal government, he wrote, "Well here it is—the test between John L and the government of the United States. I have no idea as to the outcome of it all. No doubt though I will be among the army of losers in the deal. I will get some rest at least." Three years later he expressed doubts about a strike against the government thinly disguised as a protest over the death of three miners that occurred while the government was running the mines: "John L says we are going to be off next week for a bit more of mourning. Would like to see the last of that kind of stuff." He often registered skepticism about whether the pay increase from a strike settlement would equal the wages lost in the strike: "I guess the little raise in pay is supposed to be a big thing, but I can't see it. It will take 6 or 8 years to make it up. . . . John L has assessed us $5 each for two months. Our raise won't help a bit." He took a short-range view of changes, however, not the long view that saw hourly rates rise from 75¢ an hour in the late 1930s to over $3.00 in the early 1960s (shortly after he retired), more than doubling the rate adjusted for inflation.

Still, like most miners, Dad took pleasure in union victories over the owners. In 1951 during an impasse over a strike that the government contended was interfering with production of war materiel, he wrote, "They found John L guilty of contempt of court [which meant the mines would be seized] and does that burn the operators up. . . . The Government is going to take over the mines and just turn over enough for the expenses of the operators." And he was displeased with the antiunion aspect of the Taft-Hartley Act; in 1947 he commented, "The bill passed; don't look good for the workingman now."

If my father was ambivalent about the union, many were devoted to it and defended it to the bitter end. Such a person was our next door neighbor, Paul Boydoh, who told me:

> I think the union took special care of the coal miner; what would coal miners have done if it hadn't been for the union? They got us all the safety procedures we have now and didn't used to have. That's how we got 'em—through the union. They keep after these rules and keep fighting for them [a generous view of the union's role in safety promotion, I argue later].
>
> John L.? Oh, I thought he was great, just great. He was a hard fighter for the common people; we need somebody like him today.
>
> Yea, I've worked in the union a good bit—been secretary of the local, been on the safety committee, been on the mine committee.
>
> It's true, there's been violence in strikes around here. I remember 1932 or 1934 when the union was fighting for recognition. There was deputies—called them yellow dogs—on great big horses and they had long sticks. They kept you in the house after dark—a quarantine, or I mean a curfew. The county sheriff made deputies of scabs who were actually paid by the company.[2]

Gerald Spragg, also a Monongah man of my generation, remembers those 1930s strikes differently. Spragg was a surveyor in Consol's engineering division and therefore not a UMWA member but a salaried employee. "Oh, yes, there was violence in those strikes. . . . I remember that nonunion miners would try to go through the picket lines to get to work while the pickets would try to overturn the cars to keep them from working. The deputies would ride around on beautiful horses trying to protect property as they patrolled. And at Mine No. 63 [Monongah] they had machine guns on the tipple and the river trestle. . . . But I don't think they were ever used."[3]

Two observers of the same events, but how different their views. One man's "beautiful horses" sent out to "protect property" are another man's "big horses" ridden by "scab deputies" who wielded "long sticks" and were "actually paid by the company." One recalls a company-imposed curfew; another, picketing and overturned cars. And so it is with the whole history of the union movement: right to strike versus right to work; a legislated eight-hour day versus "liberty of contract"; labor racketeering and labor representation. A Paul Boydoh can cite as achievements of "his" union the miner's increased wages and reduced hours of work, safety committees, union weighers to check the honesty of company weighing of the coal loaded, dispute arbitration, portal-to-portal pay, health and retirement programs financed by coal royalties. Antiunionists point to the times when leaders sold out their own followers, sabotaged union democracy, lied and distorted the truth on black lung, abandoned the rank-and-file members in collaborating with coal corporate leaders to let mechanization take place without even talking about the consequences for displaced miners, played fast and loose with money in a union-owned bank. Some leaders fattened on expense accounts and practiced nepotism with abandon; at their lowest they resorted to thugs to assault dissenters at union conventions and ultimately hired murderers to maintain their positions of power. It is simply beyond denial that at times the union has served the membership's goals, but sadly also the members have been used for the well-being of the union and especially of its leaders.

Indeed, in surveying the history of labor unions, one might almost say that the only thing worse than labor unions is no labor unions at all, and the history of the mine workers' union is a vivid illustration of this proposition. Even as it served to protect the miner, it simultaneously became an instrument to serve the leadership at the expense of the dues-paying membership. If it is spiritually uplifting to see the well-meaning efforts of the best leaders of the union, it is depressing to see the misuses of power not only by the worst leaders but also by many whose careers included some admirable achievements. Happily, the recent trend of the union is more democratic and responsible and more oriented to the well-being of the miners.

Origins of the UMWA

In the beginning of efforts to organize the coal workers of America, one leader set forth in idealistic terms the function of a miners' labor union. Daniel Weaver, like many early U.S. mine organizers, was born in England, worked there as a young miner, and learned his first labor organizing lessons in British mines. In 1861 he sent this letter to a newspaper, addressing it to "the miners of the United States":

> The necessity of an association of miners, . . . having for its objects the physical, mental, and social elevation of the miner, has long been felt by the thinking portion of the miners generally.
>
> Union is the great fundamental principle by which every object of importance is to be accomplished. Man is a social being and if left to himself, in an isolated condition, would be one of the weakest creatures; but associated with his kind he works wonders. Men can do jointly what they cannot do singly; and the union of minds and hands, the concentration of their power becomes almost omnipotent. . . .
>
> Men have learned the power and efficiency of cooperation, and are, therefore determined to stand by each other. How long, then, will miners remain isolated—antagonistic to each other? . . . Our unity is essential to the attainment of our rights and the amelioration of our present condition: and our voices must be heard in the legislative halls of our land. There it is that our complaints must be made and our rights defined. The insatiable maw of Capital would devour every vestige of Labor's rights; but we must demand legislative protection; and to accomplish this we must organize. Our remedy, our safety, our protection, our dearest interests, and the social well-being of our families, present and future, depend on our unity, our duty, and our regard for each.[4]

Weaver and others before and after him tried to establish miners' unions, but despite their noble sentiments and valiant effort these struggling associations all foundered in the sea of animosity of mine owners and the difficulty of persuading miners to unite and collaborate in the face of the harsh penalties the owners could bring to bear. Mine operators resorted to criminal conspiracy laws under which organizing a labor union was considered a criminal offense. They also demanded that miners sign "yellow dog contracts" as a condition of employment: the miner had to swear not only that he was not a member of a labor union but that he would not join one while in the employ of the mine owner; if he did join, he was subject to immediate dismissal. And since the political power of the operators gave them control over state laws and courts, the individual miner had little chance to prevail in either civil or criminal law matters (such as suits over injuries suffered while at work, or charges under the criminal conspiracy law). Under these circumstances early labor unions failed one after the other.

The first effort to organize miners came in 1849 and was called "Bates' Union" after its founder, John Bates; it did not last very long and is said to have failed when Bates was seduced by the operators in the course of a strike, leaving behind him a bitterly disillusioned rank and file who would "hear no more talk of unionism for years to come."[5] In 1861 the first national coal union, the American Miners Association, was formed, but it died seven years later when it lost a long strike in Pennsylvania. In 1868 a union leader named John Siney persuaded a number of local unions in Pennsylvania to join in creating the Workingmen's Benevolent Association. At that time railroads were entering the coal industry, especially the anthracite field, and Siney led a successful strike against them in 1869. In 1873 he got anthracite and bituminous miners together in a convention at Youngstown, Ohio, where the Miners National Association of the United States was formed. In due course Siney and an associate were charged with violation of the Pennsylvania criminal conspiracy law. At their trial the prosecutor told the jury that the defendants had sought to create a "combination of miners, for the purpose of raising wages, and it is your bounden duty . . . to bring in a verdict of guilty."[6] Although the associate was sentenced to a year in prison (a sentence commuted by the governor), Siney was acquitted. But his union did not survive the panic of the mid-1870s. As blacklisted miners were fired and the failure of the Miners National Association became apparent, Siney was ousted from the leadership of the dying organization in 1876.

Meanwhile, another coal workers' association was making a name for itself, an infamous name that long survived the actual group. The Molly McGuires took their name from a band of Irish rebels who violently opposed English landlords and oppressors for centuries in Ireland. They were associated with the American version of the Ancient Order of Hibernians, although that society was in no sense a sponsor. Wayne Broel, author of the leading study of the Molly McGuires, emphasizes the historical roots of opposition to British oppression, particularly the great famine that killed millions while people by the hundreds of thousands "walked to the ports around the coast of the island, got passage in whatever vessel they could find, and emigrated. And they carried with them the accumulated grievances of hundreds of years of serfdom, ill treatment, and degradation. They brought with them deep, bitter, black resentments, resentments that could only be erased by time. And before they were completely wiped out, these resentments were inexorably destined to come to the surface again."[7]

Those buried antagonisms surfaced in response to the oppressive working and living conditions of the anthracite coalfields where Irish miners resented their treatment and took out their anger by harassing mine owners, coal company bosses, and the police. Their retribution against their oppressors included even murder, often preceded by "coffin notices," and their terror campaign aroused such fear and anger that the organizing efforts of legitimate unions were made more difficult than ever. But the mine owners had means for dealing with terror; they resorted to private police organizations, such as the Pinkertons, that specialized in infiltrating union organizations. An "official" history of the Ancient Order of Hibernians quotes the "actual words" of Franklin Gowen, a coal mogul *and* president of the Reading Railroad, who instructed the Pinkertons to invade the ranks of the Molly McGuires:

> I control the means of communication and transportation to and from the district; I want you to send a man to Schuykill County to join the Mollie McGuires and become its leader. I want this man to gain the confidence of the Irish miners, become an officer of their organization and start them out on a crusade of crime. I want him to precipitate strikes against the several mines and make the lives of mine managers a burden. I want him to

lead bands against the English, Welsh and German miners and mine bosses, beat them and kill them off until the collieries will be unable to run for want of competent men. That course will force the rest of these independent operators to sell out to me at my own figure. Finally, I want this man whom you send to turn informer on his associates, hand them over to the authorities—and I will do the rest. With the execution of these fellows two results will be accomplished: I will be looked upon as the savior of the coal region—the supreme preserver of the peace—and organized labor will be given a black eye from which it will never be able to recover.[8]

Whether these are in fact Gowen's actual words, they describe what did take place: an informer named James McParlan successfully infiltrated the ranks of the Mollies, rose to a leadership position, fomented terrorist acts, informed on the leaders, and with his testimony helped send twenty of them to the gallows. And Gowen did buy up 100,000 acres of land for the Reading Railroad between 1871 and 1874, and he organized a market-control scheme that secured him a dominant position.

While the Molly McGuires were wreaking havoc in anthracite country, a totally different union was gaining followers; by the 1880s it would have 700,000 members. This was the utopian society called the Order of the Knights of Labor of America and the World, given to secrecy, passwords, fraternal handgrips, and obscure initiation rituals. Originated among the needle trades in Philadelphia in 1869, the Knights soon opened their ranks to all and organized in so-called assemblies that were not based on particular occupational skills but accepted all workers equally. They accepted women as well as men, blacks alongside whites, inexperienced immigrants and skilled natives, professional people (teachers and doctors), craftsmen (such as carpenters), laborers (such as coal miners), small businessmen, and farmers. They all sat in the same assembly meetings, heard the same high ideals preached, and in some cases no doubt were commonly mystified by the secret rites. The Knights believed in temperance, popular education, and democracy; they were apprehensive about the power of capital and the evils of monopoly. They opposed strikes and violence, advocating concili-ation and arbitration of labor-management disputes. As a secret organization they were unjustly compared with the Molly McGuires and feared, even though they were peaceful and nonviolent as well as idealistic. Nevertheless, their numbers grew steadily.

In 1883 the Amalgamated Association of Miners of the United States developed in Ohio as a result of the most common impetus to labor organization: the reduction of wages. A strike over that wage cut led to the demise of Amalgamated, but in 1885 still another attempt at national organization blossomed. The National Federation of Miners and Mine Laborers soon got support from a newly generated force, the American Federation of Labor, founded in 1886 by Samuel Gompers. The Knights, recognizing the threat of the new AFL, and over the objections of some of their leaders, set up a special unit for coal diggers—Assembly 135. A rancorous dispute raged between the two unions, but when it became clear that the conflict was only helping the operators, a unity meeting was arranged in January 1890. After much heated debate a mutual agreement was reached on January 25, a historic date for American coal miners, for it marked the birth of the United Mine Workers of America.

In its early decades the UMWA was unstable and the tenure of its leaders anything but secure. When John Mitchell came to the presidency of the union in 1899 at the age of twenty-nine, he was the fifth incumbent in nine years. (By contrast John L. Lewis took the reins in 1920 and held office for forty years, a familiar tenure pattern in American labor unions in the twentieth century.) Under Mitchell's leadership the union grew—by the turn of the new century there were more than a quarter of a million members, with anthracite miners the bulwark of the mine work force—and in 1900 he prevailed in a strike to win union recognition in anthracite territory. But a more difficult strike was to come two years later, the famous 1902 strike that found the unyielding operators unwilling to participate in the effort to settle the dispute through White House intervention.

President Theodore Roosevelt recognized the potential political power that public attention bestowed on the presidency, and most of his successors used that potential in dealing with crippling strikes. But in 1902 the owners, unimpressed with the public attention the White House could bring to bear, remained confident in their commanding power and arrogant in their attitude toward both unions and presidents. One of those arrogant owners expressed his God-given right to rule in a letter that became world famous. Said George Baer, president of the Philadelphia and Reading Railroad, "The rights and interests of the laboring man will be protected and cared for—not by labor agitators, but by Christian gentlemen to whom God has given control of the property rights of the country and upon the successful management of which so much depends." Baer is also reputed to have said that miners "don't suffer. Why, they don't even speak English."[9]

Labor Violence

Small wonder, then, that during the first third of the twentieth century, violence between coal companies and miners was as devastating as it was frequent. Hundreds were shot and killed on both sides.[10] As miners by the thousand joined the United Mine Workers of America, operators resorted to all manner of tactics to keep the union out. Many insisted that their employees sign yellow dog contracts as a condition of employment. They hired thugs who ruthlessly evicted union participants from their houses, and the worse the conditions (inclement weather, predawn hours, destruction of furniture and other possessions, pregnancy of a miner's wife), the better it seemed to suit the operators. Mine guards, paid by the owners but officially acting as deputy sheriffs, came to coal camps equipped with rifles, sawed-off shotguns, machine guns, hand guns, and clubs. Companies hired detectives from agencies such as Pinkerton and Baldwin-Felts, and their injuring and killing of miners (and their wives and children) was not only common but permitted without so much as an official investigation let alone arrest and trial.

All these activities were facilitated by company control over state and county government, making it possible to declare martial law and try miners before military tribunals—even though civil courts were open and operating—and to bring in the state militia to reinforce the other forms of force and compulsion.

Although they were at a disadvantage, the embittered miners rallied their counterforces with a united passion. They bought hunting rifles by the thousand. Skilled in the use of dynamite, they resorted to it with devastating effect. They knew the woods, and like Indians resisting white settlers they melted into the scenery to attack from ambush, killing hundreds of mine guards. They were also frequently helped by local nonminers who, in their dislike for the mine owners, allowed strikers to pitch tent cities on their land and otherwise aided them.

From 1900 to 1935 in southern West Virginia, the UMWA fought for recognition against a recalcitrant band of operators who fiercely resisted what mine owners in other regions were coming to accept. Mines in the Midwest and in Pennsylvania were successfully organized long before those in West Virginia; even northern West Virginia mines signed contracts with the UMWA while those in southern part of the state—and in Kentucky, Tennessee, and Alabama—held out staunchly.

Among the most tumultuous of struggles in the nation's labor history were the strikes against the mines on Paint Creek and Cabin Creek in 1912–13. They began in the Paint Creek area, where the union had a foothold. The issue in dispute was a contract provision regarding the elimination of "cribs" built on coal cars, requiring coal loaders to provide five hundred to one thousand pounds more coal per car than they were being paid for. Nonunion miners joined unionists in shutting down the Paint Creek mines. They were soon followed by 7,500 Cabin Creek miners who were not union members but were aroused by the actions of the owners in the area. Upon being evicted from their company houses, striking miners moved into tent colonies, which became targets of gunfire from mine guards and Baldwin-Felts men. The companies had an armored train constructed to import strikebreakers and used it also for raids on union positions; the "Bull Moose Special" consisted of a locomotive, a day coach, and a baggage car, each protected by iron plating, and with machine guns mounted in the side doors of the baggage car. One night in February 1913 this menacing tank on train tracks pulled into a tent village in Holly Grove. The machine guns opened fire on the tents strung out on both sides of the tracks, and from the coach windows a coal operator and nine mine guards began shooting with rifles. One miner was killed.[11]

When the strike continued despite the terror of such raids, and the owners began to lose money, they resorted to the resource they could always call on: the state government and in particular the governor of West Virginia, who proclaimed martial law and sent the state militia to the strike region. At first the miners assumed that the militia had come to separate the two sides and bring peace, but it soon became apparent that they were there to break the strike. The governor did violence to the U.S. Constitution by banning all "congregating" and ordering the arrest of anyone who attended a meeting. (Among those swept up under this edict was the labor agitator Mary "Mother" Jones, who read—or tried to read—the Declaration of Independence to an assembly.) Under martial law, arrested persons were summarily tried in military tribunals and given long prison sentences. This was done despite the U.S. Supreme Court's ruling in *Ex Parte Milligan*, a Civil War decision holding that civilians cannot be tried in a military court when normal civil courts are open and functioning—as those in West Virginia were.[12] Under these conditions the writ of habeas corpus is supposed to apply—but not in West Virginia, as the state Supreme Court found that a "state of war" existed.[13] An example of the result was a miner who was arrested on one day, tried the next, and sent off to the penitentiary for five years on the third day. His offense: arguing with a soldier in a train station.

Then a new governor took office in 1913. Henry D. Hatfield—nephew of "Devil" Anse Hatfield, patriarch of the family in the Hatfield-McCoy feud—proposed a compromise to settle the strike. Although the compromise ignored vital issues such as union recognition and abolishing the mine guard system, both UMWA leaders and the operators accepted the settlement. Delegates from union locals were chosen to consider ratification of the deal, and with the intervention of the governor in arresting and detaining sixteen delegates known to oppose the new contract, it was approved. When a large number of miners continued to reject the compromise and vowed to continue the strike, the governor's response was a thirty-six-hour ultimatum: return to work or be deported from the state. To enforce the edict he sent "soldiers into the coal fields to question each worker and then escort him back to the mine."[14] Facing that, the rebels gave up the fight—but only temporarily, for as an investigation by the U.S. Senate on the whole West Virginia situation got under way, the rank-and-file miners resumed the strike.

The violence resumed as well: there were pitched battles with mine guards, mines were dynamited, and tipples were burned as local unions defied district and national officers of the UMWA. Inadvertently, the governor overplayed his hand and strengthened the position of the strikers when he sent soldiers to smash the presses of two dissenting socialist newspapers and jailed their editors. That turned the political situation around and aided some U.S. senators who were outraged at the state's conduct. The Senate investigation brought to light the convictions under martial law, making such good publicity for the strikers that the resolve of the owners faltered, and they agreed to grant the original demands of the union—in particular, recognition of the UMWA. Moreover, in the words of David Corbin, "the Paint Creek-Cabin Creek strike also created a situation in which violence was accepted as a necessary, justifiable, and, at times, pleasurable tool to be used against the operators and mine guards who had adopted the use of terror earlier."[15]

Violence in the southern West Virginia coalfields over the next ten years included the murder of eleven Baldwin-Felts agents in the town of Matewan in Mingo County ("Bloody Mingo") in 1920, agents who had come to the town to evict striking miners from company houses and, as usual, had terrorized the community in the process. Among the dead were two brothers of the head of the Baldwin-Felts organization. Police Chief Sid Hatfield (who had been a miner) and Matewan's Mayor Catell C. Testerman were involved in the argument that preceded the showdown with the agents. Hatfield was tried for murder but acquitted; then he and a fellow member of the UMWA were killed in a retaliatory shooting by other Baldwin-Felts agents.[16]

The murder of Sid Hatfield and the mayor of Matewan, the oppressive Cossack-like use of mine guards and Baldwin-Felts agents, the countless and ruthless evictions of miners from company housing, the insistence that employees sign yellow dog contracts (operators in the area at one time were estimated to have the signatures of 50,000 miners on such contracts)[17] all combined to enrage and motivate thousands of southern West Virginia miners to retaliate. So did the one-sided courts: judges readily granted injunctions to operators against strikers, but when the union sought injunctive relief from operators, they found that judges could hear only one side in labor litigation. A former state attorney general recalls that one judge presided over a case in which the union sought an injunction against mine owners, even though the judge's family was earning $60,000 a year as lessor to one of the companies involved. Said the judge, the family's interest "entirely escaped my memory at the time of the hearing."[18]

Among the counties in southern West Virginia most staunchly resisting UMWA organizing efforts was Logan County, where the local political machine was controlled by Sheriff Don Chafin (whose net worth was said to be $350,000 on a $3,500 annual salary). Chafin had hundreds of armed deputies derisively called "Logan County's Standing Army"—which was severely tested in 1921 when the Battle of Blair Mountain erupted.

Miners' grievances against Logan County treatment were of long standing. In August 1919 some five thousand of them went on the march but were persuaded to disband by promises from the governor and his threat to call for federal troops unless they desisted. The marchers yielded and submitted their list of grievances to the governor—to no avail. The summer of 1921 brought a renewed drive. Within a week of Sid Hatfield's murder, thousands of miners at a meeting in Charleston were addressed (or harangued, depending on the point of view) by Mother Jones, whose saintly-grandmother appearance juxtaposed with her coal miner's profanity delighted militant miners.

Mother Jones spent most of her adult life—till she was nearly a hundred years old—promoting union causes; wherever miners went on strike, Mother Jones could be expected soon. In her autobiography, she said, "There is never peace in West Virginia because there is never justice." And she promised, "When I get to the other side, I shall tell God Almighty about West Virginia."[19] Well known to the operators and their tame politicians, she was often jailed to keep her quiet. Coal managers spoke of her as "the old hag" and many wives and mothers of miners, including my own mother, recalled not so much her battles for workingmen as her "bad language."

Although her standard comment was, "Pray for the dead and fight like hell for the living," Mother Jones often tempered her radicalism, and on this occasion—expecting the worst—she urged the men to resist the call to arms. They rejected her plea and headed for Logan County, gathering cohorts as they went, ultimately assembling 15,000 to 20,000 miners and sympathizers. Led by veterans of the Spanish American War and the First World War, this hastily organized but fairly disciplined fighting force headed for Blair Mountain, a twenty-five-mile ridge around Logan and Mingo Counties.

Despite the well-equipped army they had to face (Sheriff Chafin and his deputies plus mine guards, state police, militia, and Baldwin-Felts men, armed with machine guns and assisted by pilots of company-hired airplanes from which they tossed ill-targeted bombs and gas canisters), the miners managed to secure half of Blair Mountain in the course of a week's intermittent fighting. The incredible amounts of ammunition expended resulted in an unknown number of dead and injured on both sides. But Chafin's army was one thing; the troops of the United States were quite another. When President Warren G. Harding ordered U.S. soldiers to the battle scene, the miners at first resisted capitulation even when urged to do so by their own leaders. Only the imminent arrival of 2,500 U.S. troops and fourteen aircraft doomed the uprising.[20]

In retrospect, the frequency and ferocity of violence in labor union-coal operator disputes, mainly over the right of unions to represent miners and promote their interests, is hard to believe; today's more orderly labor relations stand in sharp contrast. In the early decades of the twentieth century, however, the place of unions—and indeed of the worker generally—was not a settled matter. Owners felt justified in resorting to extreme measures because they perceived the union movement as a challenge to their right to profit from their investments. Unionists, equally convinced that the battle for recognition would determine a way of life for themselves and their successors, were prepared to use almost any means to secure their right to participate in making basic decisions about their work conditions and life-style. Both sides were as ready to resort to illegal and often lethal measures as militants today have been to blow up a federal building in Oklahoma City and Muslim terrorists to bomb the World Trade Center—in pursuit of a vision of rights claimed and wrongs avenged.

One could cite a lengthy catalogue of violent actions of miners. One example is the Herrin (Illinois) Massacre of 1922: after some strikers were murdered, seventeen scabbing miners were rounded up as "prisoners" and shot in cold blood; a mine superintendent who tried to surrender became one of twenty-five who died that day. Elsewhere, unionists dynamited mines in which strike-breakers were working; squirrel-rifle marksmen ambushed and killed countless deputies, mine guards, and Baldwin-Felts and Pinkerton agents; union men reduced to rubble millions of dollars worth of mine equipment and buildings.

But whether these acts of violence made the miners more sinners than sinned against is difficult to say. Mine owners not only were equally committed to and certain of the rightness of their cause, but had the resources to acquire manpower and artillery for mayhem and the blessing of the law to sanctify their behavior, not to mention the willing cooperation of governors, sheriffs, prosecutors, and judges whose authority could cover the tracks of violence and free perpetrators of the nuisance of prosecution. A fracas in Ludlow, Colorado, illustrates the free hand operators had to exert deadly force. In 1914 the Colorado Fuel and Coal Company faced a strike for union recognition, and like the operators of West Virginia who used state government to back up their coal domains, the Colorado owners (among them John D. Rockefeller, owner of the Ludlow mine) played rough and relied on the state militia to protect their interests. As the militia commander had said during an earlier strike, "It is the intention of the mine owners to stamp out unionism. . . . The troops will remain there until this is done."[21]

He personally arrested Mother Jones and twenty-seven union leaders. Another tactic involved an attack on a tent colony sheltering a thousand members of miners' families who had been evicted from company housing: one morning in April—without warning or provocation—mine guards, militia men, and Baldwin-Felts agents opened fire on the area. Occupants retreated to holes they had dug under the tents for warmth, but many were hit before they reached safety. When darkness fell, the tents were set afire, and more perished in the flames. In all, twenty died in the attack: one striker, eleven children, and eight women. No militia man, mine guard, or agent was ever punished for those deeds.

It is not only the violent actions of thousands of mine guards, deputies, detectives, and undercover agents in the employ of mine owners that must go on the balance sheet, but also the thousands of miners' deaths by preventable accidents. The ignominy and abuse heaped upon families by the reckless behavior of eviction agents must also be laid at management's door. And cannot the agony of more than 100,000 black lung victims struggling to death's edge for a breath of air be rightly declared an act of violence? Do not years of sitting up in a chair through nightlong bouts of sleepless and debilitating coughing count as violence? No plea of ignorance of the damage done to human lungs by coal dust will suffice: British officials and doctors had published their evidence; the truth was available to any who wanted to know and who desired to find a way to prevent the disease instead denying its existence in order to maximize profits.

The Radical Challenge

When it became clear that unlike its several predecessors the UMWA had a chance to survive, its size—300,000 members in 1905—made it a prize plum to be plucked, and competitors for the opportunity to represent miners schemed to take over. Among the suitors were some radical movements seeking to muscle in on the union. One was the International Workers of the World (IWW), or, more popularly, the "Wobblies." Committed to revolution they were, but they never got far with miners or anybody else, except a fringe following, because they were so given to words, words, words rather than concrete action. Doctrine has never gone over well in the American labor movement, and the Wobblies suffered as a result of that impatience.

To the left of the IWW were the systematic anarchists, who got even less attention from most miners; in fact, they scared the working class as much as they did the owning classes. Not only were they overwhelmingly led by immigrants from the continental Marxist movement (and therefore suspect among native Americans); they were also true revolutionaries, advocating violence and backing up their words with direct early action. Conventional ballot-box politics held no appeal for anarchists. And the press was quick to scare the daylights out of average citizens with publicity about such a book as one published in the 1880s by Johan Most, titled *Science of Revolutionary Warfare: A Manual of Instructions in the Use and Preparation of Nitroglycerine, Dynamite, Gun-Cotton, Fulminate of Mercury, Bombs, Poisons, Etc., Etc.* No wonder these fiery advocates were seen as the long-bearded, wild-eyed bomb throwers so familiar in cartoons of the period. Despite the violence described above, few accepted the anarchist doctrine that a "pound of this stuff [dynamite] beats a bushel of ballots all hollow." For a time it was debatable whether ballots really could replace bullets, but ballots prevailed, especially after the discrediting of radicalism during and after the Great War.

Before that war, however, there was also a democratic socialist movement with considerable standing in the populace, and not least in the ranks of miners.[22] In the early years of the new century three different political courses of action were promoted for the unions: to develop a labor party; to develop a socialist movement party; or to back candidates from major parties who endorsed labor's goals. The first alternative tended to be the line taken by recent arrivals from Great Britain, where by the turn of the century a labor party was growing into a viable political force. But in the United States there was no fertile soil for that seed to germinate in, and it withered and died. The second alternative attracted more followers within the ranks of miners. But the doctrines behind it were born of the continental Marxist model, and that did nothing for its popularity. Still, until the boom was lowered on radicals in 1917–23, the socialists got healthy voting support from miners: in 1912, when Eugene Debs hit the high-water mark for Socialist Party presidential votes, miners were among his reliable supporters; moreover, many Socialists were elected to state legislatures with strong miner backing. But only the third alternative remained viable; the radical alternative withered—or, perhaps, was poisoned—on the vine.

The high fever of war sentiment was the death of the Socialist Party, no doubt partly because the powerful were apprehensive about Debs's showing in 1912. Debs himself went to jail on a trumped-up charge of opposing the draft in a public speech. Hastily enacted sedition laws were used to close radical journals, and the Supreme Court approved these steps as within the powers of Congress to meet a "clear and present danger." The Court again and again applied sedition law to situations that were not dangerous, certainly not presently and immediately so, but only a minority admitted that this was a sham intended to wipe out insignificant opposition. When the war ended, the government continued the attacks on leftists with the Palmer Raids, named for Woodrow Wilson's attorney general, who ordered massive efforts to sweep up and deport aliens suspected of radical thoughts. (The raids were a training exercise for J. Edgar Hoover and gave him his first taste of antiradical action.) American union politics has never been the same since the World War I antiradical pogroms.

Nevertheless, an element of the UMWA remained opposed to capitalism in the coal industry and urged nationalization of the mines. Among strong advocates was John Brophy, who was born in England, came to the United States as a child, and went to work as a miner in Pennsylvania at the age of twelve. An intelligent, articulate, and self-educated man, he rose in union ranks and became president of a UMWA district in central Pennsylvania, where he led a drive for endorsement of nationalization in the district convention of 1921. That body, after debating and approving the idea, issued two pamphlets on the plan. "Competition," said one of them, "is a luxury which we can no longer afford. Private interest must give way to public welfare. Private competitive ownership in coal must go." The rights of miners were being trampled by wrongs to miners—slack work, low wages, disease, bad housing, overhard and unnecessary labor, accidents, sudden and violent death—"and we say these ills are incurable while profits rule the lives of men."[23] The second pamphlet laid out the nationalization proposal in specifics, calling for democratic operation of the industry, collective bargaining, fair pricing of coal, a six-hour day, and a five-day work week.[24]

In 1922 the national convention of the UMWA took up the nationalization idea. John L. Lewis, then newly president of the union, might have been expected to oppose the plan, given his generally conservative orientation. But he was also one who took close account of the way the wind blew, and so the convention approved the appointment of a Nationalization Research Committee with John Brophy as its chairman. That committee came up with another pamphlet, *How to Run Coal,* which proposed that the government buy all coal and rights to coal then in private hands and establish a federal commission on mines to set budget and general policy. The commission would be appointed by the president and by professional and industrial associations, and it would be headed by a cabinet-rank secretary of mines. Wages would be set by collective bargaining and the mines administered by a national mining council composed of representatives from three groups: industry administrators, miners, and consumers. The pamphlet estimated the fair price of the buyout at $4.5 billion, and ended by comparing British and other plans for nationalization, noting that "the British coal owner has been more advanced in his concessions than the American miner has been in his demands."[25] Therein must lie at least part of the reason why Britain adopted nationalization in 1946 and the United States has yet to consider the issue seriously.[26]

John L. Lewis

John L. Lewis maneuvered his way into the presidency of the United Mine Workers in 1920 and thereby marked a turningpoint in the organization's history. The union had had eight presidents in its thirty-year history, and in their brief tenures none dominated the institution—certainly not in the way Lewis took absolute control during his forty-year reign. He tolerated no competition in running the union, ruthlessly putting down anyone who threatened or seemed to threaten his leadership. As his suspicion and fear of competition undermined the respect he once had for most of the men who occupied other key positions, he saw William Murray, Philip Green, John Brophy, and even less prominent leaders as enemies and ran them out of the organization. U.S. presidents with whom he had had alliances became his reviled adversaries: Woodrow Wilson, Herbert Hoover, Franklin Roosevelt. He was a domineering leader who had the courage to take on any opponent, no matter how formidable; during World War II he led the miners in two strikes that must have made Americans hate him more than anyone else outside the Axis nations.[27] It apparently did not affect him in the least.

Lewis was a unique personality who seemed always to be consciously acting. He could be pompous, dogmatic, sarcastic, abusive, caustic; he was given to classical and biblical allusions that sometimes made no sense but sounded grandly Victorian and rolled on the tongue. He could mesmerize an audience by bellowing or modulating his powerful voice; his biographers say that he "crooned and cursed, . . . charmed and cajoled, entertained and taught, . . . agitated and pacified . . . his listeners."[28] In a 1937 radio speech he denounced Roosevelt for stabbing labor in the back, saying, "Labor, like [the Biblical] Israel, has many sorrows. Its women weep for their fallen, and they lament for the future of the children of the race. It ill behooves one who has supped at labor's table and who has been sheltered at labor's house to curse with equal fervor and fine impartiality both labor and its adversaries when they become locked in deadly embrace."[29]

Early in his tenure Lewis turned his full rhetorical artillery on mine owners who resisted a raise in pay after World War I: "During this crisis from out of Macedonia comes the cry: 'we gentlemen stand here with spotless robes and white mantles and are ready to negotiate a wage scale . . . except as affects our mines.' In God's name we expect consideration to be given those 452,000 human souls who are asking for bread and have been given a stone."[30]

One thing that more than any other provoked Lewis to verbal onslaughts against coal operators was the wanton waste of human lives in accidents— yet it must be acknowledged that he was more a speechmaker than a performer where safety was concerned. When the record is examined carefully, it becomes clear that the UMWA has historically not fought for safety where it mattered most—at the bargaining table and in Congress. Nevertheless, in the Lewis era much was said that heightened the public's awareness of the cost of neglecting safety practices, and nobody put it more dramatically than John L. himself. Speaking to Congress after a mine explosion in West Frankfort, Illinois, which killed 119 men just before Christmas of 1951, he declared that something had to be done about this "slaughter unequaled in the civilized world," and went on:

> It is something to go down the rows of a hundred burned and dismembered and blackened corpses lying on the floor of a gymnasium in a public building and look at them and know that a few hours before they were walking about in the form of men, even as you and I, and that there they lay, disfigured, changed from the form of human beings to something beyond imagination, and then be expected to emerge from that scene of horror with patience and with tolerance for the men who come before this committee and say, "Don't pass any legislation. Let me continue to do as I will. I hope some day to be able to operate my mine without killing so many men. But don't rush me. Don't rush me."[31]

It is suggestive and helpful in understanding Lewis to compare him with Winston Churchill. Both were nonconformist in behavior, both given to old-fashioned rhetorical flourishes, capable of conscious ranting and raving, power hungry, and ready to use their positions to the utmost for both their personal goals and the almost inseparable objectives of the institutions they commanded. Each could be outlandish, domineering, good at pretense and deception, ready to publicly denounce someone at one minute and privately forget the seeming animosity the next. Both, that is to say, were superb politicians, leaders who sought and won large objectives.[32]

As one sizes up the career of John L. Lewis, how does he stand? That he made contributions to the well-being of miners there is no doubt. It was his effort at the bargaining table that helped make American miners the best-paid coal diggers in the world and, for a time, better paid than any other American industrial workers. Not that it was Lewis alone who put the American miner out front in the world and at home. The comparative wealth of America itself helps account for the relative position of U.S. coal miners internationally, and the demand for coal historically has something to do with the fact that American miners are still well paid in comparison with other trades. And miners themselves helped pay for the high wages—in strikes that cost them heavily in income lost and, not least, in lives lost in strike-related fighting. The fact remains, however, that John L. Lewis was a powerfully effective representative when contract-haggling time came. For in part the bargaining process is a matter of public relations, and Lewis was a master at persuading the public of the reasons why the miner deserved the demands being made of the operators. He managed to win such major concessions as "portal-to-portal" pay, for example: that is, payment figured from the time miners entered the mine until they left it, meaning they were earning while riding the mantrip (or walking) to and from their work place. Before that, miners often spent hours in dangerous travel without any compensation.

Lewis contributed much to the development of unions in this country—not only the UMWA but the whole CIO movement. Although early in his career he had been an organizer for the American Federation of Labor and a trusted assistant to its founder, Samuel Gompers, he became devoted to industrial as opposed to the AFL's craft unionism—favoring, that is to say, unions composed of all workers in a given industry rather than those that organized workers according to their craft specialties. The UMWA was an industrial union, and Lewis was a leading figure in the origination of the Congress of Industrial Organizations in the 1930s. He was also instrumental in the development of the United Automobile Workers and the United Steel Workers as key constituents of the CIO. But Lewis broke with the rest of the leadership over the reelection of Franklin Roosevelt for a third term; he threatened to resign if union members did not follow his lead and support Wendell Willkie in the 1940 election. They didn't, and Lewis quit as CIO president; in 1942 he took the UMWA out of the CIO as well.

Lewis also contributed much to the establishment of the UMWA on firm ground during his tenure as its president. In the 1920s it nearly foundered—in West Virginia its membership declined from 10,000 to 600—but with the NRA and the Wagner Act as legal protections for unions, the UMWA reestablished itself as a strong and viable organization. Yet if Lewis helped the union to grow, he also ruled it with a dictatorial hand. He rode roughshod over conventions, using preemptive tactics that quashed dissenters' initiatives. He reduced the democratic control of UMWA district organizations: in 1940 only four of twenty-three districts retained self-governance; Lewis had put the others under trusteeship by alleging some shortcoming in the operation of a district's affairs. And once trusteeship was declared, it had no set time limit but commonly lasted for years or indefinitely. This gave the president control over the union's International Executive Board, and, that plus the powers of the president under the union constitution, assured his authoritarian rule. Lewis made the most of his political opportunity. So complete was his command that he had no serious opposition for reelection to the presidency after John Brophy's failed challenge in 1926.

One of John L.'s proudest achievements was the establishment of the miners' Welfare and Retirement Fund in 1946. Financed by royalties from each ton of coal mined under union contract, the fund was run by three trustees: one from the union, one from the operators, and a third neutral person. For as long as he was in office, Lewis was union trustee, and the "neutral" trustee was Josephine Roche, one of his close associates from the 1920s; he thus retained effective control of the fund's operation. With income from the royalties, ten modern hospitals to serve miners were established. They proved so costly to operate that they were sold in the early 1960s, but other fund clinics remained open where miners with "health cards" got free service for themselves and their dependents. The trouble was, however, that many who had been miners and union members for decades, even if disabled in mine accidents, were arbitrarily ruled to be ineligible; in 1960, miners who had been unemployed for a year were denied health benefits.

The shortage of funds that led to such cutbacks was partly due to irresponsible management of resources. One instance was the practice of placing fund money in non-interest-bearing accounts in the National Bank of Washington, which the UMWA effectively owned. The operators' representative complained, but Lewis could not be persuaded to change a procedure that benefited the union by permitting the bank it owned to invest the money in those accounts elsewhere and retain the earnings. The potential income thus lost to the welfare fund would not have materially altered the shortages it ultimately had to face, but it was not insignificant. When a retired miner brought suit against the trustees for misuse of funds, the judge of the U.S. District Court that eventually heard the case, noting that the practice had gone on for twenty years, concluded that Lewis and Roche had chosen to "advance the interest of the Union and the Bank in disregard of the paramount interest of the beneficiaries who were entitled to receive the benefit of prudent investment of their funds."[33]

Manipulation of health and retirement funds through the union's bank showed Lewis's willingness to put the interests of the union ahead of those of coal miners needing health services and retirees in need of pensions. But his secret dealing with coal companies on the issue of mechanization during the 1950s, which ultimately drove hundreds of thousands of miners out of their jobs, was the worst neglect of the fundamental interests of union members in the history of American unionism. Lewis, who had spoken of coal operators as "leeches" and reviled them in gaudy language during every bargaining season for more than thirty years, fell silent in 1950 and struck a clandestine deal with his erstwhile adversaries, the Bituminous Coal Operators Association (BCOA). The deal was essentially this: if the BCOA increased its royalty contributions to the welfare fund and fattened wages, the union would eschew strikes and not resist the mechanization of coal mining whereby the operators could hold down production costs.

By the end of World War II the place of coal in the economy was fundamentally different from what it had been for the better part of a century. Where once coal had stoked the boilers of thousands of locomotives in the world's longest rail system, diesel engines had taken over the hauling task. In the early 1940s most homes and other buildings had been heated with coal, but tending a coal furnace was a dirty, demanding, and time-consuming task; frequent strikes made coal supplies undependable; and amassing a reserve was sometimes difficult and expensive. Natural gas, on the other hand, was cheap, clan, and abundant, and oil was in ample supply following development of oilfields to feed the machinery of a world at war and the creation of a worldwide oil transportation system that the war had established. Moreover, oil companies, which had grown into economic giants to fuel the universal automobile, began to undercut the coal industry with their oligopolistic tendencies. In addition, the production of coal was expensive when it depended on human power to get it out of the ground. Underground mining, where the UMWA dominated, faced two challenges: the enormous capital costs of mechanizing deep mining, and the rise of low-cost and manpower-cheap strip-mining.

Recognizing these fundamental shifts in the underlying economic strata, Lewis set about to remedy the situation. In essence, the UMWA became a coal operator. The union's possession of the National Bank of Washington gave what the *New York Times* called the "richest labor union in the land" a handy tool to execute its invasion of the industry: The trustees of the Welfare and Retirement Fund expanded the bank's available capital by the manipulations just discussed, and then John L. Lewis, trading his trustee cap for his union one, used that cash to make loans to coal companies in order to influence the structure of the coal trade.

The program had several phases. One involved pumping $25 million into a large nonunion coal producer, West Kentucky Coal, with the cooperation of railroad tycoon Cyrus Eaton. Soon after the union put up the cash for Eaton to buy his way into the company, West Kentucky signed a union contract and set about garnering a significant share in supplying the nation's largest coal user, the Tennessee Valley Authority (TVA). This was done secretly; when it became public knowledge, the union sold out with a loss of $8 million. But in the meantime the UMWA-Eaton team had acquired the Nashville Coal Company (with $7 million from the union) and by 1960 was the country's third largest bituminous producer.[34]

In his fervor to become a capitalist coal operator, then, Lewis sacrificed his commitment to the miners who, he always claimed, had his first allegiance. To expand his operations in Tennessee and Kentucky, the union chief made deals with small mine owners, entering "sweetheart" contracts that allowed them to pay a wage scale far below the national rate and lower royalties—or none at all—to the welfare fund. Worse still, under federal law the smallest mines were exempt from certain safety requirements that larger mines had to provide (see chapter 4). This accommodated companies that were unable to pay for machinery to modernize their operations or to meet the provisions of the national contract. But what was happening was that mechanization put hundreds of thousands of miners out of work in the 1950s and left them adrift, unemployed and isolated in Appalachia or working for starvation wages and in grave danger to life and limb in these doghole mines. (Again, contrast the way the British handled their automation layoffs: there the proud claim of both the National Coal Board and the National Union of Miners was that as long as possible, every affected miner was given early retirement or transferred to other mines—after visiting various collieries with his family to choose the most suitable location.)

Lewis played the capitalist's role to the hilt in the 1950s by reducing the open competition and conflict between the union and the operators. No longer the flamboyant speechmaker denouncing the owners, now Lewis dealt privately with such men as Harry Moses, George Love, and George Humphrey (who had formed the BCOA in 1950 to deal with Lewis) and, unknown to the miners, negotiated agreements with his coal corporation counterparts. Lewis, the man of affairs and conservative mien, would leave his UMWA experts back at the office and meet his rivals / collaborators in secret sessions to make deals. Men like George Love, scion of the family that owned most of the Pittsburgh Consolidation Coal Company, were comfortable with Lewis, and together they formed an alliance that sold out the miners who would be prime instances of massive downsizing (long before that ill-begotten term came into currency). Accordingly, Lewis was feted at the industry's American Mining Congress in 1958 by magnate George Humphrey, who called him "a friend of coal." Lewis, in turn called for the cooperation of all elements of the industry, and in 1961 he became head of the National Coal Policy Conference; fittingly, George Love succeeded him in office the next year.

Finally, Lewis entered into so blatant a conspiracy with Consolidation Coal to drive competing mines out of business that both the union and the company were found to have acted in restraint of trade in violation of the Sherman Antitrust Act and were penalized with triple damages for their actions. Numerous suits were brought by companies affected—and often bankrupted—by the conspiracy, and though there were many appeals and varying judicial interpretations of the facts and the law, the end result was a finding that Lewis and Consol had in fact *sought* to drive competitors out of business, rather than that the bankruptcies and closings were incidental consequences of their actions.[35]

Curtis Selzer summed up Lewis's career in this comment on that colorful life: "What irony! Here was a Republican conservative spearheading the nation's most militant labor union . . . Lewis, the huckster of federal planning, was a free-market capitalist as ideologically firm as any pinstripe on Wall Street. Lewis, the organizer of the unorganized, had purged John Brophy, the UMWA's most articulate organizer. . . . Lewis, the miner's cosmic hero, had done his utmost to deny them genuine participation in their union's affairs. Lewis, the free-enterprise advocate, bore the wrath of the very capitalists he was trying to rescue."[36]

W. A. Boyle

Not the least of the shortcomings of Lewis's career was his failure to take seriously the recruitment of able subordinates to succeed him in power. The selection of William Anthony ("Tony") Boyle certainly has to rank as one of his most egregious blunders. When John Brophy once asked Lewis how he would select and train future union leaders, the chief's response was that "whenever I see a bright young fellow I pick him out and place him on the payroll of the union"; this, said Brophy, "was his conception of how leadership was developed."[37] That was exactly what Lewis did with Boyle, whom he brought from Montana to Washington in 1948 to serve as his assistant. A close relationship developed between the aide and the senior leader, and on his own retirement in 1960 Lewis had Boyle appointed vice-president; this put him in the presidency two years later when Thomas Kennedy had to step down because of his health.

Boyle was wholly unsuited for the job—intellectually inadequate, paranoid, and insecure. Trevor Armbrister, whose book *Act of Vengeance* portrays him better than any other, says that Boyle was imprisoned by his mentor's heroic stature. Armbrister quotes a UMWA secretary who thought Boyle lived in the "old man's shadow. . . . Those who counseled with Lewis found themselves on Tony's black list. 'You know who I am, don't you?' he would say to me. 'I control this organization. I can fire anyone from the basement to the sixth floor.'"[38] Boyle was insignificant and uncertain where Lewis was firm and commanding. One can see the striking difference between the two men by comparing them at the sites of two disasters: Lewis at the West Frankfort explosion in 1951, and Boyle at Farmington in 1968. Lewis put on a miner's hard hat, went below for a personal inspection, and emerged—blackened—to be photographed in a historic shot that caught his grief, as did his words. Boyle resisted going to Farmington and, when his appearance became inescapable, asked his aides what he should say. Then he made the infamous and often quoted comments on the inevitability of explosions and Consol's virtuous cooperation in safety matters (see chapter 4). The Lewis photo "just had to make coal miners feel so proud," said Jock Yablonski. "But that sonofabitch Boyle. With those people dead in the mine, how could that bastard stand up and praise the company's safety record the way he did?"[39]

Boyle's lack of concern for the well-being of miners was clear in 1969: with two battles in progress—one for federal legislation on health and safety, and another to persuade the West Virginia legislature to recognize black lung as an industrial disease—Boyle managed to be on the wrong side in both. He was forced to back the act that ultimately passed Congress, but he did so halfheartedly and only in response to the pro-safety campaign of Jock Yablonski, who was then running against him for the UMWA presidency. More characteristic of Boyle was his vow in March 1969 not to "destroy the coal industry to satisfy the frantic ravings of self-appointed and ill-informed saviors of coal miners." He later told a congressional committee that "the UMWA will not abridge the rights of the mine operators in running the mines. We follow the judgment of the coal operators, right or wrong."[40]

The campaign for legislation on black lung in West Virginia was unusual in several respects. For one thing it was conducted by a spontaneous miners' organization, the Black Lung Association; for another it led to a strike of 42,000 of West Virginia's 44,000 active miners, shutting down nearly every mine in the state. Moreover, the campaign was directed against the legislature, a most unusual tactic because it is difficult for a diffuse and hastily organized association of workers to present a sufficiently unified front to conduct intricate negotiation over legislative language. But the miners were adamant on the black lung issue and were pulled together in part by the fact that the national union was opposing the independent move; Boyle denounced the "black tongue loudmouths" and ordered the strikers to go back to work, which they refused to do. Yet when they won the day, the UMWA claimed credit for having got the law passed.

In the congressional battle over the 1969 Coal Mine Health and Safety Act, Boyle often sided with opponents of health and safety measures—until Yablonski took the opposite position; then Boyle would switch sides, as he did with respect to the Coal Mine Safety Board of Review (which was eliminated in the bill passed by the Senate). The Board of Review, created by the 1952 safety law, had the power to review and overrule decisions made by the Interior Department to close mines and take other actions against companies. It was composed of five members: two miner representatives, two from industry, and a "neutral" chairman usually drawn from the ranks of industry, giving the operators effective control. Boyle favored retaining the board, but when Yablonski came out for its elimination, Boyle suddenly reversed his stance.[41]

Other aspects of the legislative contest over the 1969 act illustrate Boyle's and the UMWA's waffling on health and safety matters. One important factor in the struggle was uncertainty about the extent of public reaction to the horror of the televised scenes of the 1968 Farmington explosion and revulsion at having to leave seventy-eight bodies underground in the raging fire that could not be extinguished. Strong public sentiment could be translated into congressional support, not only in open roll call votes but in committee or other behind-the-scenes maneuvering, and possibly enable the passage of legislation on both health and safety; weaker public attention would likely reduce the prospects for one or the other.

The UMWA leadership believed that getting both was out of the question; they expected operators to say, "You got the safety provisions so you can't expect to get health now too." Congressman Ken Hechler refused to capitulate without a fight and drafted a strong and inclusive bill, but few agreed with him. Most coal region members of Congress were accustomed to playing the game in the limited UMWA style. Senator Jennings Randolph of West Virginia, "errand boy" for the UMWA leadership, introduced a bill that conceded the single- versus the two-issue strategy without a contest. Taking the floor of the Senate to perform the customary rites of extravagant praise for the supreme wisdom of the union's leaders, Randolph lambasted the "critics of the United Mine Workers . . . leadership, . . . critics who falsely claim that the men who work in the coal mines lack for adequate union attention to their health and safety needs. They are in error. History will not support such allegations; neither will current events."[42] In fact, not only would history fully support the critics of the UMWA's leaders; it would hang out to dry the likes of Jennings Randolph. His blind faith would lead him to support a murderer whose panic over a threat to his hold on the union's presidency led to the most infamous crime in the history of American unions.

Boyle was known for resorting to "rough stuff" both in the Montana District from which he came and later in Tennessee and Kentucky, particularly in UMW District 19, which had a reputation for violent union politics. That district was the home base of the "Jones Boys," a gang of thugs who with guns, dynamite, and incendiary materials terrorized coal operators and area residents generally; when charged with crimes, they were acquitted, as witnesses conveniently "forgot" damaging evidence. The reputed boss of the Jones Boys was Albert Pass, secretary-treasurer of District 19 and the man in charge of "security" for national conventions in the Boyle era, which meant the bloody suppression of dissidents, with Boyle's approval. The security forces were known as Pass's "storm troopers," and Pass became Boyle's trusted confederate. Accordingly it was to Pass that Boyle turned when Jock Yablonski threatened the tenure of the union president in the 1968 election. Six months before the election he talked with Pass and the president of District 19—in a hallway outside a meeting of the International Executive Board in Washington. The district president later testified that Boyle had specifically ordered them to get rid of Yablonski: "We are in a fight. Yablonski ought to be killed or done away with." Then Pass said, "If no one else will do it, District 19 will. District 19 will kill him."[43]

To finance the assassination a bogus "research" committee was set up, manned by retired miners who merely signed their "research" payment checks and returned the cash obediently and without question. Even though Yablonski lost the race by a considerable margin (partly because of corrupt conduct of the balloting), three thugs were paid $5,000 to commit the crime; at about 1:00 A.M. on the last day of 1969 they crept into the Yablonski home and shot and killed Yablonski, his wife, and his daughter. The assassins, the union officials who arranged the murder, and Boyle were all eventually found guilty of murder in the first degree.

Arnold Miller

In 1972, in a Labor Department–supervised and therefore at least minimally honest election, Boyle, despite having been charged with murder, won 44 percent of the vote but lost the union presidency to Arnold Miller. Two more different men can scarcely be imagined: where Boyle was a braggart given to violence, Miller was a soft-spoken and peaceful man. It is true that both were insecure and apprehensive about their associates, but their ways of showing that insecurity were strikingly different: Boyle turned to abuse and violence or threats of it; Miller would withdraw and avoid confrontation. These words from Miller's inaugural speech catch the character of the man and his personal commitment to the miners and their safety:

> I'm sick of these things—telegrams of condolence, letters from people saying they're sorry—I'm sick of it. There's just too much plain irresponsibility in the coal industry, and the former leadership of the Union has been too close to the industry to see it or fight it. That's over.
>
> I've seen more than my share of needless suffering in my lifetime, but I have never before been in a position to do very much to stop it. Now that has been changed, and I want you to know there will be no peace in the coal industry until this bloodshed ends.
>
> Every coal miner will know this is his union. It no longer belongs to one man. . . . We're going to go out and resolve the problems we have and make this union the greatest union in the country, as it once was.[44]

Brave and hopeful words—words that promised more than Miller could deliver, for the universe of problems the union had to face were not simple but complex and not readily resolvable. Still, the number of coal mine fatalities did decline during Miller's years (1972–79) as compared with Boyle's (1962–72). In the 1960s the number of fatalities in underground mining was 2,383; in the Miller decade it was 1,210. The number of miners killed in explosions was 258 in Boyle's era and 78 in Miller's.[45] These figures, though still high compared with those of other countries, at least move in the right direction. How much of the reduction was attributable to the change of union presidents is impossible to say; too many other factors were involved. One was the number of miners at work, which has generally declined since 1950; interestingly, however, although the number of miners went down from roughly 200,000 to 130,000 during the 1960s, it increased about equally in the 1970s (see figure 2). But other factors such as the gradual results of applying the rules contained in the 1969 Health and Safety Act undoubtedly served to improve the situation. Boyle could not claim much credit for that turn of events, having opposed some key aspects of the law. Miller may have helped stiffen the backbone of enforcement during his years, but inferences based on that must at best be guarded. Nevertheless, when he died at age sixty-two the *New York Times* obituary credited him with having changed the attitude toward safety both among operators and at union headquarters.

That Miller wanted to do something about the pain and suffering of coal miners there can be no doubt. He had himself known enough pain to feel sympathy. He had spent months in army hospitals, undergoing twenty plastic surgery operations after being hit in the face with machine gun fire in Normandy in 1944. From his years in the mines he had contracted black lung disease and knew nights when sleep was possible only while sitting in a chair, if then. He was among the original organizers of the West Virginia Black Lung Association and a founder of the Miners for Democracy (MFD), which had developed from the BLA. He had been president of his union local and, in a more democratic union, might have moved up the hierarchy and acquired some training in organizational leadership. But under the circumstances he came to the chieftanship of the union with hardly any training at all. He had been little prepared either in school (which he left for the mine at age sixteen) or in his workplace to cope with men experienced in the conduct of large corporate entities or the carefully trained negotiators who sat on the operators' side of the table.

His lack of negotiating skill got him into serious difficulty with his own rank and file, who voted down by a two-to-one margin a contract he offered them in 1978. The company representatives wanted to alter the way health benefits were financed. Instead of the funds originally established at the insistence of John L. Lewis in 1946, they wanted an insurance system that would let operators arrange their own deals with insurers, thereby saving them money and increasing their control over the system while diminishing that of the union; in effect, they proposed to swap that advantage for a 37 percent raise in wages and other benefits. But the miners had already expressed different contract preferences: health and pension benefits were their first and second desired goals, ahead of increased pay. Thus, when the contract came to a vote, they repudiated Miller in unmistakable terms. Even the staid *Wall Street Journal* agreed editorially with the miners, saying that Miller had given away the health plan they had had for thirty years. With its characteristic concern for tax breaks the *Journal* pointed out that the miner did not have to pay tax on money that went into the fund as royalty payments, whereas they would pay taxes on the deductibles that would now come into the system. The editorial writer concluded by saying that a Taft-Hartley eighty-day "cooling off" period was needed not by the workers but by the negotiators.[46]

Not only had Miller lost touch with his own miners; he was also failing to communicate with his own staff experts. He had alienated most of the specialists who had come to union headquarters with the Miners for Democracy movement (displacing or augmenting the Boyle crew), and they had resigned or been dismissed. It is illustrative of the distance between Miller and other officials of the national union that his own bargaining council turned down the contract. In fact, so withdrawn had the president become that at first he refused to appear and convene the council to consider the contract; he simply disappeared and was reported to be driving alone on the Washington Beltway for hours at a time to avoid confrontation. The end was in sight for Miller. He had had an earlier contract rejected in 1974, and though he won reelection after that fiasco, he got only 40 percent of the 1977 vote in a three-way race. After a stroke and two heart attacks he was persuaded to step down following the 1978 contract dispute, and his vice-president, Sam Church Jr., took over.

Church, like Miller, was a former miner, untrained in the management of a large organization and inept in his own way as negotiator. A bulllike man who chewed copious jawsful of Red Man tobacco, he had a tendency to express his disagreement with colleagues and subordinates by flooring them with a ham-sized fist. His macho mentality reflected the true miner, but as a union president he left much to be desired.[47]

The miners rejected Church's only contract by a better than two-to-one margin and struck for eleven weeks. The following year Church's term ended, and he failed to achieve reelection. Even his old-fashioned redbaiting, accusing his opponent of having hobnobbed with radicals, did not get him far. Nor did his allegation that his opponent, a young lawyer named Richard Trumka, had not worked for five years in a coal mine, as required by the union constitution; Trumka claimed that he *had* fulfilled the requirement, though some of the work was part time, to finance law school. At age thirty-three Trumka won the union presidency two to one, aided no doubt by many miners' belief that Miller's and Church's problems stemmed in some degree from their lack of education and inability to comprehend the issues of contemporary coal mining. In interviews they said such things as "We had enough dummies," and "Rich [Trumka] and Cecil [Roberts, the vice-presidential candidate] know what they're talking about. That's what's been wrong with the UMW for years: We've got the body but not the head."[48]

Richard Trumka

In his years of presiding over the miners' union (1982–95), Trumka changed the basic strategy of contract negotiations. Instead of meeting the whole industry head on in an attempt to force concessions from all the major operators in one concentrated campaign—and striking against them all if necessary—the new approach focused on hammering out a contract with one or a few major companies and then persuading the remaining producers to accept it.

This has been essentially an accommodation to the changing status of the union. Instead of dominating the industry and being able to cut off most of the country's coal supplies in the course of a strike, UMWA miners now produce only about a quarter of the country's coal. With coal readily available from nonunion mines, both underground and surface, the UMWA cannot apply the same pressure in negotiation as in the past. Moreover, some operators have adopted a contracting-out strategy: a company that has accepted the union contract for its main operations may contract with nonunion operators to run some company-owned facilities, thus reducing the costs of the contract by running both union and nonunion operations at the same time.

Although Trumka had some success, such as winning key strikes against the Pittston and Massey coal companies, such undertakings are now difficult and expensive. For one thing, the courts have levied millions in heavy fines and damages on the union (such as for violating strike-breaking orders during suits brought by operators); for another, providing strike support for thousands of miners' families—as much as $225 a week—is very hard on the once affluent UMWA treasury. (Of course, standing off the UMWA can be expensive for the operators too, as Pittston discovered in the course of a 270-day strike that cost tens of millions and ultimately forced the company to concede the battle.)

Another union problem is the miners' frequent resort to wildcat strikes. Traditionally, the picket line has been sacred among miners; they almost never cross one. So when wildcat strikes break out, there is not much the union leadership can do about it. The more democratic the union, the more difficult it is for the leaders to break a wave of wildcats, and under Trumka the once autocratic UMWA became one of the most democratic of the major unions. District officers are elected by the membership, not appointed and fired by the national leadership as in the days of Lewis and Boyle. The UMWA is one of two major unions that elect their leaders in direct balloting by members (the other is the United Steel Workers of America). There is also a way for members to express their preferences on contract issues before negotiating begins, and the membership ratifies or rejects a contract in direct voting.

Clearly, the UMWA faces difficult days ahead. Whereas it once had half a million members and was the strongest and richest union in the land, it is no longer either. An indication of how times have changed for the union can be seen in the standing of coal miners among hourly wage workers. For decades, miners led the pack or were among the highest paid; in 1980 coal miners' pay was second only to that of steel workers. But by 1994 other occupations had moved into the top dozen, and coal miners ranked thirteenth (tobacco workers were first).

The shift is attributable to many things, not least that miners are in surplus and that mostly nonunion strip-mined coal is pressing hard on UMWA-mined deep coal—facts that appear at the bargaining table implicitly or explicitly. It is not necessarily a sign of union weakness that miners are no longer at the top of the wage scale; when Lewis was doing business with business in the 1950s, wage increases were a way of keeping dissent from developing—though from the vantage point of the miner displaced by mechanization or denied a health card, high wages meant nothing. Today the leadership of the UMWA is more responsible and responsive than in the long darkness of the late Lewis and Boyle dictatorship.

It says something positive about the UMWA's leadership that when in 1995 the AFL-CIO sought to revive itself and stop the decline of unions in the United States generally by electing a more militant and aggressive leadership, one of the three top-ranking officers chosen was Richard Trumka. As secretary-treasurer of the new AFL-CIO he faces a challenge, but the record of his thirteen years as president of the UMWA suggest that he is up to the task. Against formidable adversaries in the Pittston and Massey strikes he drew significant cooperation from other unions and won important victories, generating considerable enthusiasm from the ranks of union activists by providing resourceful, energetic leadership.[49] It appears that in Trumka the union found a president who believed in democratic unionism, was not overpowered by sophisticated bargainers, was in sympathy with the values and goals of the working and the retired miner, and most of all did not sell out the members for political advantage.

Now that Trumka has moved on, what are the chances his successor will deliver competence, honesty, and good faith? Cecil Roberts became vice-president of the union in 1982 in the same election that brought Trumka to power. Before that, he held several positions in his local union and then rose to national visibility as an outspoken vice-president of southern West Virginia's District 17, the UMWA's largest district. He has a family history of mining: he is a native of Cabin Creek, West Virginia, the site of a major strike in 1912–13; his father was a miner; and both his grandfathers were killed in mine accidents. Veteran of the Vietnam War, Roberts came into the union at a time when revolt was stirring against Boyle's autocratic rule. By the time Trumka arrived on the scene in 1982, Roberts was ready for a national role. How he will cope with the ominous challenge today's miner faces remains to be seen, but the omens are certainly more promising than they were for three of his four predecessors: Boyle, Miller, and Church.

Reviewing the long history of the UMWA, one must admit that the union often ill served the interests of the ordinary coal digger, yet it also brought many benefits and improvements into the miner's life, especially the innovative health service. And though it is true that the leadership at times sold out the membership for some presumed tactical advantage or for security in the competition for union political position, it is also true that thanks to the Miners for Democracy movement the union now promotes the right of rank-and-file members to participate in making important decisions.

Even so, more democracy does not guarantee success in dealing with the challenges ahead—particularly in light of the power in the hands of corporate leaders.

7

The Problem of Externalities

Mᴏᴅᴇʀɴ ᴄᴏʀᴘᴏʀᴀᴛɪᴏɴs, with all their complexity, size, and isolation from accountability, operate in ways that have many side effects which they are not "charged" for and can ignore in calculating their prices, executive salaries, and profits.[1] Economists call these "externalities," the incidental costs of business conduct that corporations pass on to others who cannot avoid paying to benefit the perpetrating corporation. A classic example is the ubiquitous coal dust that smothered the coal town of yesterday: the coal company passed to the housekeeper the labor and the cost of cleaning materials to keep down the dust and debris incidental to the movement of coal into the channels of commerce. Externalities are hard to deal with effectively because there is no ready way to provide a cost accounting; neither the producer nor the consumer can be accurately assessed for their contribution to community dirt. That doesn't mean there is no way to deal with these problems as public policy matters, but as long as they are basically ignored, we will never come up with answers to the unasked questions. Let me then at least raise some leading questions.

The list of externalities for the coal industry is long and imposing. Air and water pollution are among the most serious and costly problems—and among the most difficult to fix responsibility for and to correct. I have already referred to the ruinous consequences of strip-mining. Then there is the danger of structural failure when heavy rains put a strain on unstable coal waste dams—with devastating results downstream. Long-term mine fires allow noxious fumes to escape into homes, with serious health results and in some cases the necessity of abandoning a whole community. Mine fires can also cause subsidence of the surface into areas where coal has burned a hole in the subsurface. Even without fires, the earth can fall into the vacant spaces left by room-and-pillar mining, sometimes destroying buildings, streets, and public utilities.

A final externality, in effect, is the impoverishment of an area after its resources have been exploited. Left behind are not only the scarred earth and crippled environment but also the erstwhile miners whose ability to make a living may be hampered by injury and disease as well as areawide unemployment. Coal corporations take the resources and run, leaving the area to cope with the results however it may.

Air and Water Pollution

One of the surprising discoveries of my first days as a miner was digging into a hunk of iron sulfide hidden in the coal seam. The small piece of con- centrated metal that gleamed dimly in the light of my miner's lamp was flint hard and curled the tip of my pick. The rotten-egg smell of the sulfur was unmistakable; I knew it well from the scent of the West Fork River, where I swam in my foolish youth. The West Fork, like all rivers border- ing the hundreds of bituminous coal mines of northern West Virginia, ran a muddy yellow, discolored by the mine waste pumped from active mines or slowly draining from abandoned ones. That dark yellow mine water was diluted sulfuric acid, and it turned the rivers into streams devoid of life of any kind. Here and there where small tributaries flowing into the West Fork drained areas without coal mines, their green, clean water penetrated vis- ibly—for a few feet; then, like all the rest of the river, it turned a sickly yel- low. I was an adult before I realized that a swimmer in clean water could dare open his eyes under water, for I had learned that sulfuric acid is sting- ingly unkind to the eye. When still much later in life I heard of acid rain I learned something more about sulfur and remembered whence it came.

Coals vary in the amount of sulfur they contain; some have very little (like that from Wyoming) and can be burned without producing sulfur dioxide (SO_2). Midwestern coal is heavily laden with sulfur; eastern coal varies from moderate to light content. Burning coal with great amounts of sulfur requires fitting smokestacks with "scrubbers" to remove particulate matter that otherwise would be sent into the atmosphere and pollute lakes and rivers downwind for hundreds to thousands of miles. Smokestack scrubbers are expensive, costing an electricity-generating plant more than $100 million. But they do work for SO_2 (other polluting substances such as nitrous oxide and carbon dioxide involve other problems).

In the years since acid rain was discovered there has been much debate about the use of sulfur-laden coal, some of it bordering on nonsense and some of it sophisticated. In 1990, for example, Senate consideration of an amendment to the Clean Air Act of 1977 evoked both kinds of discussion. Some senators showed a remarkable command of the scientific concepts and language of environmental matters; others babbled almost incoherently. Senator Max Baucus of Montana observed that in 1970, debate on a clean air act took two days; in 1977, three days; in 1990, to that point, 21 days or 150 hours. "Not only has debate been long, it has been complex. . . . [The] complexity is inevitable. . . . the regulatory process is complex; the technology is complex; the chemistry is complex; and, of course, the politics are very complex." He went on to say that for all its complexity the bill was very much worth the effort: "Let me tell you why. As we speak, 150 million Americans are breathing dirty air. This year, between five and ten million will get sick, or die prematurely, because of dirty air. And then there are economic costs—rising health care expenses, lost workdays, crop damage, and structural erosion. . . . Strict controls . . . will reduce SO_2 emissions by ten million tons a year."[2]

The most dramatic contest in the course of considering the 1990 bill was the campaign led by Senator Robert Byrd of West Virginia to provide relief for miners who would be left unemployed by legislation to curtail coal smoke pollution. The Byrd amendment was based on a prediction that within five years 3,000 to 5,000 miners of high-sulfur coal would lose their jobs because of the act, and another 10,000 to 11,000 in the following five years. He proposed that miners put out of work by the legislation be given unemployment compensation amounting to 70 percent of their pay in the first year of unemployment, 60 percent in the second, 50 percent in the third, and that a retraining and educational program be instituted.

The senator's prediction of disaster in the coal industry proved prescient. Five years after the Clean Air Act of 1990 became law about 1,000 mines had shut down (leaving 2,500) because coal prices were low, demand for sulfur-laden coal was off sharply, and profits were in decline; electricity-generating companies could not afford the scrubbers that were made mandatory under the law if they burned high-sulfur coal. Accordingly, disaster of Depression-like scope hit the affected coalfields of northern West Virginia, western Kentucky, Illinois, Indiana, Pennsylvania, and Ohio. In fact, the senator's estimate of job loss was far too low: mining jobs in the affected regions declined from 37,000 to 26,000, a reduction of 11,000 jobs, in the first five years. (It is no coincidence that West Virginia had the highest unemployment rate in the nation as of early 1996.) It does not necessarily follow that all 11,000 jobs were lost because of the Clean Air Act—some cutbacks may have been attributable to the new competitive position of western strip-mined coal—but certainly the new pollution rules accounted for a major portion of the loss. It was not caused by a decline in total demand or total production; in fact, total production for 1995 was expected, for the first time, to exceed a billion tons, the difference being made up by strip mines in Wyoming and Montana and, to some extent, by increased output of low-sulfur coal in southern West Virginia and eastern Kentucky.

In regions such as Marion County, West Virginia, where I once lived, the crisis is as real as Byrd forewarned. Where mines once burrowed beneath most towns in the county, there are few now, and only one of the large mines still operates. Service companies are feeling the pinch: the county has lost 400 retail jobs and 27 of its 355 stores. Unemployment stands at 9 percent. Miners who were earning $50,000 a year, who had bought cars and homes and made plans to finance their children's education, wonder what kind of jobs they can find now that they have been turned out—or expect to be when the tide reaches them. True, unemployment compensation is available for six months and will continue if one is in training for a new kind of work, but there is little prospect of finding jobs that pay half as much as coal mining, even after retraining. The *New York Times* quoted a miner who has had three years of college and who was laid off four months earlier: "I'm scared to death. I'm 44 years old. I'd like to live another 50 years. What am I going to do?"[3]

Some observers thought Byrd was exaggerating the problem and being small-minded on behalf of his constituents—playing politics. But the problem is a real one, and it merits better than the sneering attitude it often gets. His proposal was dismissed as a quaint, cracker-barrel Byrd performance, and, admittedly, graduated compensatory payments over three years was not a very imaginative approach to a chronic problem. But it surely was as sensible as another feature of the legislation that did survive. It is interesting to note that a plan to shift some of the burden from the miner was rejected, while a way to let corporations profit was accepted. I am referring to the scheme that permits companies to sell authorized but unused rights to pollute to another polluting coal user: electric utilities are assigned specific allowable-emissions quotas and may sell any unused portions on the open market.[4] It hardly sounds like a way of reducing pollution to arrange for futures speculators to wager on whether pollution permit prices will go up or down.[5]

Still, the scrubbers installed on plants burning fossil fuel have significantly reduced the acidity of rain falling on sampling locations across the country. The U.S. Geological Survey reported in September 1993 that sulfates, which contribute to acid rain, declined in a statistically significant way in 26 of 33 collecting stations from 1980 to 1991. But other aspects of the findings are less positive. One is that the actual acidity of rivers and lakes has increased because of nitrates combined with the sulfates still emitted from smokestacks. The quantity of sulfates has gone down by 30 percent since the enactment of the first Clean Air Act in 1970, but nitrates are down by only 6 percent since 1978. And the expectation is that "nitrogen oxide emissions from automobiles and new power plants and factories are likely to increase [total] emissions by early in the next century." Further, the apparent decline in buffering particulates in the atmosphere—calcium, magnesium, and other base materials—will reduce the neutralization of acidity in waterways, even though the amount of pollution is somewhat decreased.[6] So, some good news, some bad news: coal still remains a cause of acid rain, despite gains from legislative action.

Another form of air pollution that results from burning fossil fuels of all kinds is carbon dioxide (CO_2), which promotes the greenhouse effect, or warming of the atmosphere. Carbon dioxide absorbs heat and prevents it from being discharged into the stratosphere. Studies of the atmosphere indicate a continuing increase of carbon dioxide, which many scientists believe may raise world temperatures sufficiently to cause melting of the polar icecaps and the consequent flooding of coastal cities, with obviously disastrous effects. Some estimates place the rise of sea levels by the middle of the twenty-first century at five to eight meters, assuming that present levels of fossil fuel use continue—or even higher, if the consumption of cheap and abundant coal increases to satisfy ever greater demand for electricity. To complicate the matter further, the carbon dioxide concentration is intensified by the clearing of tropical jungles, which is taking place around the world at a rapid pace.

Although coal promoters tend to play down the danger of a greenhouse effect, the threat is apparently not illusory. A panel of 2,500 scientists advising the United Nations estimated in 1994 that the atmospheric concentration of carbon dioxide will be double the preindustrial level by the end of the next century, even if the global emission rate is reduced below 1990 levels. That much heat-trapping gas would, they say, lead to raising world temperature by 3 to 8°F. "By way of comparison," writes a *New York Times* reporter, "various estimates say the earth has warmed by five to nine degrees since the depths of the last ice age. This magnitude of warming, many climatologists say, would at the very least upset the earth's climate by altering atmospheric circulation patterns that determine where it is hot and cold, where and how much rain falls, where and how often storms strike and how violent they are."[7]

Strip Mining

Strip-mining represents one of the most devastating of externalities because dealing with its aftermath is so expensive and restoration so difficult to achieve. As noted earlier, stripping in the East poses a problem for reclamation because steep hillsides and frequent heavy rains often result in severe erosion and the flooding of streams silted with runoff debris. In the semi-arid West the lack of rainfall prevents the growth of plants capable of restoring land to something like its pre-stripped condition. Although state and federal agencies require restoration of stripped land to its preexisting contours, achieving compliance is politically as well as physically difficult. Strip-mine companies make formidable adversaries, for surface mining is commonly profitable enough to encourage owners to organize and battle against conservationists. In West Virginia, for example, after Congressman Ken Hechler opposed strip-miners vigorously and proposed legislation to curtail stripping sharply, the operators succeeded in driving him out of Congress. John D. Rockefeller IV, when he was governor of West Virginia, had to back off from his campaign to regulate surface mining because the combined strength of strip-mine operators and workers was sufficient to threaten his political future. Some measure of the spirited self-defense of strippers is evident in the comment of the vice-president of Consol in a 1968 speech denouncing conservationists as: "stupid idiots, socialists, and Commies who don't know what they're talking about. I think it is our bounden duty to knock them down and subject them to the ridicule they deserve."[8] Getting strip-mining regulations put into law has been difficult to impossible in some states. Indiana enacted an official joke by requiring a $25-an-acre performance bond![9]

It is hardly surprising that some orders to reclaim spoiled surfaces get no response. Very often the owners are small-time operators; they have little invested as compared with underground operators and, being more fly-by-night, are not subject to the pressures that influence more established mine owners. Reclamation is often advertised with color photographs in which bucolic "after" scenes replace the barren gullies of "before," but as in most advertising the evidence is carefully cultivated. More commonly than not, the gullies and gashes are still there.

Congress passed surface mining laws in 1977, but reclaiming mines once abandoned is as difficult under federal law as under that of the states. Not only are the strippers powerful politically, but enforcers in the Reagan-Bush years were told to take it easy on offenders (consequently, an investigation of the former director of the Office of Surface Mining, Reclamation and Enforcement began in 1993 in the Department of Interior). How much such officially sanctioned nonenforcement had to do with the lack of effect of the law is difficult to say, but the House Appropriations Committee reported that only 1.5 percent of abandoned mines were cleaned up from 1977 to 1991 and estimated cost of reclaiming the rest at $61 billion.[10] But why should taxpayers be burdened with the cost of restoring stripped terrain to viable condition? The beneficiaries of the stripping were the corporations that profited from cheaply produced coal and the consumers of cheap electricity; they gained and now everyone pays the bill. Is that the free market we hear so much praised?

Mine Spoil Dams

Coal comes from the earth "dirty" and must be cleaned before it is shipped off to be burned. In earlier times, cleaning was left either to the loader, who could have his car of coal dumped without pay if it contained what the bosses considered too much slate, or to "breaker boys" who sat in a cleaning area and picked out debris by hand. The waste formed the familiar slag heaps that were common to most mining communities, burning from spontaneous combustion and polluting the air with an acrid smell and perpetual smoke.

Today, however, "preparation plants" use vast amounts of water to remove slate and other debris; the waste in uncleaned coal can amount to as much as one-fifth its weight. And since a single mine may use as much as half a million gallons of water a day for this purpose, the leftover culm, or gob, or slag (the names vary from region to region) now comes in handy for damming streams to form reservoirs where used coal-cleaning water can be returned, the dirt allowed to settle out, and the water reused. And therein lies a danger to the people who live downstream from such a dam.

In Logan County, West Virginia, the Pittston company had eight mines that delivered coal to be cleaned in a preparation plant near the company's three dams on the Middle Fork tributary of Buffalo Creek. Made entirely from solid mine spoil—waste matter—that in places was burning, these unstable dams gave way after heavy February rains in 1972, and a 21-million-cubic-foot wall of water up to thirty feet high went roaring down the narrow valley at a speed of about thirty miles an hour. The torrent took the lives of 150 residents, destroyed 1,000 homes, and shattered the psychological peace of hundreds of victims who saw members of their families swirled away by the black, greasy current. One man tried desperately to pull his pregnant wife onto the roof of his house. He was holding their two-year-old son with his right hand and trying to keep a grip on his wife's hand with his left when he fell himself. His wife was swept away, and he sank again and again into the murky and freezing water: "I was thrown from side to side and crushed—my insides was crushed so hard that it just seemed like my eyeballs was trying to pop out, and my breath, I just couldn't get my breath at all. Somewhere along there I lost that boy of mine. I don't know where." Another man watched helplessly as a house trailer floated by with three women standing at "a picture window, a big window. They were standing in the window and I saw their mouths moving. I gathered they were hollering. Now where the houses done jammed up against the bridge, the mobile home hit those houses and I guess the pressure and the impact was rolling under and that mobile home with the three women in it just vanished underneath all those houses and I never did see no more of the mobile home."[11]

In the aftermath of the flood, Pittston was sued and settled for $13.5 million. But the implications of the policy that had led to the construction of the flimsy dams seemed not to register with either the company or West Virginia officials. Said a representative of Pittston: "It was an act of God." Said Governor Arch Moore, the dams were "logical and constructive" and kept dirty water out of Buffalo Creek—but they did *not* keep 21 million cubic feet of very dirty water out of Buffalo Creek, a point that seemed to have escaped the governor.[12]

Mine Fires and Subsidence

To the uninitiated it would seem a simple enough matter to extinguish a coal fire underground: pour on water and seal out air to cut off its oxygen. But it is not that easy. Coal fires have been known to go on burning for as long as eighty years despite strenuous effort and millions spent.[13] They are more likely to occur and harder to extinguish in anthracite than bituminous coal, because anthracite seams are steeply pitched, allowing heat and gases to circulate more freely—thus sustaining the fire—than in the flat beds of bituminous coal. And when coal companies—particularly in anthracite regions—go bankrupt or close down for other reasons, there is no organization with an assignable responsibility for putting out a fire or dealing with its consequences.

Mine fires are not rare; they occur in all major coal states. In West Virginia in the 1980s eight underground mine fires were burning, and 1,200 acres of surface waste was afire. A major fire burns under a quarter of the city of Scranton, Pennsylvania, and in that state's anthracite mining area there are dozens of smaller fires in progress. A state agency makes some effort to assist towns facing this unseen danger, but in 1985 the state estimated that $15 billion was needed to cope with abandoned mine problems—in Pennsylvania alone.

The fire under Centralia, Pennsylvania, a town formerly of about 1,100 people 190 miles due west of New York City, is a long-term, complex, social, political, scientific, and economic problem. It began in 1962 when the town fathers burned a garbage dump and thought they had extinguished the fire at the end of the day. But the trash pile was deep and kept smoldering until it ignited the underlying coal bed. Then, so to speak, the fat was really in the fire, and for decades it has gone on burning. Nothing done by the local council, the state government, Congress, the U.S. Office of Surface Mining, or the Bureau of Mines (some of whom evaded doing anything constructive) has been able to stop it though millions have been spent in the effort.

The consequences for the town have been virtually intractable. Noxious gases, especially carbon monoxide, infiltrated homes and made people ill; buildings and roads were damaged; houses directly over the fire had to be purchased with public funds and demolished. In fact, almost all of Centralia's residents have now been relocated. Subsidence, of course, became an ongoing hazard, as was well illustrated by the experience of a twelve-year-old boy who fell into a gaping hole near his grandmother's house on February 14, 1981. Todd Domboski told an interviewer

> I saw a little smoke a couple of yards from where we [he and a cousin] were working on a motorbike. So I went over and brushed away some leaves 'cause I thought someone had thrown a match and I wanted to make sure there was no fire. And the ground just started giving way, and I went down to my knees, then my waist, and kept going. I grabbed for some roots and was screaming for my cousin. I couldn't see him; there was smoke everywhere. I just heard him screaming, "Put your hand up! Put your hand up!" I was in over my head when he finally grabbed me. It smelled like sulfur. It was unbearably hot, and it sounded like the wind howling down there.[14]

Young Domboski later learned that the hole was three hundred feet deep and its temperature 350 degrees. "Ever since," he said, "I've had terrible nightmares about falling in that hole." No wonder.

Fires are by no means the only cause of subsidence. Pillars left behind to shore up the top in worked-out mines slowly decay from ground water seepage, or they crumble when the clay they are standing on gets wet, and each pillar that gives way vastly increases the weight on adjacent pillars. In West Virginia alone the state estimated in 1980 that 89,000 acres of land within its borders were in danger from subsidence.

I remember from my youth many hillside gashes where deep gaps were left open from the sinking of coal land. In Fairmont, only six miles from Monongah, the city's subterranean mines are caving in gradually, threatening the city with major structural damage. When the sinkholes appear, buildings are twisted and crumpled as foundations are left unsupported. In 1978 an apartment building and three houses were affected. Said one homeowner, "The gas lines pulled apart, the electric lines snapped. The doors wouldn't shut and the cabinet doors wouldn't open." Within a few weeks the buildings were condemned and vacated. In Fairmont the federal government spent nearly $1 million in 1979–80 alone to prevent subsidence destruction and was seeking $3 million more to shore up a church and a large part of the downtown business section. The Office of Surface Mining reported that between 1980 and 1995 it expected to spend $5 billion to correct mine subsidence.[15]

Corrected for inflation, all such estimates become much larger, and it is the taxpayer who must subsidize the absent owners of former mines, for there is no way to reach yesterday's profits to cover the costs of today's subsidence. Once again, coal corporations get away with the gains and leave the losses to plague the region's future.

8

Coal and Corporate Power

THE AMERICAN BUSINESS CORPORATION is a wildly ambivalent institution. It has been an agent of unparalleled growth and a major factor in producing a national wealth unmatched in history. It has amassed and controls unimaginable amounts of capital and has put together the world's most productive manufacturing and service-providing system. It can fairly be said that no institution in American life has done as much as the corporation to shape the economic and to a large extent the social character of the society. But then, neither has any other institution done so much to generate gross inequality, to visit blind-eyed viciousness on its victims, or to avoid being held accountable for its actions.

It is true, of course, that in all societies small groups of powerful persons make basic and crucial allocative decisions. Corporate leaders have persuaded us to call our way of making these determinations "private enterprise" with "market mechanisms" guiding allocations—a system in which "consumer sovereignty" controls. This is about as persuasive as the fiction that in Stalin's version of socialism (an "authority" system) the well-being of the masses was the guiding light, not the preservation of the system itself.

If in all societies there is an inescapable tendency for the powerful few to control the purse strings of national wealth and, operating from hidden recesses, to take actions that affect all but that most are either unaware of or unable to prevent, then surely the coal industry is a prime example. It is corporate power running amok both historically and contemporaneously. If any point has been demonstrated by the evidence adduced in these pages, it is that coal barons made millions while despoiling the environment and sacrificing the lives of accident and disease victims whose suffering was never entered in their account books. Perhaps we can get a handle on the problem of unaccountability by looking hard at the coal corporation.

Corporations and How They Grew

Corporations grew with American society; feared at first but ultimately worshiped, the limited stock company was perfectly fitted for a country that was in love with business and economic expansion. The nineteenth century was made for corporate hegemony. With capital in short supply and high demand, corporations proved able to gather resources, on the whole, efficiently. At the opening of the 1800s there were only 335 business corporations in existence, but they doubled and redoubled with great speed; today there are 3.6 million. The Civil War was a fervent call for corporate creation, for it was the first war of production, a war of numbers—huge numbers. Millions of troops needed millions of dollars worth of supplies and services: coal, iron, manufactured goods, railroads. Thus corporations expanded and became fundamental units of the economy, but they were still under restrictions historically placed upon them by common law.

Overcoming those barriers was a slow process, but in the end the game went to the corporate moguls, and laws like the Sherman Antitrust Act of 1890 were effectively negated by court interpretation. For example, in *U.S. v. E. C. Knight Co.* (1895) the Supreme Court took the ridiculous position that the monopolization of the sugar refining business did not involve interstate trade and therefore the antitrust law did not apply—yet the company controlled 95 percent of all sugar refining in the United States. With regard to state laws that regulated business, the Court held that a corporation was a "person" within the meaning of the Fourteenth Amendment's protection of a person against the denial of due process of law. In *Lochner v. New York*

(1905), due process was tortured to mean "liberty of contract," which forbade a state legislature to regulate hours of labor in a bakery. The argument was that such a law denied a workingman the "liberty" to contract for more than a sixty-hour work week. Thus a provision intended to protect newly freed slaves was used by corporate interests to put shackles on workers. Interestingly, however, the Court rejected the coal companies' challenge to hours-of-work legislation for coal miners, in *Holden v. Hardy* (1898), accepting the argument that there is a relationship between long hours of coal mining and safety. But what the courts usually did in that era was to abrogate labor laws, not approve them.

Early twentieth-century corporations were small, at least as compared with the giant companies that dominate many areas of the economy today in this era of freedom for corporations to consolidate through mergers and buyouts. During the 1980s the merger-acquisition fever ran high. In 1980 1,889 such deals were approved; over the next six years the average annual rate jumped to 3,336; and in 1988 their value reached a record $335.8 billion. After a slowdown due to the junk bond episode the merger process regained strength, and in the first ten months of 1994 a Wall Street research firm reported deals involving $284.4 billion, probably making 1994 the second biggest merger year in history.[1]

A measure of the freedom for corporate consolidation now allowed by the Justice Department, even where there is potential conflict of interest between the elements being joined, is the "explanation" offered by government attorneys when CONOCO (Continental Oil) bought Consol in 1965. They told an inquiring congressional committee that they had approved the deal because "only insignificant amounts of Continental's gasoline is sold in Consolidation's market area." (Since Consol is not in the gasoline business, that seems a strange "explanation.") They noted that fuel oil "can sometimes compete with coal" but that the two companies did not sell in the same areas. ("Sometimes compete"? Strange language when one recalls how often coal executives complained about oil undercutting coal in the post–World War II era.) They said they were aware that Consol was trying to develop a synthetic gasoline from coal, but presumably that would be sold in the West Virginia and Kentucky areas where it would be made.

(Had these bright lawyers never heard of fleets of highway oil tankers and miles of railroad tank cars?)[2]

It is not the merger process alone that has produced the enormous resources of capital in the hands of corporate bosses. According to *Fortune* magazine's 1991 accounting, the ten largest companies had combined assets of $893.3 billion, far larger than the 1989 Gross National Product of all but five countries in the world (the United States, France, West Germany, the Soviet Union, and Japan). That total, it should be noted, includes the assets of only the largest industrial corporations; it omits all the hundreds of billions controlled by the nation's financial institutions—banks, brokers, insurance companies. Four of the ten largest firms in the *Fortune* list were oil companies, three of which also owned coal mines; eighth among the big ten was DuPont, which in 1981 had bought the tenth largest oil company and then largest coal producer—CONOCO, which already owned Consolidation Coal.

The significance of corporations to the development of American economic and political life generally is clearly demonstrated where coal mining is concerned. Corporations schemed to get mineral rights or land itself to exploit the rich lodes of coal that lie in such abundance beneath American soil. Corporate decisions determined the fate of hundreds of thousands of miners in the roughly 150 years of extensive coal operations in this country. Corporate officials used their economic power to gain control of governmental policy in order to bury safety legislation, to fend off laws for the prevention or treatment or compensation of black lung. They committed fraud on a massive scale to hide their failure to comply with the law stipulating dust controls. Their actions damaged the environment, crushed competition, and conspired to advance coal interests with little regard for other consequences. Coal corporations make the critical determinations on capital allocation and take all the decisive actions that set the fate not only of the corporate owners but of their employees and a widely affected public.

Coal companies vary greatly in size, wealth, ownership, and control. Some are owned by an individual or a family and employ perhaps half a dozen miners; these very marginal doghole mines may earn workers a bare living and the owner not much more. Other small operations can be a source of considerable income, depending on the mine, the demand, and various random factors. At the other extreme are huge corporate giants worth billions of dollars which operate hundreds of coal enterprises, are often owned by major oil companies, and control large portions of the mineral rights and resource reserves of the country. But whatever their size and the amount of capital invested or available, coal companies have common features. They all work within the confines of the market—demand, the cost of capital acquisition, competition, the pressure of employees (whether organized or unorganized but always potential union workers)— and of governmental regulations.

Historically, however, American coal corporations have had a wide-ranging discretionary authority to operate as they see fit, free to decide the fate of their employees and to walk away once the coal has been removed. If the surface of the land caves in after the coal is gone, or if a fire rages underground for years and noxious fumes seep into people's homes, the company has often refused to accept responsibility. If a once beautiful mountain is decapitated, leaving a raw and exposed wound on the body of nature once strip mining is completed, "so be it" is often the attitude of the company that profited from the scarring of the earth. When overloaded coal trucks damage a public highway, it is the public that pays the repair bill, not the destroyer of the public domain. In the past, companies denied responsibility for disasters such as the Monongah explosion, calling them "acts of God." It is becoming more difficult, though, to get away with that kind of evasion. The Pittston Coal Company was found liable for damages when a dam made of mine spoil gave way in 1972 and created havoc downstream; formerly, the act-of-God explanation would have routinely been accepted, and the victims would have borne the cost alone.

Yet if in some respects greater accountability prevails today, the reality of the situation leaves little cause for cheering, for the coal industry is adept at creating the illusion of accountability. Take the black lung case as an example. Although there was the appearance of action to reduce the floating dust in the workplace to safe levels after a specific upper limit was legislated, testing was left to the industry itself, and as we saw in chapter 4, some companies resorted to massive fraud by reporting conditions falsely. And although operators lost in Congress and a compensation program was instituted, and in fact half a million miners or their widows were paid some (nearly all temporary) awards, winning approval of a claim was made more difficult after the first few years of the program when coal companies were given a role in determining eligibility. In the early 1980s, for example, 94 percent of all claims were rejected.[3] And the chief ground for rejection has been the insistence on the use of X-ray evidence, despite the findings offered for decades that black lung can exist in the lungs without showing up in an X-ray. Clearly, appearance of accountability and real accountability are not the same thing.

The sheer size and wealth of modern corporations complicates the task of making them accountable. They are shielded from scrutiny by having the money to buy attention to their point of view in the political process. For example, the 1996 elections set a record for campaign expenditures for federal office: $2.2 billion. Much of it came in the form of "soft money" (contributions to political parties, nominally to promote such activities as "getting out the vote" but in reality to support candidates) via political action committees. Labor PACs were seven of the ten largest contributors, mostly to the Democratic Party. But business PACs gave more money than did unions, the bulk of it to the Republican Party. Of the ten most lavish corporate givers (averaging $1.2 million) the two biggest were tobacco companies, and four were in communications—two fields in which important legislation was pending.[4] In this way often without public awareness, corporations win tax favors and subsidies, kill regulatory efforts, and accomplish myriad other political coups. Try as reformers ardently may to modify the laws of campaign financing, cash remains a political force of great significance.

Indeed, the peculiarity of this form of political power is that it requires no overt action on the part of business to have its effect. As Charles Lindblom has illustrated, business clout ensures that other actors in the political process must take account of potential business reaction to any proposed regulatory action. A change may have a depressing effect on the economy, "because the businessman may perform his role less vigorously since he expects negative effects from the regulation. Because a market system is not a 'command' system but an 'inducement' system, any change or reform that they [businessmen] do not like brings to all of us the punishment of unemployment or a sluggish economy."[5]

The very possession of enormous wealth, then, wins the huge modern coal company a certain deference from other political performers. In a market system, money talks and big money roars. The greater the amount of capital available for company managers to distribute, the greater the inclination to believe that what the disposer of big money hints or threatens has to be taken seriously. We are so much in the habit of deferring to corporate power that no thought is given to alternative ways of managing affairs. When, for example, Lockheed and Chrysler experienced serious setbacks and asked for governmental aid in recovering their profitability, no one seemed to give serious thought to what obligation they might owe in return. No government official or political leader suggested that some part of those corporations "belonged" to the United States. And when John Kenneth Galbraith made the sensible suggestion that corporations mainly involved with making armaments ought to be owned by government so as to prevent corporate use of national resources for their own gain rather than for promoting the reasonable military needs of the country, his idea was no more than noted in an occasional book review, not given the broad attention it might have received in other societies. Corporations are empowered by the widespread assumption that they are a "given" in this society, accepted routinely rather than routinely challenged.

In striking contrast to today's huge corporations, coal companies of the past were small, individually owned and operated. Katherine Harvey's study of early U.S. mining shows how small operators struggled in the middle decades of the nineteenth century in western Maryland, experiencing constant failure, bankruptcy, and continuous absorption of the smaller by ever growing larger, combined companies. The Consolidation Coal Company had its origins in those chaotic times. Formally organized in 1864, by 1870 it had, through mergers and outright acquisitions, achieved control over half the coal in the western Maryland region and all the local railroad facilities.[6] From there it went on to take over faltering operations in

West Virginia, Pennsylvania, Kentucky, and elsewhere until it became the largest coal producer in the nation. In 1965 Consol itself was taken over by CONOCO, and in 1981 both were bought by E. I. Du Pont de Nemours, the giant maker of explosives and chemical products, in a $7.6 billion deal.

But before the day of astronomical transactions that beggar the imagination, there was the era of what Harry Caudill calls the reign of the "Moguls." In West Virginia and Kentucky particularly, a handful of coal operators in the last quarter of the nineteenth century and the first quarter of the twentieth dominated the development of coal mines and made themselves millionaires in the process. The Watsons, Camdens, Flemings, and Haymonds in West Virginia (known as the Fairmont Ring) not only owned countless mines; they also occupied political offices—governor, U.S. senator, U.S. congressman, state legislator, judge—and unashamedly used those offices to advance the interests of coal operators. In Kentucky, John C. C. Mayo rose from poverty to plutocracy with his coal investments. Starting with a little borrowed money, before his untimely death at age fifty he had amassed an enormous fortune and reigned over a vast empire of coal and cash. But most of these names have long since been forgotten— perhaps, says Caudill, because they did so little for the regions that sustained them. They liked to call themselves philanthropists, but little of their beneficence came to the hill country. How many small coal cities got libraries, hospitals, parks, or schools named for these entrepreneurs? Caudill adds, "Their successors have been equally stingy. The whole land therefore lies barren of cultural facilities without which life must remain relatively sterile and true education impossible. Their cupidity made the moguls eminently forgettable."[7]

The great day of small-time local operators is long gone; a few remain, but the bulk of the industry is in corporate hands. Some observers have a romantic vision of the small, local owner as someone who tried to look out for local people and the well-being of the community. No doubt there were such owners, but they were outnumbered by tough-minded entrepreneurs who either failed in the fierce competition or sold out to large corporations. As Caudill points out, the Moguls were stout defenders of business prerogatives; no softhearted community values hampered their style. As one of them instructed his brother, who was about to take over as superintendent of one of the family mines, he must maintain tight discipline: "We are not running a Sunday School."[8]

Absentee Corporate Ownership

Even if there were evidence that some early-day coal men were community minded, that can scarcely be said of the absentee corporate owners who succeeded them. Controlling at least three-quarters of eastern coal mining, owning vast amounts of land and mineral rights to still more land, they still maintain tight discipline, though no longer by firsthand involvement. Now the flow of information via computers and other technology allows coal business bureaucrats in distant New York or Pittsburgh to see exactly how many persons worked how many hours to produce exactly how many tons of coal with how many machine breakdowns keeping how many miners idle how long, last Tuesday—with correlations to show how one mine compares in cost-effectiveness with others. Computers facilitate control—minutely.

The absentee corporate mine official is concerned with data of that kind, not with how the Marion County economy is faring or how many families will be cast into turmoil by the latest wave of mine closings. (One commentator on the progress of corporate disregard for worker welfare, reporting on the devastating impact of massive downsizing by IBM, notes the unusually high proportion of ex-employees needing psychiatric care.)[9]

The actions of absentee corporations has meant the impoverishment of coal country, despite the richness of its mineral wealth. In their concern for salaries, profits, and freedom from accountability, businessmen have exploited the coal states mercilessly. How have they turned native wealth into state penury? Here is what appears to me to have happened.

The remaining locally based coal operators in this country are definitely in the minority; most mining operations are controlled by absentee corporations that own most of the mines, the land that has coal under it, and the mineral rights to as yet untapped coal reserves. In the eastern coal states at least three-quarters of all coal mining is controlled by relatively few, very large corporations. The history of these corporate giants is not a tale of concern for the residents of coal country; the mineral riches of these states—Kentucky and West Virginia in particular—have not enriched but impoverished the residents, while out-of-state executives and the stockholders share in the wealth that departs the state immediately upon being realized.

West Virginia and Kentucky, the two states whose economies are most dependent on coal mining, rank among the lowest five of the fifty states in all but one of the usual statistical measures of economic well-being. In per capita personal income West Virginia in 1994 ranked 46th; Kentucky, at 42d, barely rose above the bottom five. In disposable personal income West Virginia ranked 48th and Kentucky 46th in 1994. In 1993 the percentage of people below the officially designated poverty line put West Virginia in 48th and Kentucky in 47th place. In average household income for 1993, West Virginia was 48th, Kentucky 46th, at $22,421 and $24,376 respectively; compare the national figure of $31,241.[10] Fleeing the conditions suggested by these statistics, enough West Virginians left the state to make it one of four that lost population in the 1980s, and the second largest loser in percentage. Eight of the twenty-five counties with the lowest personal income in the country are in Kentucky (six) and West Virginia (two); of the twenty-five U.S. counties with the highest unemployment in 1991, West Virginia had five and Kentucky two.[11]

Absentee corporations contribute to this poverty in several ways. They manage to avoid or hold down taxes on their extensive property holdings. If schools are run down and public facilities are decrepit, one reason is that taxes duly owed by big out-of-state corporations are either not levied or not paid. In 1970 a study of seven West Virginia counties showed that all had more than half their property owned by corporations, and local tax assessors turned blind eyes to the fact that these landholdings were endowed with coal riches. In Marion County, coal land worth from $25,000 to $40,000 an acre was assessed at 50¢ per acre; although state law says that property must be assessed at a minimum of 50 percent of actual value, the state tax commissioner paid no attention to this flagrant violation. Why? The deference to corporate power and the consistently demonstrated ability of big business to control local officials—either through outright corruption or through political organizational manipulation—both help account for the sweet deals the big mules (to use a common southern expression) buy for themselves. This report was said to have come from unnamed "young people" and therefore might appear suspect.[12] Yet it was fully confirmed in an extensive and thoroughly professional inquiry a decade later.

The survey that corroborated the limited early study was done by the Appalachian Land Ownership Task Force, financed (at $130,000) by the Appalachian Regional Commission (an agency representing the federal government) and thirteen state governments.[13] A large group of paid and volunteer researchers scoured the tax rolls and land records of eighty counties in six states: Virginia, West Virginia, Kentucky, Tennessee, Alabama, and North Carolina. Their 1,800-page report showed that almost half the land in those eighty counties was owned by coal, timber, and oil companies. In addition, several railroads and other companies owned and leased coal acreage to mine operators; one was leasing 75,000 acres of virgin coal lands to an oil company. The Norfolk and Western Railroad (now Norfolk and Southern) owned 178,481 acres throughout the eighty counties, but that put it third among major landholders in the region. Second in standing with 218,561 acres was Bowater Company of London, England. Other owners of more than 100,000 acres were headquartered in Pittsburgh, in Portland, Oregon, and in New York City. Only 1 percent of the local population owned tracts in excess of 250 acres.

Three-quarters of the owners of mineral rights were paying less than 25¢ an acre in property taxes; those in twelve counties of eastern Kentucky paid a grand total of $1,500 in property taxes annually. Overall, the average tax per ton of known reserves in major coal areas was an astonishing one-fiftieth of a cent. All this left the local landowner paying a disproportionate share of the taxes; had taxes been equitably collected, the eighty counties would have taken in an extra $16.5 million each year (about $200,000 apiece). The evidence from the eighty counties went on and on. Of the 50 largest landowners, 46 were corporations. Of the 15 largest mineral rights owners, not a single one was headquartered in Appalachia, but collectively they held rights to 1,238,454 acres.

Such concentrated ownership prevents economic diversification, since land is unavailable for alternative uses—and possible jobs. It also means a lack of locally controlled capital for investment in other productive lines and, given the minuscule taxes levied on extraction of natural resources, insufficient infrastructure to attract new industry and businesses. The scarcity and resulting high cost of land for home building, and therefore of housing, also make it difficult to attract investors. Coal "busts" have the same impact as failure in one-crop economies: when the one industry on which all depend gets into difficulty, there are no stable alternatives to support the economy. The only choice for many is outmigration, and the survey found a high correlation between the degree of corporate ownership of a county and heavy outmigration during the 1960s, a time of coal decline. State and federal government ownership of large tracts in Appalachia complicates rather than eases the situation, since governments too do not pay taxes commensurate with those of average taxpayers. Moreover, by occupying 8 percent of the land, state and national parks and other tourist attractions exacerbate the shortage.

The survey also reported on the expansion of oil companies into the coal industry. Before 1960, no coal companies were owned by oil interests; the oil invasion began in the 1960s as Continental acquired Consol; Occidental Oil took over Island Creek Coal; Standard Oil of Ohio got Old Ben Coal Company; Exxon, Mobil, Texaco, Ashland Oil, and others acquired smaller coal units. In the 1970s big oil expanded and consolidated its coal operations. Soon Gulf Oil, Standard of California, and Ohio Standard got into coal; others owned reserves and were poised to enter.

The survey's review of fifteen West Virginia counties found that eight large oil companies owned 340,000 acres of mineral rights and 50,000 acres of land. In Logan County alone, 35,000 acres of coal reserves were owned by oil companies. And so on across the region. The increasing role of oil interests in deciding which energy sources to develop and how rapidly is important because, as international corporations, they have great independent power and do not respond to local interests that may not want to see hundreds of acres of strip-mining become thousands of acres, with grim consequences for local communities. The huge oil company is absenteeism raised to the nth power as its concern for energy development in line with its particular corporate concerns crowds out local (or even national) concerns.

The clout of oil interests is nicely illustrated by the defeat of a bill seeking to curb the ability of oil companies to acquire coal and other energy reserves. By a vote of 62 to 30 the Senate in 1977 rejected the proposal, offered by Senator Edward M. Kennedy. Oil lobbyists argued that the bill was tantamount to a divestiture move, forcing companies to get rid of energy reserves already acquired. Although Kennedy insisted that the bill did not do so, the oil companies prevailed. The Massachusetts senator said there was "a wholly reasonable fear the oil and gas industry will bring to bear the same [noncompetitive] tactics in the coal and uranium industries" that they use in oil and gas. Indiana Standard said in a bulletin on the bill that it "would make no economic sense for any company to withhold or manipulate any fuel in today's economy, when doing so undoubtedly would forfeit market position."[14] Perhaps that was true in the days of the oil embargo (although there is evidence of manipulation of supplies in that "shortage"), but what oil companies would do to protect their interests in a different market situation is perhaps less modest. One thing at least is clear two decades later: no one would trouble to offer such legislation now; it would be a sheer waste of time.

The story of coal in America is the story of corporate successes and excesses generally. Granted, the coal corporations' accomplishments in productivity are unparalleled. They have raised vast amounts of capital and developed mining technology that the rest of the world's coal industry has envied and bought and emulated (not that this has been a one-way street; Americans have adopted innovations from other countries, such as longwall mining techniques). But they have also inflicted cruelty on their own employees to a degree unequaled in advanced nations, caused more environmental damage, and exhibited more flagrant conflict of interest (such as oil interests buying heavily into coal operations). And the industry leadership has been so deferred to that not only has it never really been threatened with nationalization; it has not even had to respond to that idea for the last seventy years. Coal companies have fought labor unions with vary-

ing degrees of success; they also worked out deals with the UMW that practically eliminated the union from participation in implementing the mechanization of coal production. They have corrupted and exploited state
and local governments for their own benefit in a broad range of policies
involving health and safety regulations, tax policy, environmental degradation, land ownership, and mineral rights.

The coal corporation is an outstanding illustration of the point made
by Robert A. Dahl and Charles E. Lindblom, discussing the independent
power of corporations, in the 1976 preface to their *Politics, Economics, and
Welfare* (written a quarter-century after the book was originally published):

> In the realm of attitudes, ideas, and ideology, we Americans have an irra-
> tional commitment to private ownership and control of economic
> enterprises that prevents us from thinking clearly about economic arrange-
> ments. This irrational commitment to private ownership and control
> conflicts with [our] underlying assumption . . . that a modern economy
> ought to be thought of and treated as a *social* or *public* economy. . . . The
> adequacy of [an economy's] performance and alternatives for achieving
> better performance require social judgments and decisions. . . . Our notion
> of a good society is one in which the members seek the ends for social
> action by means of a public economy that is subject to the final say of a
> democratic government.[15]

The coal corporation has been free to make important social and economic determinations that are tantamount to political decisions for the
whole society. The society has little or nothing to say about those decisions,
but society suffers from floods like the one on Buffalo Creek, mine fires like
that in Centralia, explosions like the one in Farmington, massive unemployment in Appalachia, acid rain in eastern waterways, and a thousand
other examples. This raises important questions that the country has given
very little thought to. How can those decisions be made in a more democratic way, one that brings more equitable results and assigns more
accountability for the actions taken? What changes in the way economic
decisions are arrived at will make them more just, fairer to all concerned?

9

Confronting Corporate Hegemony

THE PROSPECT OF curbing excess corporate power is dubious for many reasons, not least of which is the reverence for corporations prevalent among Americans. We shall accomplish little unless we can shake the firmly rooted acceptance of the divine right of corporations to rule the roost. Two of the 1996 Republican presidential aspirants—Bob Dole and Pat Buchanan—marginally challenged corporate downsizing by companies when profits (and, they might have added, executive salaries) were at an all-time high. But those little outbursts could not compare with the glowing adulation for the market system, pleas for freedom from regulation, and the glorifying of privatization that abound in this era of the defeat of Marxist doctrine.

The way in which deeply held ideas (capitalism, racism, scorn for immigrants) take precedence over statesmanlike gestures is well illustrated by what came of one of the most striking political system changes of the century (or so it seemed at the time): the enfranchisement of millions of African Americans in the deep South. Potential voters who had been barred from the polls by one device or another were, under the 1964 Voting Rights Act, granted the ballot, and within a few years the barriers were largely eliminated. I argued at the time that this would bring to the political arena citizens who would express in the voting booth their resentment at their long exclusion from society, their oppression and enforced poverty, and would thus have a decided impact on national politics. That long-denied people with an antiestablishment orientation, given the right to participate, would change the balance of politics by placing a new weight on the scale seemed an inescapable conclusion—but it did not materialize in practice.

There has been some effect, to be sure, but nothing like the revolutionary impact I expected. Some blacks went to the House of Representatives, and their opportunity to stand up and tell the nation via C-Span the wrongs or rights of this or that proposal was important in its way, but it did not change the power orientation of the country. The underlying racism and economic power of the Big Mules continued as always. It is ironic that only a few years later the prevailing racism of the nation and of the Deep South in particular came surging through to elect a majority of southern Republican congressmen who were hostile to black aspirations. Who predicted that the Voting Rights Act would enable a Newt Gingrich not only to win a House seat from Georgia but to become Speaker to boot? Certainly not I.

The case of black enfranchisement is a warning of how powerful beliefs and prejudice can be. Hence, the renewed enthusiasm for capitalism is in itself reason to be on guard. We can ill afford to turn a blind eye toward an agency that has the performance record of the coal establishment. Our deference to corporations generally and our headlong rush to privatize and place under corporate control everything from health care to the welfare and school systems carry grave potential consequences.

Sources of Corporate Prestige and Power

The way corporations are seen is not a matter of indifference to the wealthy. Today television is the dominant or sole source of news for two-thirds of the public, and that in itself approximates a conspiracy to keep the citizenry uninformed about corporate and labor affairs, for the communications media are themselves owned increasingly by supercorporations: Westinghouse owns CBS, Disney buys ABC, Ted Turner's CNN joins Time Warner, Rupert Murdoch adds Fox to his empire. Newspapers decline in number; most of those remaining are owned by great chains, and both papers and news magazines reflect their corporate ownership. Sports and fashion are given sections of their own, but what newspaper has a labor section? Editors and, more important, publishers do not think of labor events as a distinct newsworthy subject.

Furthermore, the wave of anti-Communism in the 1950s and 1960s gave socialism and nationalization such a bad press that many people actually feared possible retribution if they so much as mentioned such matters. In the 1950s, when Senator Joseph McCarthy was bullying witnesses and riding high, an aircraft worker came to me in desperation when I was a state senator in Connecticut. He told me he had been barred from his job and escorted off the premises by armed security personnel but had never been able to discover what he was supposed to have done or who had charged him. The only possible cause appeared to be that his father subscribed to a foreign-language paper from an East European country. Tales like this were commonplace, and the blacklisting of writers and performers scared the timid, turning radical thought into forbidden doctrine. The mood of the 1950s no longer prevails, it is true, but the aftermath of that redbaiting continues to inhibit thought, as one notices in talking with Europeans who freely discuss what Americans are silent about. A whole spectrum of social outlook and programmatic politics has been eliminated from the American forum. Fervor for free enterprise is by no means only incidentally related to the antiradicalism of the society.

Politics and money are also prominent factors. In the course of the twentieth century, governmental effort to curb corporate excess has put some limits on previously independent corporate power by regulation of the stock market, environmental curbs, protection of workers' rights to organize and strike, a coal mine safety role for the federal government, and other intrusions. The corporations' response has been to wade into the turbulent currents of politics and fight back, and their prestige and cash have been invaluable sources of political strength. The New Deal restrained antiunion activities through the Wagner Act, but the business community counterorganized and curtailed union actions through the Taft-Hartley Act. Deregulation became a battle cry—even before Thatcher-Reagan-style politics arrived—in the deregulatory campaign of Democrat Jimmy Carter, thanks to the power of business PACs and lots of money poured into the coffers of both major political parties.

At the state level, corporations sponsored "right-to-work" campaigns and other antiunion legislation that invited manufacturing companies to relocate in the southern nonunion, low-wage, right-to-work states to such an extent that twenty-two of the twenty-five counties with the highest percentage of employees engaged in manufacturing in 1990 were in the South, including five in North Carolina and four each in Mississippi, Tennessee, and Alabama. But the twenty-five counties with the lowest unemployment rates included only four southern counties, all of them in Texas. The only southern counties in the top twenty-five for per capita personal income were four Virginia counties adjacent to Washington, D.C.[1] In brief, manufacturing companies flocked to the South in the 1960–90 decades, but did not bring prosperity along with the jobs. And large numbers of the concerns seeking low-wage workers have begun leaving the South for Third World countries with even lower-paid people to be exploited, a movement speeded by the North American Fair Trade Alliance (NAFTA).

Control over investment in manufacturing plants and other commercial ventures is translatable into cold profit with a little manipulation of the local and state industry-recruiting agencies. Special dispensations—forty-year exemptions from taxes, no-cost highway construction and rail connections, free electrical power, and other bait—are dangled before corporate officials in a game of "What can we offer to get you to relocate?" Competition is heated among politicians who want fancy jobs-I-recruited feathers for their campaign caps. The location of the General Motors Saturn plant in 1985 in Tennessee is a vivid illustration of the point: thirty-eight states and more than a thousand communities had vied for the 6,000 jobs the plant was supposed to involve, offering incentives as lucrative as $1 billion worth of free hydroelectric power for twenty years.[2] Whether such competition serves the welfare of the people who have to pay for the inducements is doubtful. The frantic bidding for professional sports franchises, too, keeps taxpayers funding new stadiums and financing in part the obscene salaries of big-time athletes, surely one of the most dubious forms of public subsidy in this budget-cutting, damn-the-poor era. Mayor Rudolph Giuliani of New York thus beats the drum for a $1 billion Manhattan Stadium to keep the Yankees in the city—while services for the sick and poor decline.

The leaders of corporations use their inside track with legislators and executive branch officials to win tax law loopholes, special subsidies for exporting their products, and various other advantages over their competitors with inconspicuous provisions slipped into legislation or executive orders. They arranged mergers that eliminate competition, as I have noted, once the Justice Department's antitrust division became a toothless tiger, not an enforcer of the law's antimonopoly provisions. Collectively, trillions of dollars in corporate cash are manipulated to maximize short-term billions in profits and long-term control over capital in unimaginable amounts. And what cannot be done legitimately is often done under the table by various forms of outright fraud (like the coal mine dust-sample cheating) or by subverting safety checks through advance warning of inspections, or very probably through deals like those in which President Ronald Reagan and his subordinates delayed enforcement of the 1969 mine safety legislation by pretending that the training of inspectors took years to achieve.

Money has been used in other ways to facilitate control: denouncing supposed government incompetence and wastefulness, when in part the wastefulness was a result of corrupt overcharges for military hardware; financing information and propaganda from conservative think tanks; supplying politicians with free corporate airplanes, plush vacation facilities, or costly seats at sporting events. After the law nominally forbade direct corporate campaign contributions, money was often gathered by assigning certain sums to be collected from colleagues whose money *could* be legally contributed to corporate-approved candidates—to be reimbursed by phony travel or other expense vouchers. Winning a Senate seat from one of the larger states, for example, requires millions in campaign funds, and the sources of that cash—often from beyond state boundaries—are hardly working-class donors.

The contemporary corporation, then, has money, motive, and much to defend: prerogatives, power, healthy salaries, and even rich retirement packages—"golden parachutes" to ease for executives the pain they lightly inflict on "downsizees." The adversary, in short, is formidable—but there are possible weapons.

Potential Restraints on Corporate Power

One possible means of limiting the freewheeling power of coal corporations is for miners themselves to become members of boards of directors. Who better to reflect their fears, hopes, and aspirations? In the presence of living human beings who are directly involved, potentially embarrassing issues would be differently discussed. Miners would represent their specialized knowledge and vital interests—and have a direct vote—in the forming of policy.

It can hardly be said in opposition that because wages and working conditions would be on the agenda, this would be a conflict of interest; no one makes that argument against the managers whose salaries and other perquisites are also settled in the board room. In Europe, and particularly in Germany, workers are represented on boards and have reportedly held down the exploitive tendencies of management. Germany's mines are nationalized, however, which no doubt makes the assignment of the miners a more natural step, whereas U.S. owners would likely resist. There might also be opposition from the UMWA on the ground that a union should work from the outside, that to join in management would fatally compromise the adversarial role that is the proper function of a union. In fact, coal companies have from time to time proposed that the union join in running a mine as a modified partnership, but this has always been voted down by the miners themselves after a trial period.

Even if both those hurdles could be cleared, there is the question of how much difference the miners' presence would make where environmental problems are concerned; they might be as much the fox in the chicken coop as the owner-managers, since the goal of retaining a job parallels that of making a profit. The same might hold with respect to taxation, public expenditures, and perhaps some externalities if the impact did not directly concern the well-being of the particular miners and their families. And the history of active miners' selling out the interests of those retired or laid off raises a further question. Could ways be devised to represent ex-miners and their special concerns, as well?

Still, worker representation could be a real asset in a wide range of issues: matters of safety, dust control, working conditions, community relations, job security, conflict resolution, and wildcat strikes. It might be difficult to recruit representatives able to cope with the probable sophistication of board members who might try to snow the less-experienced miners unaccustomed to computer printout, but by the same token a corporate executive with a Harvard law degree who does not know one end of a roof bolter from another could be misled by a miner.

One can imagine other problems and other benefits, but on balance the idea seems a positive one. Interestingly, in a recent book on the corporation around the world, Anthony Sampson quotes a former head of Britain's largest chemical industry, Sir John Harvey-Jones—"Management [of corporations] has never been so powerful or so unaccountable"—in arguing that some form of counterforce is necessary, and he suggests worker board membership as a potential restraint on the great power of corporate chief executive officers.[3]

Is there something to be said also for better representation of shareholders? The typical annual meeting as described in the press leaves the strong impression of a farce in which the wily management, bearing bags of obedient proxy votes, silences the clamorous dissent of frustrated minor shareholders. Occasionally, when such issues as civil rights in the 1960s and South African apartheid arise, institutional shareholders may mount a non-investment demand and make it stick, but those unusual victories are the exception that demonstrates the rule—and have tended to be accomplished by large institutional investors, not individuals.

Of course, some shareholders, like some coal miners, might sacrifice the environment for profit as quickly as corporate leaders—and perhaps such humane issues as black lung prevention or compensation and safety matters as well. But they already do raise a voice of dissent about the salaries, stock options, and bonuses that executives award each other in a generosity that researchers claim has little relationship to the performance or size of the company. One study found a company that in 1994 suffered a loss of $7.9 million on $72 million in revenue but paid its chief executive $15.5 million for bringing home no bacon. In the large companies investigated, salaries ran as high as $30.5 million; even in the smallest ones the average was over half a million. In the big companies one-quarter of the pay corresponded to size and performance; in the smallest only 10 percent was "justified."[4] To say the least, the salary issue is one that shareholders and workers might go after with some enthusiasm.

Robert Dahl, in his magisterial *Democracy and Its Critics*, argues that "stockholder democracy" is a self-contradictory term, since democracy's one person, one vote rule would require a holder of one share to be counted as equal to the holder of a million. Moreover, to operate a corporation on a democratic basis would mean giving each person working in the firm a single unit share of the venture, entitling each worker to a single vote, and only one vote. In practice, says Dahl, there would be difficulties in running the internal affairs of a firm as a democracy—maintaining sufficient technical information and expertise, for one thing—but that is true of the state as well: "Just as we support the democratic process in the government of the state despite substantial imperfections in the process," he concludes, "so the citizens of an advanced democratic society would support the democratic process in the government of the economic enterprise despite the imperfections that surely would exist in practice."[5] Would it be possible to rein in the wild horse of corporate management with anything less than complete democratic control of the corporation? The answer is necessarily speculative, but I doubt it—just as I doubt the practical feasibility of transforming the corporation into a democracy.

Neither miner nor shareholder representation on boards of directors will provide a strong enough counterforce to contain the power of coal companies. Countering the accustomed, preemptive authority of an entrenched group requires a strong power base from which to mount retaliation in case of confrontation or deadlock, and as matters now stand, neither group has a power base that would provide any wallop in a fight. The UMWA, down from a peak of 600,000 to about 70,000 members, is weakened, struggling to grow and to win reasonable contracts and to fight off the company practice of contracting out their mines to nonunion operators so as to evade the UMWA's wage scale and benefit costs. At best, the union is marginally effective in its traditional role; to expect it to perform a revolutionary new task is to ask for the unlikely. Change in external conditions of the fight would have to come first. And since a change in attitude would have to precede any form of miner representation, I keep the idea alive only for the sake of the argument.

The ability of shareholders to function as a restraint seems even more problematical. Unorganized, scattered, and sharing only common ownership of securities, stockholders have always been difficult to persuade to do more than retaliate by selling the company's stock and reducing its value. Management may be highly conscious of the price of its markers on Wall Street, but shareholders are not an organized or directable form of opposition. Therefore, I see shareholder control as minimal pressure that might be enhanced under the right circumstances: for example, a mood of public outrage with the acts of corporate leadership sufficient to invite formal means of counterforce on policy matters.

Grassroots Organizations

What is the potential for citizens' spontaneous grassroots organizing to oppose corporate policies that affect the environment, jobs, health and safety, externalities, or conservation of resources? Despite the preference of most people to avoid involvement in social issues, there is no denying that mass movements have often influenced our history. What else was the abolition movement but a citizens' uprising? Slavery was for most people no burning issue prior to the Civil War, yet abolitionists persisted, faced death in opposing slavery, and finally became politically significant in a confused country. Among other examples are the civil rights movement of the 1950s and 1960s, the Black Lung Association, the Miners for Democracy.

Although the civil rights movement did not achieve its economic equality goals for the average African American, it did accomplish the seemingly impossible elimination of all the legal basis for Jim Crow—no small success in the long view of history. Without those college-age rebels, the uneducated but deeply committed Fanny Lou Hamer and Rosa Parks, the Freedom Riders, the lunch counter sit-ins, the organizers who dared recruit black voter registration and those who bravely tried to sign up, it could not have happened. Similarly, but for the grassroots BLA, when would anything have been done about black lung? From both coal management and UMWA leaders came sneering and abuse and belittlement of the BLA doctors and the living (and dying) evidence of the suffering that black lung involved (miners seeking help were said to have "compensationitis"). How likely was it that such a motley movement could bring about a strike that closed nearly every mine in West Virginia, defying a back-to-work order from the national union, to support a drive for enactment of a compensation law by the state legislature? Improbable as it may seem, an unlettered mob negotiated with seasoned politicians and came out with sound legislation. Better laws were later drafted and passed, but they stood on the shoulders of that first victory.

Likewise, the Miners for Democracy faced an entrenched, wealthy, and ruthless opponent (one prepared after all to commit three murders to hold power) and a quiescent Labor Department that preached union reform and self-discipline but in practice was unwilling to move a hand for election supervision or to take action against the Boyle regime's disregard of the law. MFD was regarded as a bit wild-eyed, too much influenced by visionaries and financed by outsiders, even "pink" when the redbaiting got going. Yet that ragtag assembly of young idealists and erstwhile Lewis sycophants and old-line union organizers—all believers in more democracy and disgusted with its subversion—pulled together a rank-and-file following that turned a union disgraced by leadership repudiation of union ideals into one of the most democratic and effective and member-oriented labor unions of our time. If the MFD and the BLA could accomplish all that, can we dismiss grassroots movements lightly?

Despite the tendency of most people to avoid involvement, a minority of hardy souls have come forth to organize for a long list of causes. Alexis de Tocqueville, that prescient observer of the American scene of the 1830s, thought that this "joining" proclivity was a basic feature of the country's politics, noting that Americans formed all manner of associations, "religious, moral, serious, futile, general or restricted, enormous or diminutive.

The Americans make associations to give entertainments, to found semi-naries, to build inns, to construct churches, to diffuse books, to send mis-sionaries to the antipodes; in this manner they found hospitals, prisons, and schools. If it is proposed to inculcate some truth or to foster some feeling by the encouragement of a great example, they form a society."[6]

But even though "in no country in the world has the principle of associ-ation been more successfully used or applied to a greater multitude of ob-jects than in America," Tocqueville saw the relation of this principle to individualism: many associations "are formed and maintained by the agency of private individuals. The citizen . . . is taught from infancy to rely upon his own exertions in order to resist the evils and the difficulties of life; he looks upon social authority with an eye of mistrust and anxiety, and he claims its assistance only when he is unable to do without it."[7]

Toqueville rightly understood that Americans thought of private politi-cal organization as a means of expressing individual political views partly because they distrusted formal authority. Historically, these associations they formed have played a significant if intermittent role in correcting the excesses of politics. But three features of such organizations must be kept in mind: first, they become major forces only when situations are extreme; second, once crises are past, they tend to wither and fade; third, it is easier to generate an organizational core than to recruit and hold a large sup-portive following.

The life and times of the anti–Vietnam War movement illustrates these points. It took a long time for a massive, organized antiwar effort to get going, but when the untenable costs of the war became so widely ac-knowledged as to undercut the sweeping support that normally backs the leadership of a nation at war—(as America First opposition to war was wiped out by the Pearl Harbor attack in 1941), it became an irresistible force. Once the main object of withdrawal from Vietnam came in 1973, the move-ment quickly faded.

The Vietnam movement illustrates several problems with grassroots op-position to unpopular policies. Getting people to move from their familiar grooves of habit is difficult. Nevertheless, at the height of the antiwar drive people by tens of thousands from all ranks of society joined forces; work-ers, professionals, students, business people, housewives, and academics boarded trains, planes, buses, and cars to make a testament of dissent in Washington. In the end the uprising contributed much to ending the war, although not before damage had been done not only to the war's victims but also to the social fabric of the country; the slowness to get organized diminished the movement's effectiveness. And facing the formidable support that exists for any war was a limiting condition. So too will any attack on corporate power face strong support for corporate freedom.

Participatory Politics

Whatever else war opposition accomplished, it stirred up considerable thought about participation in political life. My political science colleagues took to the participatory notion as a parched camel does to water, endlessly debating its fine points in countless department meetings. One colleague drafted an exemplary plan for university-wide governance, greatly increasing the participation of all constituent elements: faculty, administration, staff, and students. Radicals saw it as a sop to the easily swayed crowd who would be deceived into believing some real change had come about, while in fact a capitalist-bourgeois elite had created a charade to give the appearance of self-rule but was maintaining elitist, authoritarian control as firmly as ever. Defenders of the plan's system of electing policymaking assemblies pointed to the possibility of control over budgets and broad planning for university conduct; they thought the election system would open the way to a democratic/participatory community led by an administration and a board of trustees but with some genuine decentralization of power. On a smaller scale, my department adopted a participatory arrangement that brought students into the consideration of courses and general departmental policy (and more endless hours of debate) yet left matters of personnel (especially tenure) decision securely in the hands of senior faculty.

The whole question of participation was a universal topic of campus conversation and debate that outlasted the Vietnam crisis. Not everyone saw the value of wide participation; one group of graduate students protested that they had come to the university to learn, not to run the institution. Doubters said, "If these Ph.D. candidates find participation outside their

With more modern equipment it is conceivable that even larger bodies of people could act in concert, replicating in a rational fashion the Greek democratic experience of 2,500 years ago. Still, today's world is not the Greek polis of Pericles' time but a series of huge and complex nation-states where participation as a means to deal with the authoritarian character of an important institution such as the economic enterprise is at best limited.

Practically speaking, mass participation even in such institutions as universities is severely restrained by the corporate money and influence in the institutional structure—whether subtle or blunt—and the mind-set of the institutional leadership. George Love, the longtime head of the Bituminous Coal Operators Association (and collaborator with John L. Lewis in the UMWA–BCOA conspiracy that set the pattern for labor relations in coal for the 1950s and early 1960s—no strikes, high wages, and mechanization), was a trustee of Princeton and a much respected alumnus. Now I am not aware that his role in personnel decisions or other measures ever directly reflected his family's ownership of the Consolidation Coal Company or his attitudes as chief of the national coal establishment for decades. But even if he remained silent, he must have had an impact through others' expectations of his views and their awareness of the possibility that he might one day direct his own or his corporate resources, or those of other wealthy potential donors, to the ever money-hungry university. This silent form of corporate power may be difficult to pin down and specify, but one ignores it at the peril of grave misunderstanding of power in American society.

The deference or respect factor—the extent to which decision-makers are aware of, think about, anticipate, and react to establishment power—is hard to evaluate. University tenure decisions, for example, are made ostensibly on grounds of the candidate's promise of future excellent performance but clearly on other attitudinal or value grounds as well—such as the question of what it might cost tomorrow if the "wrong" candidate is promoted today. How much I was personally affected at Princeton by the fact that I came to that upper-class institution from a coal company town and not from an absentee owner residence I find it hard to say. I don't think I was intimidated in my support for anyone in a tenure decision by any sense of threat from people I clearly perceived to be from the other side of the track, even though no less than J. Edgar Hoover was once drawn by conservative alumni into a denunciation of me as a much more radical figure than I am in fact. About the worst they could do was report that two of my children had been to Cuba to cut sugarcane; it was true and I was proud of them, so the revelation had no impact on me. I don't mean to say that I was some kind of fearless defender of the radicals of the academic world; I wasn't, but neither do I think I was intimidated by my working-class background. Some, I knew, thought less of me for that reason, but others talked me into becoming chairman of my department, an honor as onerous as any I was ever unfortunate enough to receive.

Outside the academy, though, one impediment to mass participation is the unequal distribution of familiarity with arcane and technical matters, inhibiting the capacity of the less informed to participate effectively. I am not saying that those who are less familiar with fancy words know less than the terminologically well equipped; in fact, the less articulate poor may, for example, comprehend more fully than a swift-speaking jargon slinger what poverty's problems are. Still, my experience with the War on Poverty in the late 1960s is a case in point. I was a member of New Jersey Governor Richard Hughes's Migrant Labor Committee, and that led me into the hardships of the state's impoverished farm workers. That many of them spoke only Spanish was the least of our communication difficulties. More troublesome was conveying, especially to local welfare bureaucrats, the basic objective of the federal Office of Economic Opportunity, which was to seek out programs that showed something new enough to be tried and tested elsewhere. When we explained the call for new and innovative approaches, the standard reply was "What innovation do you want?"[8]

It follows that only with the utmost difficulty can representatives of miners, stockholders, or any other concerned group (environmentalists, coal users, communities near mines, local and state government) have a restraining influence on coal corporations. To send them forth against such a well-endowed foe is to send David against Goliath sans slingshot. All the mice in the old fable agreed that they would be safer if the cat wore a bell, but who would bell the cat? It will be possible to bell the coal cat only if the depredation becomes severe enough to invite countervailing organized opposition, and getting up the dander of a nation is no commonplace event.

10

Democracy and Corporate Power

WHAT PROSPECT IS THERE of an uprising of disadvantaged and outraged people against the abuses of corporate power? And if it should happen, what principles ought to guide the restraining or remedial effort?

My candid answer to the first of these questions is, I don't know. The coal industry has shot itself in the foot often enough, as the evidence shows, yet nobody has for decades been able to mount a successful campaign to trim its suzerainty. Will the distress caused by downsizing trigger a reaction? With half a million coal jobs gone, and the union helping not at all—indeed it collaborated—there has been no more than growling resentment on the part of the victims. Of course, coal companies blamed mechanization on competition from oil and later from western strip-mined coal. Will the loss of millions of jobs in other corporations that can offer less reason for the cuts result in a backfire on grounds that it was done when corporate profits were at an all-time high?

In the 1991 winter quarter, corporate profits amounted to $415.7 billion; for the 1995 summer quarter, a reported $609.6 billion, a rise of 46.6 percent. To make even more, the following large companies announced these cuts over the same four years: AT&T, 123,000 jobs; General Motors, 99,000; Boeing, 61,000; IBM, 35,000; Sears, 50,000; Lockheed-Martin, 29,000; and ten others collectively, 178,000. On the basis of survey research the *New York*

Times reported that one person in ten said they or some member of their family had lost a job, precipitating a major life crisis. About 3 million people are laid off from their jobs every year, and many of the new jobs created tend to pay little above minimum wage, hardly equivalent to the lost salary of an accountant, middle manager, or technical worker. Almost no effort has gone into easing the blow of unexpected layoffs, little thought given to the emotional, not to say financial, crisis of the $100,000 a year manager who must resort to bagging groceries or pumping gas or clerking in a liquor store, if even that work can be found.[1]

Coal miners by the hundreds of thousands are all too familiar with the hopelessness and frustration that are becoming the lot of many white-collar workers. For the distraught coal miner, lacking skills other than mining, and for the local community suffering the loss of coal mines, there is not much chance to recover economic equilibrium. The case of dismissed IBM technicians may be less threatening, because they have education and a skill, but to have been a loyal and apparently appreciated employee and then to be cast out as useless surely generates enormous marital, psychological, and financial problems.

If the past is any guide, conditions generating considerable dissent will develop within the next decade or so. The path we seem destined to follow with respect to the communications/computer revolution will likely result in some new technologically sophisticated jobs, but terminate others as computerized robots and various forms of automation displace human workers in information-related and other kinds of economic activity. Meanwhile, many heavy manufacturing (as in steel) and delicate production jobs (such as making television receivers and VCRs) will be done in foreign countries, paying peon wages. This process will be speeded up by ending tariff barriers with Latin America and Europe through arrangements analogous to NAFTA. The result will be a probable net gain in jobs but a loss in income for those forced out of goods-producing jobs into service industry work at lower pay. We have lost an astonishing 43 million jobs since 1979, and although we have added more than that, the new ones have been mostly of two kinds: well-paying but technologically complicated work that few of the displaced are prepared to do, and service jobs at the low end of the wage scale. A joke I picked up somewhere puts the moral of the story well: President Clinton tells a voter that his administration has created several million new jobs, to which the man replies, "Yes, I know, I hold three of them." Family income is down overall, even though half of all men hold two jobs or both husband and wife have to work to make ends meet—and it is likely that more corporations will begin downsizing in anticipation of boosting their profits as the forerunners have done so spectacularly. Downsizing may even accelerate, particularly as productivity outpaces growth of the economy, which is likely if the Federal Reserve Board continues to dictate moderately high unemployment as a hedge against inflationary pressure.

It is an open question, then, whether (1) something like an innovative job relocation program will be adopted, at corporate or government expense, to deal systematically with indiscriminate downsizing; or (2) victims of downsizing and others outraged by injustice will rise to fight for more equitable treatment, curtailing corporate discretion in the process; or (3) the outrage will be moderated by the belief that these sufferers are merely paving the way for the good of all in higher profits. Don't bet the farm against option (3).

Coal miners will be a special case—as they have been so often. We might have expected decreased demand for coal in light of concern about sulfur dioxide pollution and carbon dioxide's greenhouse effect. But the development of smokestack scrubbers and the use of low-sulfur coal from western strip mines has meant that total annual coal production—which leveled off at 800 to 900 million tons in the early-1990s—passed one billion tons in 1995. Given the insatiable demand for electricity, if the CO_2 "earth warming" issue can be coped with (or should prove to be a false alarm), coal demand could balloon.

Guessing about the future of coal employment is more complex than that, however. One the one hand, there may well be need for an oil substitute. By 1993 estimates, the United States had ten to twenty years of oil in reserve and the rest of the world enough for forty-five years, whereas coal reserves are good for 250 years in the United States at present rates of use, and 230 years in the remainder of the world.[2] No one has yet devised an economically viable technology to convert coal into oil (Germany did it in World War II because war deprivation changed all pricing considerations), but with a decline in oil reserves and higher crude oil prices we can expect a concerted renewal of government subsidies to finance more research on conversion. Federal research money flowed during the 1970s oil shortage and the Arab embargo but ceased when the scarcity disappeared. Conversion seems scientifically feasible, and its development would of course boost coal demand.

On the other hand, breakthroughs in the pursuit of renewable, nonfossil fuels or of ways to lower energy use would surely reduce coal demand. The so-called E-Lamp (electronic lamp), a new kind of incandescent bulb, operates on one-third less electricity; the Environmental Protection Agency believes it would reduce by 232 million tons the CO_2 now belched forth every year. Photovoltaic cells convert sunlight directly into electricity, but that process is expensive so far, costing 20 to 30¢ per kilowatt-hour, compared with 4 to 6¢ for conventional power. Wind energy at an average of 8¢ per kWh, is of course practical only where winds are strong; windmills are being widely tested in California. Fuel cells, currently used on spacecraft for power supply, are also likely to become economically practical. "Biomass utilization" is another way to say "burning trash," and municipal refuse (17 percent in 1993) is being incinerated to supply electricity, as are wastes from wood processing and pulp mills. Geothermal heat too is a potential source of energy for power generation and heating purposes.[3]

And lingering in the background is atomic fusion, which, if it can be safely and economically developed, will change the energy picture entirely, providing enormous amounts of power with essentially the same process as the heat of the sun involves. But research for ways to tame the process is very expensive, and funds have been cut back. It may be decades before it comes on line, and it might turn out to repeat the wild predictions for cheap, safe, and simple energy generation through atomic fission. In practice, safety concerns have stopped the increase of atomic generating facilities in the United States and some other countries. The tragedy at Chernobyl in the Ukraine is in the minds of many planners, and that plus the difficulty of getting rid of atomic waste has brought a halt in new American plants.

Depending on the scientific possibilities of these sources of energy, the demand for coal could go up or down; either way, problems for miners and the environment can be safely predicted.

Suppose that either option (1) or option (2) comes the fore. The first may be called "industrial policy," whereby government and business would co-operate in assisting displaced workers with retraining programs and sup-porting research and development.[4] This is in part what Robert Reich, during his tenure as secretary of labor, proposed in suggesting tax conces-sions to corporations that take an interest in worker and community well-being. The second refers to the rise of a popular movement incited by outrage at injustice and inequity to try to force corrections, much as the civil rights movements went after Jim Crow.

I want to suggest some criteria in the light of which the proposals of ei-ther option might profitably be debated. If it seems inconsistent of me to argue for some things that stand in mutual opposition, that is not because of oversight; it is quite intentional. I do mean, for example, to urge na-tional-central government use of planning *and* to encourage the decen-tralization of power that would permit representation of grassroots interests. I have company in my dualism in the framers of the Constitution, who (partly without intent) set up a government that marched off in these two directions at once.

My criteria for evaluating proposed changes are these: democracy, lo-calism and popular participation, humaneness and economic rights, na-tional oversight, and a productive economic system.

First, any solution should be subject to democratic control: it must allow for the power of the populace through fair, open, and *publicly funded* elec-tions. Like holding mock elections in praise of dictatorships or self-appointed commissars, placing full power over an industry in the hands of self-appointed boards of directors will not pass muster. Nor should politi-cal elections be financed by those who have much to gain from "buying" candidates from both parties with corporate-controlled money. I know the Supreme Court has held that freedom to try to buy elections is a constitu-tional right, but the rich already have sufficient power to defend their rights, and nothing should prevent a Ross Perot or Steve Forbes from entering a campaign on the same publicly financed basis as a poor person. Incumbents resist public financing as an invitation to opposition candidates who might otherwise never become a threat, but that ground for resistance under-cuts the openness of elections. And if public financing sets up successful opponents, better that exit door for the overstayed welcome than a blind term-limit rule that fails to see the difference between the able legislator[5] and the time-serving special-interest promoter.

Democratic equality cannot be absolute, owing to the differences that we are born with. Robert Dahl observes that a society totally dedicated to an equal distribution of resources would have to regulate social and eco-nomic affairs so minutely that it would allow the regulating officials to em-bellish their own power and privileges, so that "what began in the name of political equality would then end as political inequality and state oppres-sion."[6] Relative equality, however, or at least the absence of extremes of dis-parity, is perhaps a practical precondition to democracy. Gross inequality gives unequal power to a privileged minority who dominate not only through larger resources, but through reputation for power or ruthlessness.

At a minimum, a democratic society would seek an equal opportunity to develop whatever talents and potential a person possesses. And that cer-tainly is not accomplished where the topmost incomes are hundreds of times those at the bottom of the ladder. Twenty years ago the highest paid CEOs earned 35 times as much as the average wage earner; today the dis-parity is 187 times—and even greater at the very top: in 1996 the income of the ten highest-paid CEOs averaged $64,600,000.[7] Today the upper 1 per-cent of the population owns 40 percent of the wealth, double its share twenty years ago. Moreover, not only has the gap been widened in recent decades by upper-rank increases, but the income and wealth of the aver-age wage earner has actually been declining. Not even the increasing num-ber of wives employed has stayed the downtrend in median family income: figures cited by Lester Thurow indicate a decrease of more than 7 percent between 1989 and 1995.[8] Further, according to Andrew Hacker, a leading scholar of U.S. income and social patterns, 13,505 people reported incomes over $1 million in 1979; in 1993, the figure was 65,656. He also found, as a measure of wealth, that whereas in 1989 there were 834,000 households with a million or more dollars in investable assets (measured in constant dollars), in 1993 the number had risen to 3,200,000.[9] Continuation of this trend, says Lester Thurow in the same series of articles on the rich in America, could undercut the political allegiance of the people who do not share in the bonanza: "If the democratic political process cannot reverse the trend to inequality, democracy will eventually be discredited. . . . A large group of hostile voters who draw no benefits from the economic system and don't think the government cares is not a particularly promising recipe for economic or political success."[10]

Should the corporation be subject to democratic governance? Robert Dahl remarks that defenders of the conventional power structure find such an idea foolish—much as democracy in government was deemed foolish until yesterday.[11] When the Constitution was written, democracy was far from being widely approved in this country; "sound" people had little faith in the ability of common people to govern anything, and the Constitution was full of limits on the power of the general citizenry: the electoral college, the assumption of restricted voting for the House of Representatives, the appointment of senators and the greater powers of the Senate. Yet over time the idea of majority rule and minority rights became so widely accepted that anyone opposed was very circumspect in saying anything openly antidemocratic.

Similarly, the idea of democratic forms for running the affairs of corporations seems impractical and visionary. But democracy inside the corporation makes the same kind of sense as democracy in government. No doubt some issues on the corporate agenda involve matters beyond the competence and interest of some employees, union members, and stockholders. But the same can be said of much of the agenda of government—even at the community level, and certainly at national and international levels. Yet that is not considered a reason to bar participation by the less informed citizen (indeed, exclusion on the basis of an expertise requirement would eliminate a good part of Congress from decision-making on any complex issue. I would argue that the illiterate ought to have the right to vote, for a deprived poor person knows where the shoe of poverty pinches in a profound way not shared by a Ph.D. uninterested in social matters. Though I share Jefferson's desire for literacy and access to a free press as means to ideal participation, even an unlettered person may have valid opinions on, say, medical insurance legislation and be able to participate in reasoned discussion on the matter.

That brings us to my second criterion, which may be called the principle of personal participation: the expression of personal concerns through discussion and open debate about policies of all kinds. Participation in one forum or another to influence policies that significantly affect the life of the individual is a desideratum of a good society, and the closer the policy-determining institution to the individual, the more feasible and effective participation can be. Localism and decentralization of authority are important in smaller arenas where not only local values and cultures but local differences in geography, economy, and social history need to be reflected. The participant in Virginia does not have to think about the snow removal regulations necessary in Maine; the way to legislate concerning beach erosion differs in Iowa and Massachusetts. Fifty state legislatures allow people like me to comprehend the simpler agenda of a small and understandable society (5,000 square miles and 3 million residents of Connecticut were challenge enough), rather than try to make laws for a whole nation with all its complexity and cultural variation. And Washington has enough to do without taking on the work of fifty legislatures.

There are of course policies that need to be made at the national level, for decentralization has some less attractive features: if benign geographic variation can be catered to in fifty states, so can racism and great economic power intrude as forms of state variation. Had black Americans had to battle each state to kill Jim Crow, they would still be petitioning unreconstructed southern legislatures. Delayed though it was, the end of legal discrimination came from the only place where African Americans could be heard: Washington. Similarly, federal action is required in such matters as coal mine safety laws, for domination by corporate power puts states through the wringer of competition to restrict taxes and provide other special treatment in their eagerness to gain or retain businesses and jobs.

The principle of personal participation applies most tellingly at the local level where one can be rid of the difficulty of representation. Rousseau saw representation as inherently undemocratic, given the diversity of constituent viewpoints and the necessity for a *community* to discuss and weigh any policy before adopting it. In a world with so many people and of such complexity, however, there is no practical way of escaping large jurisdictions; the sweeping scope of the United Nations has its place, even as has the monthly assembly of a neighborhood block association. But it is usually the case, particularly in economic matters, that the larger the enterprise the more complex the issues at stake; therefore, if discussion and personal input are to have an influence, they must begin with participation in a small-scale institution—*precisely because it is comprehensible.*

It may be that lower-scale issues seem too routine to challenge some potential activists, and the danger of boredom lurks beside ordinary disinclination to participate in matters outside one's more pressing private concerns. That does not obviate the importance of small-scale organizational activity; it merely faces up to the inherent difficulties of an important kind of participation—in a mine safety committee or a corporate workplace supervision body at the local community level.

My third criterion for judging potential steps toward corporate control is the humaneness of any proposal—by which I mean the extent to which individual social and economic well-being are taken into account. The dismissal of employees in wholesale fashion without regard either for worker performance or for the economic and social costs does not qualify as a humane act. A program aimed at saving labor costs would demonstrate humane qualities if it did not place the sole burden on the individual employee but provided alternative employment in the company or job retraining before the firing started, or placed loyal service in the scales of calculation about who stays and who goes, or allowed employees to join in trying to develop constructive alternatives to mass layoffs.

Another way of looking at the humaneness idea is to compare the political, legal, and economic rights of individuals. The first we proudly and rightly proclaim as an important feature of American democracy. Four of the first ten amendments to the Constitution are devoted to the protection of citizens against misuses of the criminal law for political purposes, for those who regretted the absence of a Bill of Rights in the original Constitution realized the importance in British history of the abuse of criminal law to punish political enemies. But there is as much need for protection of economic rights as for political or legal rights. Free expression is vital to democracy because denial of that freedom is bound to stifle open discussion of issues and render free choice of candidates and policies impossible. Similarly the chance to develop one's potential and to meet the obligations of one's family responsibility requires the opportunity to have gainful employment. If rough equality is a prerequisite of democracy, then the opportunity to earn a living is a basic building block of democracy. Why should the right not to be forced to testify against oneself or not to be subjected to cruel and unusual punishment be given precedence over the right to a decent job? Ask a working man or woman whether self-incrimination or gainful employment is the more important consideration in his or her life, and I think there is little doubt what the answer will be. Most of us never expect to be in criminal court, but with downsizing and productivity layoffs, who is not concerned today about keeping a job or getting a new one?

Lest I be misunderstood, I am not urging economic constitutional safeguards; it is not judicially provided rights we need but practical assurances that we will not be forced into poverty and social disruption or subjected to welfare and public scorn because of someone's arbitrary power to decide the fate of employees. We need a right enforced by countervailing power to control corporate officials who are authorized to make, or delegate the power to make, such determinations.

The fourth criterion is national rationality, or a concern with country-wide considerations that run in the opposite direction from localism. Participatory, locality-oriented involvement stresses smallness of scale and problems that are local and regional in character, involving climatic, agricultural, environmental, and cultural variation. National rationality, the other side of the coin, takes account of the ways that localism can threaten the common good by ignoring the effects, for example, of dirty air downwind of a polluting source such as the burning of sulfur-laced fossil fuel. Conservation of resources and environmental protection, the development of common policies that eliminate competitive bidding among states and municipalities in wild self-destructive efforts to attract or hold businesses and jobs, the creation of uniform rules and controls to curb the runaway corporation—those and other decisions acknowledging the interdependence of regions are important policy desiderata for which planning on a national scale is needed.

In the American experience, planning has long standing as a business practice, but planning by government has acquired a bad name in this country—partly because it is associated with socialism and attempts to allocate resources in a rational manner that is not dependent on the price system. This is illustrated by the brief life of the Temporary National Economic Committee (commonly called TNEC), set up in 1933 by a joint resolution of Congress to investigate monopolistic practices and cartels. This combined congressional-executive venture promised much but delivered little, and the animosity aroused by its planning proposals killed it in the early post-World War II years.

Nevertheless, national foresight and coordination of policies continued to be advocated among those who questioned the sanctification of corporations. One commentator has proposed national planning as a way of curtailing the excesses of the coal industry. Curtis Selzer advocates planning that is "responsive to the electorate," based on democratic ideas rather than the profit motivation that prevails in the operations of the big coal firms: Whereas "no corporation invests its capital on what is best for the American public," planners would develop "energy choices for America as a whole." Granting that such planning can go wrong and succumb to special interests, Selzer believes that it would at worst err in the name of all, not "in the name of making a buck." Public planners could assist in working out sensible transitions when coal demand fluctuates, or mines run out of coal, or productivity causes problems. They would be "more inclined to invest in controlling environmental and social costs . . . [and] should be better able to harmonize coal supply and demand," improving our capacity to make "more efficient use of our capital, labor and managerial resources."[12]

Selzer may be unduly sanguine about national planning, and certainly the decentralizers would be skeptical about the degree of national control implicit in his scenario. But somewhere along the line between central planning and participatory localism lies the correct path to one result I strongly believe we must achieve: namely, control over the broad discretionary, profit-bound policies of coal (and other) corporations.

Finally, with regard to the criterion of a productive economic system, one consideration in particular is of vital concern: whether the system envisioned will be sufficiently productive of goods and services that poverty does not overtake the whole society. I do not mean to suggest that any system that reduces gross national product is inherently flawed; some in-novations that reduce the wealth of the most affluent and aid the poor but result in a net reduction of GNP might be acceptable because they are more just than the status quo, whereas a plan that aids the rich more than the poor but increases GNP would be undesirable because the result would be distributionally *un*just.

The overall economic well-being of the nation is a favorable criterion for change, then, only insofar as changes are just, and they cease to be just when they increase inequality between the richest and the poorest sectors of the population. Thus a proposal to terminate profit as a motive for cap-ital investment, or to spend money for workers' and their families' health care, or to ensure safety on the job is neither positive nor negative with re-spect to economic justice on its face; operationally it could be either, for what counts is not whether the product is larger or smaller, but whether it is more fairly distributed. A proposal that risks the working of the market/price system is not better or worse on the basis of output alone, for in practice the market system is never wholly applied; there is always interference with the price mechanism, as Adam Smith lamented in the eighteenth century when he denounced businessmen for their eternal scheming against competition. And certainly they continue trying to take advantage of competitors today. Producers lie about their products and do all they can to subvert consumer sovereignty; corporations use their polit-ical clout to manipulate the market; monopolies exist to exploit the absence of competition. The price system is what is left after the corporation has done its damnedest to eliminate competition's uncertainties. If therefore in assessing policy proposals the weight of the price system is taken as pro-visional, there are good reasons behind the devaluation.

I do not dismiss the utility of the price system for producing goods and services, some of which do come to the least well off. But the questions that must be asked are what part of that gain goes to the richest people? What is the *relative* distribution of the extra production? And what power does the corporation wield in a democratic system as a result of its com-mand of or influence over money and jobs and socioeconomic policy? I can do no better than repeat the words of my mentor, Charles E. Lindblom, who closes his landmark study of world economic and political systems with these words: "The large corporation fits oddly into democratic theory and vision. Indeed it does not fit."[13]

The reasons corporations in practice do not fit into democratic theory are many and complex, but one outweighs all others: their control over major capital resources of nearly the whole world. With newly developing corporations in former Communist countries and booming new corporations of exploding Third World economies added to the rich and long-established old-line corporations around the world, we are looking at institutions with discretionary authority over tens of trillions in investment capital. According to an accounting by *Fortune* magazine the 500 largest corporations in the world—the "global 500"—had nearly $30.9 *trillion* in assets as of 1994.[14] Those who have power to allocate such sums have a dominant position in the economic-political world. The likelihood that their disfavor will produce ill effects and their approval a bounty means that their demands will be heard. We who seek jobs, goods, fair taxes, protection, self-advancement, and opportunity to develop our potential have to accommodate to those who control wealth.

A shortcoming in nearly all the literature on ethics and democracy is the failure to grasp the importance of the control of investment resources. The rights to vote, to speak, to dissent, to participate are self-evidently instrumental to democracy, but all these democratic elements operate within distributional parameters set inevitably by those who control and determine where the jobs will be, who will earn millions and who little or nothing, who will be advanced and who held back—and these matters are largely decided by the allocation of investment. Today that is done—increasingly so with each passing year—by corporations. What we consume, whatever economic security we have, what medical care we get—all that and more depends on corporate decisions. Even much of what we think, say, believe, and defend or oppose is significantly shaped by the manipulations of corporate leaders.[15]

I readily admit that I have not dealt adequately with the problem of wealth control. The most I can say is that at least I recognize the primacy of the problem.

Verses

Duane Lockard

Pictures at the Pit Mouth

When first black diamond lumps were found
Beneath the ancient Appalachian ground
A scene that none expected to see
Became as common as common can be
Stunned, the crowds quietly assemble
Kinfolk gather, watch, and tremble
Waiting, waiting weary hours
Near the silent tipple towers
Against all odds they vainly hope
Some miner will walk that blackened slope

For over forty years Sofie wept
And her daily slag heap vigil kept
Dragging home another sack of coal
Lost, mindless, hopeless soul
Seeking signs she'd never find
Of him she had lost in Monongah mine
When it blew up and killed five hundred
Or even more as earth was sundered
Leaving Sophie, immigrant bride,
Surviving widow, ghost inside

Precariously teetering, the wretched shack
Is home to a miner they call Jack
Twisted, warped, and decayed
Man and house worn and frayed

Jack no older than fifty years
But ancient, bent, beset by fears
His back cross-hatched and decorated
Where black coal dust had perforated
He wheezes and gasps for every breath
As he slowly suffocates to death

At Number Nine

Bathhouse baskets hang,
With clean clothes, locked on high
To take them down
Would admit the awful truth
And that is out of place
At Number Nine

But that mine was safe
Consol laments;
Come, Sisters, pray
The Preacher says to pray:
Abide it, come what may
At Number Nine

Union guy, he bites his lip
Seems to hold back tears
He says I know
I know just how you feel
But that's the risk you take
At all the Number Nines

Rules in his hand
Chill in his soul
Inspector says I looked
I saw the drifted dust

But lacked the clout to close
Old Number Nine

The tragedy is not
The seventy-eight who died
Or tears of bewildered wives
Nor wail of frightened child
We see/hear all by TV's eye
On Number Nine

What hurts still more
Is how easily they lie
How those with power accept
That nothing could have stopped
This blow or the next at tomorrow's
New Number Nine

Whitwell, Topmost, Bergoo

Have you heard the latest news?
From the Whitwells, Topmosts, and Bergoos
Did you see TV tapes flashing by
Or did their time on screen miss your eye?
Two blew up and a roof caved in
A Christmas gift for next of kin
In the thought of Reagan-time
By a logic all sublime
No connection could be found
Between striking down
And cuts in inspectors' ranks
To lower spending for rich folks' thanks
And if those hewers at coal's deep banks
Complained it proved they were just cranks
Who failed to comprehend
The Reaganomics dividend

The How and Why of Shorty Farrell

My old Buddy we called him Shorty
Tough as rock and not yet forty
But when the slate began to fall
Toughness mattered not at all
Timbers of oak, thick and sound
Keep no roof from falling down
When dead weight causes coal to snap
What use then is a safety hat?
His ribs popped out like staves of a barrel
And that was the end of Shorty Farrell

Hill and valley caked in dust
Coaltowns rotted, tipples in rust
Miners, blacklunged, left to die
Women, widowed, left to cry
Economy shattered on bust and boom
Rules for safety, dead in law's backroom
A whole society prostituted
Ruthlessly wrecked and uprooted
By greed and grab, unholy plunder
Once green hills torn asunder

And a hundred thousand Farrells wasted

Jack Nottingham, Scab

Jack had one eye and two wives
Never washed all the coal dust
From his black-rimmed eyes
The strike had lasted twenty days,
But Jack's mascara was still in place
A proud out and out scab was Jack
And it led to fists beside the spring
    Where a boy hid behind the sycamore

On his way home from the company store
Scared to see two grown men fight

Lambert was as union as Jack was scab:
Damn the company for hiring thugs
Pretend they're County Sheriff's Men
But don't the bosses pick up the tab
Buying men and clubs and shotgun slugs
Cars were toppled over hills
Conflict deepened, men were killed
 The kid looked on as Lambert caught
 Jack with a blindside hook
 Knocked him out—lesson taught!

Lambert left, Jack got up and cussed
Loudly vowed that he would bust
All those striker bastards
Washed away the blood and muttering
Curses still remembered so long afterwards
He headed up the path toward home
Where a pair of wives awaited . . .
 The boy forsook his hiding place
 And, his groceries tightly clutched
 He took the path at measured pace

Jack's front porch presented a tableau
With Jack wildly waving a thirty-eight
Screaming curses, saying he *would* go
On his left arm there hung a mate
Another clung tight to his right—
Both shouted: don't go, Oh, no don't go
While Jack roared on, a wounded bear
Go, he didn't for both survived
 The kid, scared completely out of his hide
 When past Jack's house ran like hell for
  home!

Steamshovel

Steamshovel, born free and black
Stout of arm and strong of back
When he came by they said in awe
"For him they overlook the law
That calls for two men at the face
So he loads coal at twice the pace."

Why does he do the work of two,
Twice what any man should do?
Was it the spur of double pay?
If not for extra, come payday,
How else explain the coal he heaved?
Perhaps it was something he believed.

Many marveled at thirty tons a day
Few wondered *why* he worked that way
And fewer still suspected this man
Was annoyed by the Ku Klux Klan
Kind of comment from white miners
Thoughtless masters of one-liners.

Working alone was the answer
Of this strong, silent panther
He was strongest of dust-eaters
A living legend, record beater
Saying wordless to the oblivious crowd
"I'm black, alone, unbowed and proud!"

Notes

Preface

1. See William Serrin's parallel tale of the abuse of corporate power in the steel industry, *Homestead: The Glory and Tragedy of an American Steel Town* (New York: Random House, 1992).

Introduction

1. What it was like to dig coal out of the seam directly is well described by George Orwell in *The Road to Wigan Pier* (1937).

2. Paul Boydoh, interview with author, 9 March 1981.

3. Tom Steel, *Scotland's Story* (London: Fontana-Collins, 1984), 263–64.

4. Lewis Mumford, *Technics and Civilization* (New York: Harcourt, Brace, 1934), 67.

1. Notes on the History of an Industry

1. Samuel H. Daddow, *Coal, Iron, and Oil, or The Practical Miner* (Pottsville PA, 1866), 100.

2. Harold M. Watkins, *Coal and Men: An Economic and Social Study of British and American Coal* (London: Allen & Unwin, 1934), 25.

3. Lewis Mumford, *The Pentagon of Power* (New York: Harcourt, Brace Jovanovich, 1970), 146.

4. Excerpts from the 1842 British Commissioner of Mines report in James Ridgeway, *Powering Civilization* (New York: Random House, 1982), 15.

5. Emile Zola, *Germinal* (1885), Eng. trans. (New York: Penguin, 1954), 80

6. Howard N. Eavenson, *The First Century and a Quarter of the American Coal Industry* (Pittsburgh: privately printed, 1942), 15.

7. Watkins, *Coal and Men,* 88.

8. Quoted in Daddow, *Coal, Iron, and Oil,* 111.

9. McAlister Coleman, *Men and Coal* (New York: Farrar & Rinehart, 1943), 332.

10. Eavenson, *First Century,* 114.

11. U.S. Bureau of the Census, *Historical Statistics of the United States, Colonial Times to 1970* (Washington DC, 1975), 356–57.

12. On the rise of these small mines in the East, see Katherine A. Harvey, *The Best-Dressed Miners: Life and Labor in the Maryland Coal Region, 1835–1910* (Ithaca: Cornell Univ. Press, 1969).

13. Two revealing novels deal with the fates of fictional families that fell on hard times: John Knowles *A Vein of Riches* (Boston: Little, Brown, 1978); and Mary Lee Settle, *The Scapegoat* (New York: Random House, 1980).

14. See Harry Caudill, *Theirs Be the Power: The Moguls of Eastern Kentucky* (Urbana: Univ. of Illinois Press, 1983), for an account of the careers of several local coal barons and their families in Kentucky and, to a lesser extent, West Virginia.

2. The Political Economy of Coal

1. James Still, *River of Earth* (New York: Viking, 1940), 200.

2. See Crandall A. Shifflett, *Coal Towns: Life, Work, and Culture in Company Towns of Southern Appalachia, 1880–1960* (Knoxville: Univ. of Tennessee Press, 1991), 105.

3. Shifflett, *Coal Towns,* 103.

4. See Robert Engler, *The Politics of Oil* (New York: Macmillan, 1961), chap. 7; David Howard Davis, *Energy Politics* (New York: St. Martin's 1978), chap. 1.

5. Curtis Selzer, *Fire in the Hole: Miners and Managers in the American Coal Industry* (Lexington: Univ. Press of Kentucky, 1985), chap. 7.

3. The Productivity Revolution

1. Keith Dix, *Work Relations in the Coal Industry: The Hand Loading Era, 1880–1930* (Morgantown: West Virginia University, Institute of Labor Studies, 1977), 77.

2. F. G. Tryon and L. Mann, *Coal in 1925* (Washington DC: Bureau of Mines, 1928), 456.

3. See Keith Dix, *What's a Coal Miner to Do? The Mechanization of Coal Mines* (Pittsburgh: Univ. of Pittsburgh Press, 1988).

4. On mining innovations, see generally J. Robert Marovilli and John M. Karhnak, "The Mechanization of Mining," *Scientific American,* Sept. 1982, 91–102.

5. See articles on longwall mining in *Coal Age Operating Handbook of Underground Mining,* vol. 1 (New York: MacGraw-Hill, 1977), chap. 2.

6. Marovilli and Karhnak, "Mechanization of Mining," 99.

7. Matthew L. Wald, "Coal Mine Robots Lift an Industry," *New York Times,* 8 Feb. 1990.

8. Wald, "Coal Mine Robots." On installing longwall machines, see John F. Brass, "Longwalling in Alabama," *Mining Engineer,* Jan. 1989, 317–24.

9. Information on Loveridge mine operation was generously provided by Denise Santee and by Denver Johnson, then superintendent of the mine.

10. Marovilli and Karhnak, "Mechanization of Mining," 99–100.

11. Fred W. Fraily, "Powder River Country," *Trains: The Magazine of Railroading,* Nov. 1989, 40–63.

12. Guy Mendes, "The Whole Country Will Be Stripped," *Newsweek,* 28 June 1971, 72.

13. See Genevieve Atwood, "The Strip Mining of Western Coal," in *Energy and Environment: Readings from Scientific American* (San Francisco: Freeman, 1975), 155–66.

14. Keith Schneider, "Coal Industry Contests Law on restoring Lands," *New York Times,* 9 March 1992.

15. Keith Schneider, "U.S. Mine Inspectors Charge Interference by Agency Director," *New York Times,* 22 Nov. 1992.

4. Health and Safety

1. See *Year of the Rank and File, 1973: Officers Report to the United Mine Workers of America* (1973), 164.

2. The President's Commission on Coal, *Staff Findings* (Washington DC, 1980), 42.

3. *Congressional Record* 120 (18 July 1974): H6725.

4. *United Mine Workers Journal,* 16–31 Oct. 1974, 11.

5. *Statistical Abstract of the U.S. 1995,* table 691.

6. International Labour Office, *Yearbook of Labour Statistics, 1973* (Geneva, 1973), 736–37.

7. Author's personal correspondence with John Brass.

8. M. W. Kirby, *British Coalmining Industry, 1870–1946: A Political and Economic History* (London: Macmillan, 1977).

9. British Coal Corporation, *Reports and Accounts, 1988–89* (London: Her Majesty's Stationery Office), 28–29; "Britain to Shut Most of Its Coal Mines," *New York Times,* 14 Oct. 1992.

10. U.S. Coal Commission, *Report,* pt. 3, *Principal Findings and Recommendations* (Washington DC: Government Printing Office, 1925), 1659. The date for this information is not provided, but it must have been in the early 1920s.

11. House Subcommittee of the Committee on Mines and Mining, *Inspections and Investigations in Coal Mines* (Washington DC: Government Printing Office, 1940), 5.

12. *The Government of Coal* UMW District No. 2 (Clearfield PA: UMWA, 1921), 21.

13. Meade Arble, *The Long Tunnel: A Coal Miner's Journal* (New York: Atheneum, 1976), 31–32.

14. Quoted in Clyde Farnsworth, "Canadian Town Grieves Again for Its Lost Miners," *New York Times,* 16 May 1992.

15. Moore and Smith are quoted in Brit Hume, *Death and the Mines* (New York: Grossman, 1971), 15–16.

16. Thomas Bethell and Davitt McAteer, "Monongah 1907" (a research proposal to the National Endowment for the Humanities; mimeo), 1.

17. Owen Lovejoy, "Child Labor in Soft Coal Mines," *Annals of the American Academy* 29 (1907): 2–34.

18. Boydoh interview.

19. Caudill, *Theirs Be the Power,* 52.

20. Frank Haas, "The Explosion at Monongah Mines, Fairmont Coal Company," *Fairmont Coal Bulletin,* no. 11 (20 Dec. 1908), is the best single source on the Monongah disaster.

21. Monongah Mines Relief Committee, *History of the Monongah Mine Relief Fund in Aid of the Survivors from the Monongah Mine Explosion, Monongah, W.Va., Dec. 6, 1907* (Fairmont WV, 1910).

22. Quoted in Caudill, *Theirs Be the Power,* 52.

23. Parkersburg Estate Journal, dated Dec. / Jan. 1907–8, in the Carter Jones Collection on the Monongah Explosion, West Virginia Univ. Library, Morgantown.

24. John Bartlow Martin, "The Blast in Centralia No. 5: A Mine Disaster No One Stopped," *Harper's Magazine,* March 1948, 193–220.

25. See Thomas Bethell, *The Hurricane Creek Massacre* (New York: Harper & Row, Perennial, 1972), 50–51, 66–69. See also *Coal Patrol,* nos. 5–6, 15 Jan. and 1 Feb. 1971. Bethell edited *Coal Patrol,* a report on coal developments published by Appalachian Information, 1970–77.

26. See House Committee on Education and Labor, *Legislative History: Federal Coal Mine Health and Safety Act,* 91st Cong., 2d sess., 1970, 6. This 1,151-page collection is a wellspring of information on coal mine safety politics.

27. House Committee, *Legislative History,* 7. On the Farmington disaster, see Hume, *Death and the Mines,* 9–17.

28. Quoted in Hume, *Death and the Mines,* 259. It is of more than passing interest that despite his call for passage of the law, Nixon contributed to the sabotage of its enforcement.

29. See President's Commission on Coal, *Staff Findings,* 43.

30. For an introductory note on black lung disease, see President's Commission on Coal, *The American Coal Miner: A Report on Community and Living Conditions in*

the Coalfields (Washington DC, 1980), 116–25. This discussion relies on the excellent work on black lung by Barbara Ellen Smith, *Digging Our Own Graves: Coal Miners and the Struggle over Black Lung Disease* (Philadelphia: Temple Univ. Press, 1987).

31. Smith, *Digging Our Own Graves,* 107.

32. Smith, *Digging Our Own Graves,* 114. The BLA was established in 1968.

33. Hume, *Death and the Mines,* 110.

34. Hume, *Death and the Mines,* 67–69.

35. House Committee, *Legislative History,* 1.

36. House Committee, *Legislative History,* 639.

37. House Committee, *Legislative History,* 702.

38. House Committee, *Legislative History,* 1100–1101.

39. Don Stillman, "The Assessment Scandal," *United Mine Workers Journal,* 1–15 July 1974, 8–11.

40. David Zielenziger, "Safety or Else: The UMWA and the Energy Crisis" (senior thesis, Princeton University, 1974), documents the nonenforcement of the act.

41. See Bethell, *Hurricane Creek Massacre,* 14–17.

42. Comptroller General of the United States, *Report to Subcommittee on Labor and Public Welfare, U.S. Senate, Problems of Implementation of the Federal Coal Mine Health and Safety Act of 1969, Bureau of Mines, Department of Interior* (Washington DC, 1971), 1.

43. Comptroller General, *Report,* 77.

44. Comptroller General of the United States, *Followup on Implementation of the Federal Coal Mine Health and Safety Act of 1969, Bureau of Mines, Department of Interior* (Washington DC, 1973), 1.

45. Harry Caudill, "Manslaughter in a Coal Mine," *Nation,* April 1977, 492–97.

46. Ben A. Franklin, "Coal Mine Safety Comes under Fire," *New York Times,* 22 Jan. 1982.

47. Franklin, "Coal Mine Safety."

48. Ben A. Franklin, "Violations Cited in Utah Coal Mine Fire That Killed 27," *New York Times,* 25 March 1987.

49. In 1994 McAteer became assistant secretary of labor and head of the Mine Safety and Health Administration.

50. Ben A. Franklin, "Mine Safety Agency Accused of Lax Enforcement," *New York Times,* 12 March 1987.

51. Quoted in Peter Kilborn, "Labor Chief Says Coal Companies Disregard Law on Miners' Health," *New York Times,* 16 April 1991.

52. Keith Schneider, "Coal Company Admits Safety Test Fraud," *New York Times,* 19 Jan. 1991.

53. Quoted in "Guilty Pleas Set in U.S. Coal Case," *New York Times,* 22. Oct. 1991.

54. Quoted in Kilborn, "Labor Chief."

55. On the use of criminal law sanctions in coal mine safety enforcement, see Marat Moore, "Mine Safety Crimes on Trial," *United Mine Workers Journal,* June 1993, 7–13.

5. The Miners' Way of Life

1. Still, *River of Earth*; Helen B. Hiscoe, *Appalachian Passage* (Athens: Univ. of Georgia Press, 1991).

2. Shifflett, *Coal Towns,* chap. 8.

3. Shifflett, *Coal Towns,* 148; Coal Mines Administration, *A Medical Survey of the Bituminous-Coal Industry* (Washington DC: 1947); cited as Boone Report.

4. President's Commission on Coal, *American Coal Miner,* 33.

5. David A. Corbin, *Life, Work, and Rebellion in the Coal Fields: The Southern West Virginia Miners, 1880–1920* (Urbana: Univ. of Illinois Press, 1981), 32–34.

6. Boone Report, 13–14.

7. President's Commission on Coal, *American Coal Miner,* 31.

8. President's Commission on Coal, *American Coal Miner,* 54.

9. President's Commission on Coal, *American Coal Miner,* 138.

10. Matt Witt, "'It's in Our Blood': Three Generations of a Coal Mining Family," *United Mine Workers Journal,* 1–15 Sept. 1975, 14.

11. Angela V. John, *By the Sweat of Their Brow: Women Coal Workers at Victorian Coal Mines* (London: Routledge & Kegan Paul, 1984), 230.

12. President's Commission on Coal, *American Coal Miner,* 190–99.

13. Ben A. Franklin, "Female Miners at UMW Meeting Denounce Sexism and Lack of Safety," *New York Times,* 11 Nov. 1979.

14. Quoted in Calvin Trillin, "U.S. Journal: Central PA, Called at Rushton," *New Yorker,* 12 Nov. 1979, 184. See also William Serrin, "The Life and Death of a Woman Who Won Right to Be a Miner," *New York Times,* 8 Nov. 1979.

15. Arnold Toynbee, *A Study of History* (New York: Oxford Univ. Press, 1947), 149.

16. Harry Caudill, *Night Comes to the Cumberland* (Boston: Little, Brown, 1963), 13.

17. Caudill, *Night Comes to the Cumberland,* 351.

18. Altina L. Waller, *Feud: Hatfields, McCoys, and Social Change in Appalachia, 1850–1900* (Chapel Hill: Univ. of North Carolina Press, 1988), 205.

19. Robert Coles, *Migrants, Sharecroppers, Mountaineers,* vol. 2 of *Children of Crisis* (Boston: Little, Brown, 1972), 199–200.

20. No one has written more poignantly about leaving the mountains for city

jobs than Harriet Arnow, whose novel *The Doll Maker* (New York: Macmillan, 1954) is an outstanding literary achievement.

21. Coles, *Migrants*, 283.

22. Coles, *Migrants*, 75; Caudill, *Night Comes to the Cumberland*, 75.

23. Coles, *Migrants*, 246, 292.

24. *Statistical Abstract of the U.S. 1972*, 91.

25. Trevor Armbrister, *Act of Vengeance: The Yablonski Murders and Their Solution* (New York: Dutton, 1975), 243.

26. Quoted in Witt, "It's in Our Blood," 8–17.

27. Joe William Trotter Jr., *Coal, Class, and Color: Blacks in Southern West Virginia, 1915–32* (Urbana: Univ. of Illinois Press, 1990), 103, 107.

28. Ronald L. Lewis, *Black Coal Miners in America: Race, Class, and Community Conflict, 1780–1980* (Lexington: Univ. Press of Kentucky, 1987), 168, 190.

29. Corbin, *Life, Work, and Rebellion*, 61; chap. 3 develops the argument fully.

30. George Wolfe to Justus Collins, 7 June 1916, Justus Collins Papers, West Virginia History Collection, West Virginia University. By permission.

31. Bill Love, interview with author, 2 March 1981.

6. Coal Miners and Their Union

1. Shifflet, *Coal Towns*, 117.

2. Boydoh, interview.

3. Gerald Spragg, interview with author, 11 March 1981.

4. Quoted in Coleman, *Men and Coal*, 38–39.

5. Coleman, *Men and Coal*, 36.

6. Quoted in Coleman, *Men and Coal*, 43.

7. Wayne G. Broel Jr., *The Molly McGuires* (Cambridge: Harvard Univ. Press, 1964), 70.

8. Quoted in Broel, *Molly McGuires*, 131–32.

9. Quoted in James Wechsler, *Labor Baron: A Portrait of John L. Lewis* (New York: William Morrow, 1944), 8.

10. On labor-management violence, see Louis Adamic, *Dynamite: The Story of Class Violence in America* (New York: Viking, 1934).

11. Howard B. Lee, *Bloodletting in Appalachia: The Story of West Virginia's Four Major Mine Wars and Other Thrilling Incidents of Its Coal Fields* (Morgantown: West Virginia Univ., 1969), chap. 5.

12. 71 *U.S.* (4 Wall) (1866).

13. *Mays and Nance v. Brown*, 71 West Virginia Sup. Ct. 519 (1912).

14. Corbin, *Life, Work, and Rebellion*, 98.

15. Corbin, *Life, Work, and Rebellion*, 100.

16. These events were the subject of a revealing movie, *Matewan*, written and directed by John Sayles in 1987. See "UMWA History Comes Alive in 'Matewan,'" *United Mine Workers Journal*, Dec. 1987, 11.

17. Lee, *Bloodletting in Appalachia*, 81, 146.

18. Lee, *Bloodletting in Appalachia*, 148.

19. See [Mary Harris Jones], *The Autobiography of Mother Jones* (Chicago: Charles Keer, 1972).

20. It is an interesting side note to the history of fighting aircraft that most of the planes sent to Blair Mountain crashed on the way back to base; the airplanes of that time were ill suited to flying over the hills of West Virginia.

21. Quoted in George McGovern and Leonard Gutteridge, *The Great Coal Field War* (Boston: Houghton Mifflin, 1972), 34. This detailed account of the Ludlow massacre was originally McGovern's Ph.D. dissertation.

22. John Laslett, *Labor and the Left: A Study of Socialist and Radical Influence in the American Labor Movement, 1880–1924* (New York: Basic Books, 1970), chap. 6.

23. UMW District No. 2, *The Government of Coal* (Clearfield PA: UMWA, 1921), 8, 22.

24. UMW District No. 2, *Why the Miner's Program?* (Clearfield PA: UMWA, 1921).

25. Nationalization Research Committee, *How to Run Coal: Suggestions for a Plan of Public Ownership, Public Control, and Democratic Management of the Coal Industry* (Indianapolis: UMWA, 1922).

26. John Brophy's autobiography gives an account of his nationalization efforts in the 1920s: *A Miner's Life* (Madison: Univ. of Wisconsin Press, 1964), chaps. 12–13.

27. Many years after the war I received a letter from a pilot in another squadron, who recalled, "I came by your barracks one day and saw you in a huge argument about the [then raging coal] strike and you were about the only one supporting the union side." My friends were not impressed with Lewis's contention that as of mid-1943 miners had suffered more casualties than combat troops in their fighting thus far.

28. Melvyn Dubofsky and Warren Van Tine, *John L. Lewis: A Biography* (New York: Quadrangle/New York Times, 1977), 65.

29. Quoted in Dubofsky and Van Tine, *John L. Lewis*, 327.

30. Quoted in Dubofsky and Van Tine, *John L. Lewis*, 52.

31. Quoted in Hume, *Death and the Mines*, 9.

32. I am indebted to Fred Greenstein, my colleague at Princeton University, for the thought of comparing these two nineteenth-century figures dropped into the twentieth century.

33. *Blankenship v. Boyle,* 329 Fed Supp. 1089 (1971) at 1100.

34. Dubofsky and Van Tine, *John L. Lewis,* 362.

35. *South-East Coal Co. v. Consolidation Coal Co.,* 434 Fed. 2d 7676 (1970); and *Ramsay v. U.S.,* 401 U.S. 302 (1971).

36. Selzer, *Fire in the Hole,* 54.

37. Quoted in Dubofsky and Van Tine, *John L. Lewis,* 210–11.

38. Armbrister, *Act of Vengeance,* 69–70.

39. Quoted in Armbrister, *Act of Vengeance,* 39.

40. Armbrister, *Act of Vengeance,* 52.

41. Hume, *Death and the Mines,* 217.

42. Quoted in Hume, *Death and the Mines,* 87.

43. Quoted in Armbrister, *Act of Vengeance,* 315.

44. From the liner notes of the record "Come All You Coal Miners," Rounder Records #1005.

45. President's Commission on Coal, *Staff Findings,* 37.

46. "The Miners Have a Point," *Wall Street Journal,* 7 March 1978.

47. See the Sam Church profile by Ben A. Franklin, *New York Times,* 24 March 1981.

48. Quoted in David Moberg, "Mine Workers," *In These Times,* 14–27 July 1982.

49. See the story on the Pittston strike by Jim Sessions and Fran Ansley, "Singing across Dark Spaces: The Union/Community Takeover of Pittston's Moss Plant 3," in *Fighting Back in Appalachia,* ed. Stephen L. Fisher (Philadelphia: Temple Univ. Press, 1993), 195–224.

7. The Problem of Externalities

1. See William Kapp, *The Social Costs of Private Enterprise* (New York: Schocken Books, 1971).

2. *Congressional Record* 136 (3 April 1990): S3750.

3. Peter Kilborn, "East's Coal Towns Wither in Name of Cleaner Air," *New York Times,* 15 Feb. 1996. Much of my discussion of the impact of clean air legislation relies on the Kilborn article.

4. James Dao, "A New, Unregulated Market: Selling the Right to Pollute," *New York Times,* 6 Feb. 1993.

5. Barnaby J. Feder, "Sold: $21 Million of Air Pollution," *New York Times,* 30 March 1993.

6. Tim Hilchey, "Government Survey Finds Decline in a Building Block of Acid Rain," *New York Times,* 7 Sept. 1993.

7. William K. Stevens, "Emissions Must Be Cut to Avert Shift in Climate, Panel Says," *New York Times,* 10 Sept. 1994.

8. Quoted in Duane Smith, *Mining America: The Industry and the Environment,* 1800–1980 (Lawrence: Univ. Press of Kansas, 1987), 144.

9. Smith, *Mining America,* 184, n. 3.

10. Keith Schneider, "Ex-Mine Official Is under Inquiry," *New York Times,* 8 April 1993.

11. Gerald M. Stern, *The Buffalo Creek Disaster: How the Survivors of One of the Worst Disasters in Coal Mining History Brought Suit against a Coal Company—and Won* (New York: Random House, 1976), 44, 46. See also Kai Erikson, *Everything in Its Path* (New York: Simon & Schuster, 1977); and a novel by Denise Giardina, *The Unquiet Earth* (New York: Norton, 1992).

12. Thomas N. Bethell and Davitt McAteer, "The Pittston Mentality: Manslaughter on Buffalo Creek," *Washington Monthly,* May 1972, excerpted in Ridgeway, *Powering Civilization,* 64–72.

13. David DeKok, *Unseen Danger: A Tragedy of People, Government, and the Centralia Minefire* (Philadelphia: Univ. of Pennsylvania Press, 1986), 32, tells of a fire at Summit Hill, Pennsylvania, that burned from 1859 to the 1940s and cost $2 million to extinguish.

14. Quoted in Renée Jacobs, *Slow Burn: A Photodocument of Centralia, Pennsylvania* (Philadelphia: Univ. of Pennsylvania Press, 1986), 9.

15. "Fairmont, W. Va., Lives in Peril as Old Mines under It Crumble," *New York Times,* 23 Nov. 1980.

8. Coal and Corporate Power

1. *Statistical Abstract of the U.S., 1988,* 504; Lawrence Zuckerman, "Shades of the Go-Go 80s: Takeovers in a Comeback," *New York Times,* 3 Nov. 1994.

2. The attorneys are quoted in Ridgeway, *Powering Civilization,* 338.

3. Smith, *Digging Our Own Graves,* 218.

4. Jill Abramson, "'96 Campaign Costs Set Record at $2.2 Billion," *New York Times,* 25 Nov. 1997; Sarah Anderson and John Cavanaugh, "The Top Ten List," *Nation,* 8 Dec., 1997, 9.

5. Charles E. Lindblom, "The Market as Prison," *Journal of Politics* 44 (1982): 327.

6. Harvey, *Best-Dressed Miners,* 166.

7. Caudill, *Theirs Be the Power,* 134.

8. Justus Collins to Jarius Collins, 18 Sept. 1896, Justus Collins Papers, West Virginia History Collection, West Virginia University. By permission.

9. Anthony Sampson, *Company Man* (New York: Random House, 1995), chap. 15.

10. *Statistical Abstract of the U.S., 1995,* tables 713, 714, 749, and 730, respectively.

11. U.S. Bureau of the Census, *County and City Data Book, 1994,* xviii–xix.

12. Don Marsh, "Free Ride No Surprise," *Charleston Gazette Mail,* 29 Nov. 1970. The "young people" to whom he refers were probably students of David McAteer, then teaching at West Virginia Univ. Law School, later U.S. assistant secretary of labor.

13. See Appalachian Land Ownership Task Force, *Land Ownership Patterns and Their Impacts on Appalachian Communities: A Survey of 80 Counties* (Lexington: Univ. Press of Kentucky, 1983), submitted to the Appalachian Regional Commission in 1981. The best succinct account of the report is Ben A. Franklin, "Appalachian Regional Study Finds Absentee Ownership of 43% of Land," *New York Times,* 5 April 1981.

14. Anthony Paresi, "Senate Vote Defeats Move to Curb Oil Companies' Ties to Other Fuels," *New York Times,* 9 Sept. 1977.

15. Robert A. Dahl and Charles E. Lindblom, *Politics, Economics, and Welfare* (1953; New York: Harper, 1976), xxvi–xxvii (original emphasis).

9. Confronting Corporate Hegemony

1. U.S. Bureau of the Census, *County and City Data Book, 1994,* xviii–xix, table 1.

2. Carter Garber, "Saturn: Tomorrow's Jobs, Yesterday's Myths," in *Communities in Economic Crisis: Appalachia and the South,* ed. John Gaventa et al. (Philadelphia: Temple Univ. Press, 1990), 175–89.

3. Sampson, *Company Man,* 311.

4. Judith Dobroyznski, "Getting What They Deserve?" *New York Times,* 22 Feb. 1996.

5. Robert A. Dahl, *Democracy and Its Critics* (New Haven: Yale Univ. Press, 1989), 332.

6. Alexis de Toqueville, *Democracy in America* (New York: Knopf, 1945), 2:106.

7. Toqueville, *Democracy in America,* 2:191.

8. On the communication problem, see Maxine Waller, "It Has to Come from the People," In Gaventa et al., *Communities in Economic Crisis,* 19–28.

10. Democracy and Corporate Power

1. See *New York Times,* 3–9 March 1996, for a series of seven consecutive articles, "The Downsizing of America." Data here are from the first: Louis Uchitelle and N. R. Kleinfield, "On the Battlefields of Business, Millions of Casualties." See also Kirkpatrick Sales, *Rebels against the Future* (Reading MA: Addison-Wesley, 1996). In 1996 the ten largest downsizers dismissed 129,000 employees, according to Anderson and Cavanagh, "The Top Ten List."

2. *The 1993 Information Please Environmental Almanac,* 73.

3. *Information Please Environmental Almanac,* 73–75.

4. See the clearly presented argument opposing industrial policy in Steve Fisher, "National Economic Renewal Programs and Their Implications for Appalachia and the South," in Gaventa et al., *Communities in Economic Crisis,* 263–79.

5. Not an oxymoron; I know many who are or were such.

6. Dahl, *Democracy and Its Critics,* 323.

7. Anderson and Cavanagh, "The Top Ten List."

8. Lester Thurow, "Why Their World Might Crumble," *New York Times Magazine,* 15 Nov. 1995, 75.

9. Andrew Hacker, "Who They Are," *New York Times Magazine,* 15 Nov. 1995, 70–71.

10. Thurow, "Why Their World Might Crumble," 79.

11. Dahl, *Democracy and Its Critics,* 328–29.

12. Selzer, *Fire in the Hole,* 218.

13. Charles E. Lindblom, *Politics and Markets: The World's Political-Economic Systems* (New York: Basic Books, 1977), 356.

14. "Fortune's Global 500," *Fortune,* Aug. 1995, F-10.

15. If that seems hard to believe, study the period 1947–60 when the Red Scare swept the country; every institution of communication was manipulated by the organized frenzy that corporate interests orchestrated and operated with the craven compliance of politicians, news media, entertainment moguls, educational officials, and governmental bodies. All that was needed to force betraying responses to the invasive question "Are you now, or have you ever been—?" was a hint or an accusation from a silly source. It was not a noble time, but it was instructive for any who want to learn about thought control.

Index

Italic numbers refer to illustration numbers.

221

Smith, Barbara Ellen, 213 nn30, 31, 32,
218 n3

Smith, Duane, 218 nn8, 9

*South-East Coal Co. v. Consolidation Coal
Co.*, 217 n35

Spragg, Gerald, 113–14

"steamshovel," 208

Steel, Tom, 209 n3

Stern, Gerald, 218 n11

Still, James, 90, 214 n1

strike breakers, 103

strikes, 113–14, 116–19, 121–24, 146–47;
Massey, 146; Paint Creek-Cabin Creek,
121–24; Pittston, 146–47, 217 n49

strip mining, 44–49, 155–56; in eastern
states, 46–47; and environment, 44–47;
restoration of land, 156; in Wyoming
and West, 45–46

"stumping out," 37–38. *See also* room and
pillar mining

subsidence, 158–60

sulphur dioxide in coal, 150–54; smokestack "scrubbers" for, 151–52

Taft-Hartley Act, 113, 177

Temporary National Economic Committee (TNEC), 200

"ten mile hole", 17

"The How and Why of Shorty Farrell,"
206

Thurow, Lester, 195, 220 n10

Toynbee, Arnold, 98

Trotter, Joe William, 215 n27

Truman, Harry, 70

Trumka, Richard, 145–48

United Mine Workers of America
(UMWA), 59, 75, 79, 110–48; decline of,
134–42; origins of, 115–27; reform of,
142–48

United Mine Workers Journal, 95

United States Steel Co., 81

U.S. v. E.C. Knight Co., 162–63

U.S. Geological Survey, 153

Van Tine, Warren. *See* Dubofsky, Melvyn,
and Van Tine, Warren

Vietnam War opposition, 185–88

violence in strikes, 120–27

Voting Rights Act of 1964, 175–76

Waller, Altina, 99–100

Walter, John K., xii

Weaver, Daniel, 115

Welfare and Retirement Fund, 134–35, 136

Wells, Dr. Hawly, 74–75

West Fork River, 150

West Frankfort IL, explosion, 69, 132, 139

West Kentucky Coal Co., 136

West Virginia, poverty of, 170

West Virginia University, 26, 51

"Whitwell, Topmost, Bergoo," 205

Wierton WV, 88

Wilberg UT, mine fire, 84

Wilson, Woodrow, 131

Witt, Matt, 214 n10, 215 n26

Wolfe, George, 107, 215 n30

women miners, 96–97

worker representation on boards, 180–81

Worthington WV, 88

Yablonski, Joseph "Jock," 139, 140, 142

yellow dog contract, 116

Zielenziger, David, 213 n40

Zola, Emile, 12–13, 209 n5

Zuckerman, Lawrence, 218 n1